Ella E. Meyers

The centennial cook book and general guide

Ella E. Meyers

The centennial cook book and general guide

ISBN/EAN: 9783744785969

Printed in Europe, USA, Canada, Australia, Japan

Cover: Foto ©Lupo / pixelio.de

More available books at **www.hansebooks.com**

1776   **THE**   1876

CENTENNIAL COOK BOOK

—AND—

GENERAL GUIDE.

(ILLUSTRATED.)

PRACTICAL RECEIPTS,

IN FOUR PARTS,

—EMBRACING—

MODERN COOKERY, IN ALL ITS ARTS,
FAMILY MEDICINES AND HOUSEHOLD REMEDIES,
FARMING HINTS AND COMPLETE FARRIERY,
EVENTS OF THE LAST CENTURY.

—BY—

MRS. ELLA E. MYERS.

PHILADELPHIA:
J. B. MYERS, PUBLISHER.
1876.

PREFACE.

THE "Centennial Cook Book and General Guide" is placed before the public solely on its intrinsic merits. To compile and issue a work of this kind that would be *perfect*, has been my particular aim, and, I believe that I have succeeded. The space allotted to COOKERY alone embraces nearly, if not quite, one thousand receipts, being the collection of over twenty years; and each receipt herein has been carefully analyzed and tested by me from time to time, and I can speak confidently of the correctness of each and every one of them. In these pages can be found some of the most elaborate and costly dishes to please the palate of the connoisseur; as also, some of the most economical ones to meet the wants of those whose incomes will not permit them to expend immoderately their scant earnings in supplying their tables. I know that vast sums of money are wasted annually by families and servants in preparing dishes, which might be saved if a few hints could be placed before them, whereby this saving might be accomplished. In order, then, to assist my friends in this object, I have endeavored in the compilation of the within receipts, to use only those ingredients which are practically necessary, and in such quantities only as are indispensable, and if my instructions are followed, there will be a very great saving indeed. It may not be perceptible, unless one will take the trouble to compare their own mode of preparing dishes with the different modes laid down in this work. I speak

PREFACE.

from experience when I say: "there is room for reform in cookery." If families will but follow the instructions embraced in the "Centennial Cook Book" in the different modes of cooking, there will be a saving of at least one-third. It is worth the trial.

The "Medical Department" of this work embraces valuable receipts for the cure of the different diseases that are common in families. They are carefully compiled and can be used by families with perfect safety. I have been aided in this department of my work principally by some of the best physicians and surgeons in this and other cities, and by the most approved works on medicine and surgery. A large number of the remedies contained herein, I have used in my own family for years, and I can speak confidently of their efficiency.

As great care is essential in the treatment of children, I have devoted several pages to this important subject. The hints and remedies herein prescribed have been approved by the leading physicians of this city, and should be followed implicitly by mothers and those having the care of infants. It is a matter of such vital importance that I have given it especial mention in this work. In fact, the greatest care has been exercised in arranging this portion of the book, and it will be noticed that I have discarded entirely the use of medical terms, and given the simple name of each ingredient, so that any child may be able to call for the article named in the receipt. It will be well for families to give this portion of the work a careful perusal, not only because of the efficiency of the remedies set forth, but there may be times when it will be necessary to act quickly in many cases of sickness, and probably before a physician could be summoned, the disease may have attained great headway.

The "Farming and Agricultural" department I have turned over to the publisher of this work, (an ex-farmer, with twenty years experience). This I have done for the purpose of carrying out my promise of making my work complete in all its details. In this department will be found some of the most valuable hints extant. As the planting and rearing of an orchard is a subject which interests the farmer, particular pains have been taken to give some minute directions in regard to the same; and the hope is that farmers, and those interested in this branch of agriculture, will give the remarks thereon a careful perusal and study. The Dairy, too, is an important matter for consideration in this work. The manner of making Butter and Cheese is here handled with great care. The matter has been taken up from its foundation (procuring the milk) to the last and concluding process, (the packing and shipping) and each process, as it is reached, is carefully and minutely described, and if the instructions are followed as laid down, dairymen will have no cause to say that their Butter and Cheese did not turn out as they had expected. The cultivation of crops has also been given particular attention herein. The rearing and care of stock, with their diseases and remedies, is another feature of this department, and, in fact, nothing has been left undone to make it complete in every particular. I think, then, that this part of my book, like the preceding ones, can be placed before the public on its merits.

In the "Miscellaneous" department will be found over one hundred of the best selected and most valuable receipts that could be found, pertaining to Art, Science, and Chemistry, and also several additional receipts of infinite value to housewives and farmers. I have made the selections with great care, and I would ask my friends and the public to read them carefully, because I believe they will find among them some of the very identical receipts that they have been looking for.

The fourth and last part of this work is devoted entirely to "EVENTS," embracing a history of Philadelphia from 1609 to the present time; with matters of interest in connection with "Our Centennial." This part is embellished with numerous fine engravings, intended to describe more minutely the progress of our city since the landing of Penn; and to give to each purchaser of this book a little *souvenir* of our nation's "Centennial Birthday;" something that may be retained by future posterity as a memento of the grand celebration in this "Centennial Year, 1876." In this part will be found engravings of all the "old landmarks" in Philadelphia—Independence Hall, in 1776 and 1876; the oldest churches; the house in which the "Declaration of Independence was written; the house where the *first* American flag was made; all the present public buildings, institutions, cemeteries, &c.; scenes in Fairmount Park, concluding with engravings of all the Centennial Exposition Buildings.

Having now fulfilled my task, I shall leave the work in the hands of the public, and they shall say, whether or not " THE CENTENNIAL COOK BOOK AND GENERAL GUIDE, is what I have labored to make it—a success.

ELLA E. MYERS.

BREAD AND BREAD-MAKING.

BREAD-MAKING is an ancient art indeed. The Assyrians, Egyptians, and Greeks, used to make bread, in which oil, with aniseed and other spices, was an element; but this was unleavened.

Somewhere about the beginning of the thirtieth Olympiad, the slave of an archon, at Athens, made leavened bread by accident. He had left some wheaten dough in an earthen pan, and forgotten it; some days afterwards, he lighted upon it again, and found it turning sour. His first thought was to throw it away; but, his master coming up, he mixed this now accescent dough with some fresh dough, which he was working at. The bread thus produced, was found delicious by the archon and his friends, and the slave, being summoned, told the secret. It spread all over Athens; and everybody wanting leavened bread at once, certain persons set up as bread-makers, or bakers. In a short time bread-baking became quite an art, and "Athenian bread" was quoted all over Greece as the best bread, just as the honey of Hymettus was celebrated as the best honey.

In our own times, bread has become an article of food of the first necessity; it constitutes of itself a complete life-sustainer, the gluten, starch, and sugar, which it contains, representing azotized and hydro-carbonated nutrients, and combining the sustaining powers of the animal and vegetable kingdoms in one product.

American Wheat Bread.
(AUTHOR'S OWN RECEIPT.)

Seven pounds of flour; two quarts of warm water; a large tablespoonful of salt; half a gill of yeast.

Put the flour into a deep pan, heap it round the sides, leaving a hollow in the centre; put into it a quart of warm water, a large spoonful of salt, and half a gill of yeast; have ready three pints more of warm water, and with as much as may be necessary, make the whole into a rather soft dough, kneading it well with both hands. When it is smooth and shining, strew a little flour on it, lay a thickly folded cloth over it; and set it in a warm place by the fire for four or five hours; then knead it again for a quarter of an hour; cover it over, and set it to rise again; divide it into two or four loaves, and bake in a quick oven. It will take one hour to bake it if divided into loaves weighing two pounds each, and two hours if the loaves weigh four pounds each. This bread need only rise once, and if made of the best flour will be beautifully white and light.

In cold weather bread should be mixed in a warm room, and not allowed to become cold while rising.

Rye Bread.

Wet up rye flour with lukewarm milk, (water will do to wet it with, but it will not make the bread so good.) Put in the same proportion of yeast as for wheat bread. For four or five loaves of bread, put in a couple of tea-spoonsful of salt. A couple of table-spoonsful of melted butter makes the crust more tender. It should not be kneaded as stiff as wheat bread, or it will be hard when baked. When light, take it out into pans, without moulding it up—let it remain in them about twenty minutes, before baking.

Unleavened Bread.

Mix unbolted wheat-meal (Graham flour), or three parts of wheat-meal and one of Indian-meal (coarse ground), with water sufficient to form a middling stiff dough. Some prefer hot water to "scald" the meal. Roll or mould the dough into a thin cake, not more than half or three-quarters of an inch in thickness, and bake immediately in a stove or before the fire. This bread-cake will be rather soft, but very sweet and perfectly wholesome. It may also be moulded into loaves of rather small size, and baked in the oven or in the old-fashioned baking kettles, or cooked under hot ashes, after the manner of roasting potatoes.

This kind of bread may be made in the same way, of different proportions of rye and Indian, or of wheat, rye, and Indian.

Indian Bread.

Mix Indian meal with cold water, stir it into boiling water, let it boil half an hour; stir in a little salt, take it from the fire, let it remain till lukewarm, then stir in yeast and Indian meal, to render it of the consistency of unbaked rye dough. When light, take it out into buttered pans, let it remain a few minutes, then bake it two hours and a half.

Graham Bread.

Take two quarts of Graham (*never* sift it) and one of flour, half a cup of yeast, one scant spoonful of salt, half a cup of brown sugar, and warm water enough to make a stiff batter, and let it rise. If you rise it over night, be sure to set in a cool place, as it sours much quicker than fine flour. It will rise in a warm place in four hours. When risen, mix with it a teaspoonful of saleratus dissolved in warm water, and flour enough to shape it into loaves; put it in the pans, and let it rise thirty-five minutes, and bake *slowly* an hour and a quarter. Make the loaves very small. Use molasses instead of sugar if the bread is eaten for constipation.

Currant Bread.

Take three pounds of flour; one pound of raisins; two pounds of currants; one pint and a half of new milk; and one gill of yeast. Warm the milk, and mix it with the flour and yeast; cover with a cloth, and set it by the fire. When risen sufficiently, add the fruits and mold it; then put it into a baking tin or deep dish rubbed with sweet-oil or dusted with flour; after it has risen for half an hour longer, bake in a moderately hot oven.

Apple Bread.

Weigh one pound of fresh, juicy apples; peel, core, and stew them into a pulp, being careful to use a porcelain kettle or a stone jar, placed in a kettle of boiling water; mix the pulp with two pounds of the best flour; put in the same quantity of yeast you would use for common bread, and as much water as will make it a fine, smooth dough; put it into a pan and place it in a warm place to rise, and let it remain for twelve hours, at least. Form it into rather long shaped loaves, and bake in a quick oven.

Potato Bread.

Boil the potatoes very soft, then peel and mash them fine. Put in salt, and very little butter—then rub them with the flour—wet the flour with lukewarm water—then work in the yeast, and flour till stiff to mold up. It will rise quicker than common wheat bread, and should be baked as soon as risen, as it turns sour very soon. The potatoes that the bread is made of should be mealy, and mixed with the flour in proportion of one-third of potatoes to two-thirds of flour.

Boston Brown Bread.

Take one quart of rye flour; two quarts of coarse Indian meal; one pint of wheat meal—all of which must be very fresh; half a teacupful of molasses or brown sugar; one gill of potato-yeast. Mingle the ingredients into as stiff a dough as can be stirred with a spoon, using warm water for wetting. Let it rise several hours, or over night; then put it in a large deep pan, and bake five or six hours.

French Bread.

To two quarts of flour put a pint of milk, a little salt, two ounces of melted butter, and one ounce of German yeast; whisk the fluids together, and add two beat eggs; mix the flour with it, handling it as little as possible; let the dough rise, and mold the bread into rolls; bake on tins, in a quick oven.

Common Sense Biscuit.

(AUTHOR'S OWN RECEIPT.)

Take as much flour as will do, and use judgment with regard to the amount of lard. Some folks like more, some less. They are neither so light nor good when too greasy. Put salt to the taste, and rub it all together, then add cold water slowly, and as little as will possibly answer. Make the dough so very stiff that you can neither knead nor beat it with any comfort until it is set away awhile—some twenty or thirty minutes, when it softens a little. Then heat it until it is very light, make out the biscuits and bake in a quick oven, which had better be too hot than too cold. Cover up the dough when set by to soften. They bake in fifteen or twenty minutes, if not too hot, and when done they feel very light.

American Biscuits.

TIME, ABOUT TWENTY MINUTES.

Mix a pound of flour with a quarter of a pound of butter. Make half a pint of new milk warm, and sweeten with a quarter of a pound of white sugar; pour it gradually into the butter paste. Dissolve the salt of tartar in half a teacupful of cold water, and add to the mixture, working the paste to a good consistency; roll it out, and cut into small biscuits. Bake in a quick oven directly they are made.

English Biscuits.

TIME, HALF AN HOUR TO BAKE.

Beat the yolks of twelve eggs for half an hour, then add a pound and a half of sifted white sugar, and whisk it until you see it rise in bubbles; then whisk the whites of the eggs to a strong froth, and beat them well with the sugar and yolks; stir in fourteen ounces of flour, and the peel of two lemons grated. Bake in tin molds well buttered, in a quick oven; but before you put the biscuits in, sift pounded sugar over them.

French Biscuits.

Three eggs; their weight in flour, and powdered sugar; half an ounce of candied lemon peel.

Whisk the whites of three eggs until they are *very* stiff, then whip in the candied lemon peel cut thin and fine, add by degrees the flour, and sugar pounded, and then whip all together, with the yolks of the eggs, until it is thoroughly blended; shape the biscuit on fine white paper with a spoon, and sift white sugar over them. Bake them in a moderate oven, giving them a light color on the top; then, with a fine knife, cut them from the paper, and put them in tin boxes to dry.

German Biscuits.
TIME, SIX OR EIGHT MINUTES.

Half a pound of dried flour; five ounces of butter; seven ounces of sugar; two eggs; two dessertspoonsful of cream; peel of a small lemon grated.

Beat five ounces of butter to a cream, and mix in the loaf sugar pounded the grated lemon peel, half a pound of dried flour, and the cream and well-beaten eggs, to form a nice light dough. Mix all well before kneading it, roll it in thin, long, narrow strips, and bake on a tin in a quick oven.

Wheat Meal Fruit Biscuits.

Mix Graham flour with just enough of scalded figs—previously washed—to make an adherent dough by much kneading; roll or cut into biscuits half an inch thick, and two or three inches square; bake in a quick oven.

Soda Biscuits.

One pound of flour, half a pound of pounded loaf sugar, one-quarter of a pound of fresh butter, two eggs, one small teaspoonful of carbonate of soda.

Sour Milk Biscuits.

Take two quarts of sour milk or butter-milk, and three teaspoonsful of bicarbonate of soda, dissolved in hot water. Mix the milk with sufficient flour (fine or coarse as preferred), to make a dough nearly stiff enough to roll; then add the soda and as much more flour as necessary; mould and bake quickly.

Orange Biscuits.

TIME, FIVE OR SIX MINUTES.

Eight eggs; two Seville oranges; quarter of a pound of flour; half a pound of butter; half a pound of sugar; and some candied orange peel.

Beat half a pound of fresh butter until it is a cream, and stir into it the same weight of pounded white sugar previously rubbed on the rinds of two or three Seville oranges. Add the candied orange peel cut into thin slices, then mix in the flour, and stir in gradually the yolks of eight eggs beaten well; whisk the whites until they will bear an egg on them, and mix them with the other ingredients. Fill some buttered moulds, pour in the mixture, sift some powdered sugar over, and bake them in a slow oven.

Ginger Biscuits.

TIME, SEVENTEEN OR EIGHTEEN MINUTES.

Eight ounces of flour; four ounces of butter; four ounces of loaf sugar; yolks of three eggs; and some ground ginger.

Beat the butter to a cream before the fire; add the flour by degrees, then the sugar pounded and sifted, and a flavoring to taste of ground ginger, and mix the whole with the yolks of three well-beaten eggs. When thoroughly mixed, drop the biscuit mixture on buttered paper, a sufficient distance from each other to allow the biscuits to spread, and bake them a light color, in a rather slow oven.

Almond Biscuits.

TIME, FIFTEEN MINUTES.

Four eggs; five ounces of beef-suet; half an ounce of almonds; six ounces of loaf sugar; two ounces and a half of flour; lemon to taste.

Beat the whites of four eggs to a froth, chop the suet and almonds separately very fine, and beat well together. Mix with the yolks of the eggs the loaf sugar finely sifted; beat well, and pour into the almond mixture; shake in the flour, and add the lemon. Bake in small tins in a quick oven.

Graham Soda Biscuits.

One quart of Graham flour; one teaspoonful of soda, dissolved in two-thirds of a teacupful of molasses; mix with milk and water.

Breakfast Roll.

Sixteen cups of flour, one half a cup of white sugar, one cup of butter, one of yeast, the whites of four eggs beaten to stiff froth, and four cups of boiled milk. Melt the butter, have the milk blood-warm, and mix the bread; set in a warm place, and rise over night; in the morning shape into long rolls, rise one hour, and bake half an hour.

Cranberry Rolls.

Stew a quart of cranberries in sufficient water to keep them from burning. Make it very sweet; strain and cool. Make a paste, and when the cranberry is cold, spread it on the paste about an inch thick, roll it, tie it close in a flannel cloth, boil two hours, and serve with a sweet sauce.

Economical Rolls.

To every pound of flour allow one ounce of butter, one quarter of a pint of milk, one large teaspoonful of yeast, a little salt.

English Cheshire Rolls.

TIME, HALF AN HOUR TO BAKE.

Two pounds of dried flour, two ounces of sugar, a pinch of salt, a quarter of a pound of butter, two eggs, two tablespoonsful of yeast, one pint of milk.

Boston Buttermilk Rolls.

Take two coffee cups of buttermilk, and stir into it one teaspoonful of saleratus dissolved in a little hot water, and stir into this about five cups of flour; beat this up lightly, and bake in French roll pans, the same as cream of tartar rolls. These are very nice. This will make two roll pans full.

Graham Rolls.

Take two coffee cups of sour milk, and stir into it one teaspoonful of saleratus, one of salt, half a cup of sugar, two eggs, one cup of flour, and Graham enough to make a stiff batter. Bake the same as cream of tartar rolls, allowing ten minutes longer.

French Rolls.

TIME, HALF AN HOUR.

One pound of flour; one egg; one ounce of butter; one spoonful of yeast; a little salt, and some milk.

Well beat the butter into the flour, adding a little salt; beat an egg, and stir it into the flour with the yeast, and a sufficient quantity of milk to make the dough rather stiff. Beat it well without kneading it; set it to rise, and bake it on tins. This quantity will make about six rolls, and when done rasp them before serving. Rolls (or any sort of bread) may be made new by dipping.

German Sausage Rolls.

Procure a quartern of dough from the baker's, knead this with four ounces of butter, dripping, or chopped suet; divide it into twelve equal parts, and use each piece of paste to enfold a beef sausage in it; place these rolls in a baking-tin, and bake them in the oven for about twenty minutes or half an hour.

Caraway Buns.
TIME TO BAKE, TWENTY MINUTES.

Half an ounce of caraway seeds; half a pound of currants; a little nutmeg; a little lemon peel; two eggs; one quart of new milk; one ounce of butter; two pounds of flour; a quarter of a pound of sifted sugar; one or two spoonsful of yeast.

Make a hole in the middle of the flour, and pour the milk in, with one or two spoonsful of yeast. Stir the dough, cover it over, and let it stand before the fire to rise for one hour. Then mix the caraway seeds, lemon peel, and nutmeg with one half, and the currants with the other, and cover all up together till the oven is ready. Make up the buns to a proper size, and put them on a tin baking sheet buttered. Beat up an egg, and brush them over with it. Cover them over again, and put them before the fire for another half an hour. Then bake them. Do not make them too large.

Tea Buns.

Make a hole in the middle of a pound of flour, in a pan, put in a dessertspoonful of yeast, and pour upon it half a teacupful of milk warmed as for buns; mix it up with about one-third of the flour, leaving the rest round the sides of the pan, and put it in a warm place to rise. When it has well risen, put in half a pound of butter, (not melted,) ten yolks of eggs, and two whites, and half a teaspoonful of salt; mix all well together with your hand. Put it into buttered teacups filling them half full; set them to rise, till nearly full; and bake them in a hot oven.

Centennial Buns.

Rub four ounces of butter into two pounds of flour, a little salt, four ounces of sugar, a dessertspoonful of caraways, and a teaspoonful of ginger; put some warm milk or cream to four tablespoonsful of yeast; mix all together into a paste, but not too stiff; cover it over, and set it before the fire an hour to rise, then make it into buns, put them on a tin, set them before the fire for a quarter of an hour, cover over with flannel, then brush them with very warm milk, and bake them of a nice brown in a moderate oven.

Citron Buns.

Take of carbonate of soda and muriatic acid three drachms each; flour one pound; butter and loaf sugar a quarter of a pound each; one egg; candied green citron peel cut into dice, six ounces; mix all thoroughly together with enough milk to moisten with, and bake it in the shape of luncheon buns; the tops being glazed with white of egg, arrange some nice pieces of green citron peel upon them.

New York Rusks.

Beat up seven eggs, mix them with half a pint of warm new milk, in which a quarter of a pound of butter has been melted, add a quarter of a pint of yeast, and three ounces of sugar; put them gradually into as much flour as will make a light paste nearly as thin as batter; let it rise before the fire half an hour, add more flour to make it a little stiffer, work it well, and divide it into small loaves, or cakes, about five or six inches wide, and flatten them. When baked and cold, put them into the oven to brown a little. These cakes, when first baked, are very good buttered for tea; if they are made with caraway seeds, they eat very nice cold.

Italian Rusks.

A stale Savoy or lemon-cake may be converted into a very good rusk in the following manner. Cut the cake into slices, divide each slice in two; put them on a baking-sheet, in a slow oven, and when they are of a nice brown and quite hard, they are done. They should be kept in a closed tin canister in a dry place, to preserve their crispness.

Muffins.

One quart of milk, one cup of yeast, nine cups of flour, butter the size of a walnut, and four eggs. Make a batter with the milk, butter, yeast, and flour; beat the eggs and stir in; set in a warm place, and let it rise four hours, and then bake in buttered muffin rings, or fry on the griddle in rings.

Corn Meal Muffins.

Take one quart of coarse ground and sifted Indian meal, two spoonsful of sweet cream, one quart of milk, one spoonful of molasses, and half a teacupful of hop or potato-yeast. Make into a thin dough; let it rise four or five hours; bake one hour in muffin rings, or in shallow pans.

Wheat meal will make excellent muffins managed in the same way.

Yankee Muffins.

One pint of milk, one cup of sugar, five cups of flour, one teaspoonful of saleratus, two of cream of tartar, two eggs, and butter the size of an egg. Beat the butter and sugar together, and then add the eggs well beaten; with this mix the milk, and then beat in the flour in which the saleratus and cream of tartar have been mixed. Bake in buttered muffin rings in a quick oven.

Toast Muffins.

Pull open the sides of the muffin exactly in the centre, about half an inch in; put the toasting-fork in it and toast it carefully. When it is done, and it should only be *lightly* toasted, pull it apart, lay a little butter on each side, and close the muffin. Put it on a hot plate and cut it in four. If more than one are required, lay them on the first done, but do not send in a great pile of muffins, as they are better served *hot*. A hot-water plate with a cover—a regular muffin plate—should be used, and *two* at the most only be sent in at a time.

"My Own" Muffins.

One quart of milk, five eggs, one tablespoonful of good yeast, if home-made three or four; a lump of butter the size of a walnut, and sufficient flour to form a stiff batter. Set it in a warm place to rise, and when light bake in muffin-rings.

Buckwheat Cakes.

Put a large spoonful of yeast and a little salt into a quart of buckwheat meal; make it into a batter with cold water;

let it rise well, and bake it on a griddle—it turns sour very quickly if it be allowed to stand any time after it has risen.

Buckwheat Shortcake.

Take three or four cups of nice sour milk; one teaspoonful of soda saleratus dissolved in the milk; if the milk is very sour, you must use soda in proportion, with a little salt; mix up a dough with buckwheat flour, thicker than you would mix for griddle cakes, say quite stiff; put into a buttered tin and bake immediately, about thirty minutes.

Buckwheat Griddle Cakes.

Take five wooden spoonsful of buckwheat, three wooden spoonsful of Indian meal, and one of wheat flour, with a pinch of salt; mix into this not quite a penny's worth of yeast, with just sufficient luke-warm water to make it thin enough for use. Beat thoroughly, and leave the spoon in the pot while it rises. When ready to bake, take up the spoonful, but do not stir the batter.

Johnny Cakes.

One cup of flour, three cups of meal, one cup of molasses, two cups of sweet milk, one of sour milk, one teaspoonful of soda, and one of salt. Bake one hour in a sponge cake tin.

Flannel Cakes.

Put a tablespoonful of butter into a quart of milk, and warm them together till the butter has melted; then stir it well, and set it away to cool. Beat five eggs as light as possible, and set them into the milk in turn with half a pound of flour; add a small teaspoonful of salt, and a large tablespoonful and a half of the best fresh yeast. Set the pan of batter near the fire to rise; and if the yeast is good, it will be light in three hours. Then bake it on a griddle in the manner of buckwheat cakes.

Corn Dodgers.

Take one pint of Southern corn meal, and turn over it one pint of boiling water, add a little salt, and one egg well beaten up and stirred into the batter when nearly cold. Butter some sheets of tin, and drop your cakes by the tablespoonful all over the pan. Bake for twenty-five minutes in a hot oven.

Green Corn Cake.

Mix a pint of grated green corn with three tablespoonsful of milk, a teacup of flour, half a teacup of melted butter, one egg, a teaspoonful of salt, and half a teaspoonful of pepper. Drop this mixture into hot butter by the spoonful; let the cakes fry eight or ten minutes. These cakes are nice served up with meat for dinner.

Indian Corn Cake.

Stir into a quart of sour or butter-milk a couple of teaspoonsful of saleratus, a little salt, and sifted Indian meal to render it a thick batter—a little cream improves the cake—bake it in deep cake pans about an hour. When sour milk cannot be procured, boil sweet milk, and turn it on the Indian meal—when cool, put in three beaten eggs to a quart of the meal—add salt to the taste.

To Make Mush.

Put a lump of butter the size of an egg into a quart of water, make it sufficiently thick with corn meal and a little salt; it must be mixed perfectly smooth—stir it constantly till done enough. This may be eaten hot with milk, which makes a very palatable dish.

Fried Mush.

Cut your mush into slices an inch thick, and fry brown in pork fat. Serve slices of fried pork with it. You can cook enough at one time for several breakfasts. If you do not wish to fry the mush, do not use the flour, and do not make quite so stiff.

Pancakes and Fritters.

Pancakes should be eaten hot. They should be light enough to toss over in the pan. *Snow* will serve instead of eggs for pancakes. It should be taken when *just* fallen, and quite clean. Two tablespoonsful of snow will supply the place of one egg. Time to fry a pancake, five minutes.

Common Pancakes.

Three eggs, a pound of flour, and a pint of milk; put the milk to the flour by degrees; a little salt and grated ginger; fry them in lard, grate sugar over them.

Rice Pancakes.

Boil half a pound of rice to a jelly. When cold mix with it a pint of cream, two eggs, a little salt and nutmeg. Stir in four ounces of butter, just warmed, and add as much flour as will make batter thick enough. Fry in as little lard as possible.

London Pancakes.

The yolks of twelve eggs, four whites, beat them well; add one quart of milk, six spoonsful of flour, two of brandy, one nutmeg, half a pound of melted butter; a little salt; for the first pancake rub the pan with a piece of cold butter; fry them without anything else in the pan; they must be very thin, clap hot one upon another for about a dozen, and cut through when eaten.

French Pancakes with Preserves.

TIME, TWENTY MINUTES.

Three-quarters of a pint of good cream; five eggs; two dessertspoonsful of flour; two of pounded sugar; apricot or raspberry jam.

Whip three-quarters of a pint of cream to a froth, and strain it. Whisk the yolks and whites of five eggs separately, and stir them into the flour and sifted white sugar. Mix gradually with the frothed cream, and pour it into shallow tins; put them into a moderate oven for about twenty minutes; and when done, place one on the other with a layer of raspberry or apricot jam between them.

The peel of half a lemon grated is an improvement.

Oyster Fritters—American Receipt.

TIME, FIVE OR SIX MINUTES.

Open a quart of oysters, strain the liquor into a basin, and add to it a half a pint of milk, and two well-beaten eggs; stir in by degrees flour enough to make a smooth but rather thin batter; when perfectly free from lumps put the oysters into it. Have some beef dripping or butter made hot in a very clean frying-pan, and season with a little salt, and when it is boiling drop in the batter with a large spoon, putting one or more oysters in each spoonful. Hold the pan over a gentle fire until one side of the batter is a delicate brown, turn each fritter separately, and when both sides are done place them on a hot dish and serve.

Potato Fritters.
TIME, TEN MINUTES.

Two large or three small potatoes; four yolks, three whites of eggs; one tablespoonful of cream; a little nutmeg; a little lemon juice; and half a wineglass of raisin wine.

Boil and scrape very fine two large or three small mealy potatoes; well beat the yolks of four eggs and the whites of three, and add them to the potato with a spoonful of cream, the raisin wine, nutmeg, and a little lemon juice. Beat this well together for rather more than half an hour. Drop a spoonful at a time of the batter into a pan of boiling fat, and fry the fritters a light color, drain them, and serve on a napkin. A separate sauce may be served with these fritters made of a spoonful of loaf sugar, the juice of half a lemon, and a glass of sherry.

Plain Fritters.

Beat to a froth two eggs, and stir into this half a pint of milk, one teaspoonful of salt, two cups of flour; beat this lightly, and drop by teaspoonsful into boiling lard, and fry a light brown.

Apple Fritters.

Make the batter as for plain fritters. Pare and core nice tart apples; cut them in thin slices, dip them in the batter, and fry brown. Peaches, Oranges, Pineapples, and any kind of fruit may be used with this same batter.

American Waffles.

Mix flour and cold milk together, to make a thick batter. To a quart of the flour put six beaten eggs, a tablespoonful of melted butter, and a teaspoonful of salt. Some cooks add a quarter of a pound of sugar, and half a nutmeg. Bake them immediately.

Plain Waffles.

Take one quart of milk; five eggs; one and a quarter pounds of flour; half a pound of butter; one spoonful of yeast. When baked, sift sugar and powdered cassia on them.

Rice Waffles.

Take a teacup and a half of boiled rice—warm it with a pint of milk, mix it smooth, then take it from the fire, stir in a pint of cold milk, and a teaspoonful of salt. Beat four eggs, and stir them in, together with sufficient flour to make a thick batter.

Buttered Toast.

Beat to a froth one cup of butter and three tablespoonsful of flour; pour over this one pint and a half of *boiling* water; set this over a kettle of boiling water for ten minutes. Cut bread in slices half an inch thick: toast brown and dip into this. Serve very hot.

French Milk Toast.

Put one quart of milk in a tin pail or basin and set into a kettle of boiling water. When it comes to a boil stir in two spoonsful of flour, mixed with half a cup of milk, one spoonful of butter, and salt to taste; let this boil ten minutes, and then put in the bread, which must be toasted brown. Cook five minutes longer and serve.

Toast Sandwiches.

Thin cold toast, thin slices of bread and butter, pepper and salt to taste.

Place a very thin piece of cold toast between two slices of thin bread and butter in the form of a sandwich, adding a seasoning of pepper and salt. This sandwich may be varied by adding a little pulled meat, or very fine slices of cold meat, to the toast, and in any of these forms will be found very tempting to the appetite of an invalid.

Egg Toast.

TIME, FIVE MINUTES.

Four ounces of clarified butter; four eggs well beaten; one tablespoonful of anchovy paste; one round of toast.

Put the yolks of four eggs and the whites of two with four ounces of clarified butter; beat them well together, then stir it over the fire in the same direction till mixed. Make a round of thin delicate toast, spread anchovy paste over it, then put on the mixture with a fork. Cut the toast into pieces and serve very hot.

Ham Toast.

TIME, TWO MINUTES.

Slices of toasted bread; two eggs; one ounce of butter; some cold ham or tongue, grated.

Cut some thin slices from a stale loaf, toast them as for breakfast, and then cut them into square pieces. Put the yolks and whites of two beaten eggs into a stewpan with an ounce of butter; stir them two minutes over the fire; spread them over the toast, and lay over them a sufficient quantity of cold ham or tongue, grated or minced, to cover the eggs: serve it up very hot.

CAKES AND CAKE-MAKING.

AS in this branch of cookery everything depends upon the degree of care you take in the preparation of the ingredients employed, it entirely rests with yourself whether a cake prove a success or a failure. The following hints will be of benefit if properly observed:

Eggs should always be broken into a cup, the whites and yolks separated, and they should always be strained. Breaking the eggs thus, the bad ones may be easily rejected without spoiling the others, and so cause no waste. As eggs are used instead of yeast, they should be very thoroughly whisked; they are generally sufficiently beaten when thick enough to carry the drop that falls from the whisk.

> "Beat with a knife
> Will cause sorrow and strife;
> Beat with a spoon
> Will make heavy soon;
> Beat with a fork
> Will make light as a cork."

Loaf Sugar should be well pounded, and then sifted through a fine sieve.

Currants should be nicely washed, picked, dried in a cloth, and then carefully examined, that no pieces of grit or stone may be left amongst them. They should then be laid on a dish before the fire, to become thoroughly dry; as, if added damp to the other ingredients, cakes will be liable to be heavy.

Good butter should always be used in the manufacture of cakes: and if beaten to a cream, it saves much time and labor to warm, but not melt it before baking.

Less butter and eggs are required for cakes when yeast is mixed with the other ingredients.

The following receipts, the author of this work flatters herself, are some of the finest that can be found in any work on cookery in the country. They have all been practically used by her, and not one of them but she can vouch for as being perfect in the composition of their ingredients.

Pound Plum Cake.

To a pound each of butter, sugar, flour, and eggs mixed together in the usual way, add one pound of grocers' currants, previously washed, then thoroughly dried, and afterwards plumped in French brandy.

Pound Fruit Cake.

Add one pound of candied citron-peel to the ingredients constituting an ordinary pound cake; do not slice the peel too thin, and only put it with the other things just before the cake is put into the oven. Sift sugar over the top of the cake to glaze it.

A Plain Pound Cake.

Beat one pound of butter in an earthen pan until it is like a fine thick cream, then beat in nine whole eggs till quite light. Put in a glass of brandy, a little lemon-peel, shred fine, then work in a pound and a quarter of flour; put it into the hoop or pan, and bake it for an hour. A pound plum cake is made the same, with putting one pound and a half of clean washed currants, and half a pound of candied lemon-peel.

Cinnamon Cake.

Take half a pound of dried flour, half a pound of fresh butter, half a pound of sifted sugar, the whites of eight eggs beaten to a snow froth, and sufficient pounded and sifted cinnamon to flavor the cake rather strongly, and to give it a pinkish color; mix all well together very lightly, put it into a buttered mold, and bake in rather a quick oven about half an hour.

Cocoa-Nut Cakes.

Grate the nut (scraping off the rind) very fine, and add half its weight in finely pounded white sugar; mix them well together with white of egg, and drop on wafer paper in small rough knobs about the size of a walnut, and bake in a slack oven. Excellent for dessert.

Velvet Cakes.

Make a batter of one quart of flour, three eggs, a quart of milk, and a gill of yeast; when well risen, stir in a large spoonful of melted butter, and bake them in muffin hoops.

Almond Cake.

Take half a pound of sweet and two ounces of bitter almonds blanched and well pounded, half a pound of finely sifted loaf sugar, nine eggs, the whites of four; the eggs and sugar are to be well whisked together very fast for half an hour; then put in the pounded almonds, and continue beating the whole half an hour longer, when put into a tin mold lined with buttered paper, and bake an hour in a brisk oven.

Almond Garlands.

Blanch and bruise half a pound of sweet almonds, mix them with half a pound of sugar and the whites of four eggs; place this in thick rings on wafers, and bake them in a slow oven.

Queen Cakes.

Mix a pound of flour, the same of sifted sugar, and washed currants; beat up a pound of fresh butter well, then mix with it eight eggs, the yolks and whites beaten separately, and put in the other ingredients by degrees; beat the whole an hour; butter tins, fill them only half with the batter, sift a little sugar over them, and bake them.

Strawberry Cake.

Mix a quart of flour with a teaspoonful of salt, four beaten eggs, and a teacup of thick cream, or melted butter. Add sufficient milk to enable you to roll it out—roll it out thin, line a shallow cake pan with part of it, then put in a thick layer of nice ripe strawberries, strew on sufficient white sugar to sweeten the strawberries, cover them with a thin layer of the crust, then add another layer of strawberries and sugar—cover the whole with another layer of crust, and bake it in a quick oven about twenty-five minutes.

Good Sponge Cake.

Beat together the yolks of ten eggs, with a pound of powdered white sugar—beat to a stiff froth the whites of the eggs, and stir them into the yolks and sugar. Beat the whole ten or fifteen minutes, then stir in gradually three-quarters of a pound of sifted flour. Flavor it with a nutmeg, or the grated rind of a lemon. Bake it as soon as the flour and spices are well mixed in.

Washington Cake.

Stir together, till quite white, a pound of sugar, three-quarters of a pound of butter, then add four beaten eggs. Stir in gradually a pound and a half of flour. Dissolve a teaspoonful of saleratus in a teacup of milk, strain and mix it with a glass of wine, then stir it into the cake, together with a teaspoonful of rosewater, and half a nutmeg. Just before it is baked, add a pound of seeded raisins.

Webster Cakes.
TIME, A QUARTER OF AN HOUR, TO BAKE.

Mix a pound and a half of flour with a pound of white sugar sifted, rub into it a pound of butter, add ten well-beaten eggs, two spoonsful of wine or brandy, and half a pound of currants washed and dried. Beat the mixture until it is light and creamy. Put it half an inch deep in square tin pans lined with buttered paper, and bake it in a quick oven; or it may be baked in one tin, and iced over.

Small Venetian Cakes.

Half a pound of flour; five ounces of sweet almonds; two ounces of bitter almonds; yolks of two eggs; peel of one lemon; six ounces of butter; a quarter of a pound of sugar; a little orange-flower water; two ounces of white sugar-candy.

Blanch and pound the almonds with a little orange-flower water to a smooth paste. Mix it with the flour and the butter broken into small pieces. Rub the sugar on the peel of the lemon to extract the flavor; then pound it fine, and mix it with the flour and almonds. Bind the whole into a paste with the beaten yolks of the eggs, roll it into small balls, and press each with your hand to form a round cake about an inch thick.

Brush them over with egg, and strew *thickly* over them coarsely pounded white sugar-candy. Bake them in a slow oven.

Vienna Cake.

Take a large round sponge cake and cut it very carefully into thin slices; spread each with a layer of strawberry, raspberry, and apricot jam, and replace them in their original form; pound and sift five ounces of sugar, and whisk it with the whites of three or four eggs until it will bear the weight of a whole one; spread this over the cake; sift sugar over the whole, and put it in a cool oven to harden the icing.

Lemon Cakes.

Take one egg, a little flour, a small piece of butter, a little rose-water, the rind of a lemon grated off with lumps of sugar, till the paste is sweet enough; then mix all well together, and roll out as thin as possible on a marble slab; cut into round shapes with a tin cutter, and bake on a tin sheet in a quick oven. Serve them for dessert.

Apricot Cakes.

Scald and peel a pound of fine ripe apricots, take out the stones, and beat them in a mortar to a pulp. Boil half a pound of double-refined sugar with a spoonful of water, skim it well, then put in the apricot pulp, and simmer it over a slow fire for a quarter of an hour, stirring gently all the time. Then put it into shallow flat glasses, and when cold turn the cakes out on glass plates, put them in a cool oven, and turn them once a day till they are dry.

Cakes a la Polonaise.

Take some good puff paste, roll it a quarter of an inch thick, and cut it in pieces four or five inches square, gather up the four corners of each, have ready some round molds, dip them in warm water, and put them inside the cakes; then put them in a quick oven. When they are three parts done, take them out, and brush them over with the white of a beaten egg, sprinkle powdered sugar over, and finish baking. When done take out the molds; whip the white of an egg and powdered sugar to a froth, and fill the cakes with it.

Josephine Cake.
TIME, ONE HOUR.

Half a pound of butter; half a pound of brown sugar; five eggs; one pound of flour; half a pound of currants; one glass of white wine.

Beat half a pound of butter to a cream, then beat in the sugar, and the five eggs well beaten. Mix it gradually into a pound of flour, add half a pound of currants washed and dried, and a glass of white wine, and bake it, when well beaten together, in a buttered tin.

Rich Seed Cake.
TIME, ONE HOUR.

Half a pound of butter; half a pound of sugar; one pound of flour; six eggs; and some caraway seeds.

Beat half a pound of butter before the fire to a cream, then stir in the pounded sugar, and beat it together for some minutes; add the yolks of six, and the whites of three eggs, one at a time; then stir in gradually a pound of flour, and a few caraway seeds to taste. Bake it in a tin lined with a buttered paper in a moderate oven.

Rich Cream Cake.

Stir together, till very white, half a pound of butter, three-quarters of a pound of sugar. Beat the whites and yolks of seven eggs separately to a froth, stir them into the cake—put in a wine glass of brandy, a grated nutmeg, and a pound and a half of sifted flour. Just before it is baked, add half a pint of thick cream, and a pound of seeded raisins.

Drop Cakes.

One quart of milk, a large teaspoonful of saleratus, dissolved in a cup of cream; to which stir in flour very smoothly until a thick batter. Then dip your spoon in milk and with it place your batter at short distances in a buttered pan. Very delicate, made entirely of cream, either with or without eggs.

Honey Cakes.

Boil one pound of honey, then put it in a dish to cool; add three tablespoonsful of sugar, the yolks of ten eggs and the whites of five to the honey; beat it for half an hour; add half a pound of flour, and lastly the whites of five eggs, which beat up well; put it into a buttered mold, and heat in a hot oven; treacle may be used instead of honey.

Chocolate Cakes.

Half a pound of finely-sifted sugar, four whites of eggs beaten to a stiff froth, four ounces of chocolate; mix all together, and put it on a tin in pieces the size of a half dollar; bake it in a moderate oven.

Little White Cakes.

Dry half a pound of flour, rub into it a very little pounded sugar, one ounce of butter, one egg, and as much milk and water as will make a paste; roll it thin and cut it out in little rounds; bake fifteen minutes on tin.

Little Short Cakes.

Rub into a pound of dry flour four ounces of butter, four ounces of white sugar, one egg, and a spoonful or two of thin cream to make it into a paste; add some currants, roll it out thin, and cut it in rounds; bake twenty minutes.

Turkish Cakes.

Pound to a paste eight ounces of blanched sweet almonds, and a good pinch of saffron; add a pound of butter, three-quarters of a pound of loaf sugar in powder, and a pound of fine flour; beat all together; break in an egg at a time until the paste is of the proper consistency. Make it up in the form of a flat cake and bake it gently.

Raisin Cake.

Mix with one pound and a half of flour a pound of fresh butter, half a pound of loaf sugar, the grated rinds of two lemons, eight eggs, a gill of raisin wine, and a pound of Valencia raisins picked from the stalks and divested of stones; beat all well together till perfectly smooth, and bake quickly in rather a hot oven.

Ladies' Kisses.

Make a paste, as for biscuits, of six ounces of potato flour; beat this very well, spread it thinly on buttered paper, and bake for nearly twenty minutes; cut them out in small rounds, and glaze them with white or pink icing.

White Mountain Cake.

Half pound sugar, half pound flour, one-fourth pound of butter, three eggs, one small teaspoonful of baking powder, three tablespoonsful of water. Bake in jelly pans. Icing for the cake: three-fourths pound of sugar. Spread the icing on each layer of the cake while warm, sprinkle grated cocoanut on each layer over the icing.

Poor Man's Cake.

Six cups of flour, four teaspoonsful of cream of tartar, two of soda, two and a half cups of sugar, four eggs, one-quarter pound butter and lard (mixed or not, as you choose), one pint milk, a little salt, and flavor with lemon, vanilla, or nutmeg. Bake three-quarters of an hour, in two pans, or drop with spoon, adding a few currants to each cake, or in jelly-cake pans and spread.

Jumbles.

Stir together, till of a light color, a pound of sugar, and half the weight of butter—then add eight eggs, beaten to a froth, essence of lemon, or rosewater, to the taste, and flour to make them sufficiently stiff to roll out. Roll them out in powdered sugar, about half an inch thick, cut it into strips about half an inch wide, and four inches long, join the ends together, so as to form rings—lay them on flat tins that have been buttered—bake them in a quick oven.

Hard Molasses Gingerbread.

To a pint of molasses put half a teacup of melted butter, a tablespoonful of ginger, and a quart of flour. Dissolve a teaspoonful of saleratus in half a pint of water, and stir it in, together with flour sufficient to enable you to roll it out. Bake it in a moderately warm oven.

Soft Molasses Gingerbread.

Melt a teacup of butter—mix it with a pint of molasses, a tablespoonful of ginger, a pint of flour, and a couple of beaten eggs. Fresh lemon peel, cut into small strips, improves it. Dissolve a couple of teaspoonsful of saleratus in half a pint of milk, and stir it into the cake. Add flour to render it of the consistency of unbaked pound cake. Bake it in deep pans about half an hour.

Ginger Snaps.

Melt a quarter of a pound of butter, the same quantity of lard—mix them with a quarter of a pound of brown sugar, a pint of molasses, a couple of tablespoonsful of ginger, and a quart of flour. Dissolve a couple of teaspoonsful of saleratus in a wine glass of milk, and strain it into the cake—add sufficient flour to enable you to roll it out very thin, cut it into small cakes, and bake them in a slow oven.

Apple Cake.

Scald some codlin apples; take half a pint of their pulp, mix it with the juice of two lemons and half a pound of refined loaf sugar, beaten and sifted. Separately whisk to a high froth the yolks and whites of six eggs; mix these with the other ingredients; add some slips of candied lemon peel, and dredge in flour enough to make the composition rather stiffer than ordinary sponge cake. Bake it in a tolerably quick but not fierce oven.

Sugar Drops.

Stir to a cream three ounces of butter, six of powdered white sugar—then add three beaten eggs, half a pound of sifted flour, half of a nutmeg. Drop this mixture by the large spoonful on to buttered plates, several inches apart, sprinkle small sugar plums on the top, and bake them directly.

Frosting for Cake.

Allow for the white of one egg nine heaping teaspoonsful of double refined sugar, and one of nice Poland starch. The sugar and starch should be pounded, and sifted through a very fine sieve. Beat the whites of eggs to a stiff froth, so that you can turn the plate upside down, without the eggs falling from it—then stir in the sugar gradually, with a wooden spoon—stir it ten or fifteen minutes without any cessation—then add a teaspoonful of lemon juice, (vinegar will answer, but is not as nice)—put in sufficient rosewater to flavor it. If you wish to color it pink, stir in a few grains of cochineal powder, or rose pink—if you wish to have it of a blue tinge, add a little of what is called the powder blue. Lay the frosting on the cake with a knife, soon after it is taken from the oven—smooth it over and let it remain in a cool place till hard. To frost a common sized loaf of cake, allow the white of one egg, and half of another

Country Doughnuts.

Take of risen wheat bread dough the size of a quart bowl; work into it a teacup of butter, two teacups of clean brown sugar, rolled fine, half a nutmeg, grated, a teaspoonful of ground cinnamon, and two eggs; work it to a smooth paste; strew some flour over a paste table and rolling-pin; put on some of the paste, and roll it to a quarter of an inch thickness; rub more flour over the rolling-pin, if the paste sticks; cut it in small squares, stars, or diamonds; fry in hot fat.

Superior Doughnuts.

Take a pound of flour, a quarter of a pound of butter, three-quarters of a pound of clean brown sugar, rolled fine, one nutmeg, grated, and a teaspoonful of ground cinnamon; mix these well together; then add a tablespoonful of baker's yeast, with as much warm milk, with saleratus the size of a pea dissolved in it, as will make a smooth dough; knead it for a few minutes, cover it, and set it in a warm place to rise, for three hours or more, until it is light; then roll it out to a quarter of an inch thickness; cut it in small quares or diamonds, and fry as directed.

Excellent Crullers.

Take half a pint of sour milk or buttermilk, one teacup of butter, two teacups of sugar, three well-beaten eggs, and a small teaspoonful of powdered saleratus dissolved in a little hot water; add a teaspoonful of salt, half a nutmeg, grated, and a teaspoonful of ground cinnamon; work in as much sifted wheat flour as will make a smooth dough; work it well together; roll the cakes to twice the thickness of a dollar piece; cut it in pieces two inches square; cut it in fingers, twist each a little, and join the ends together, and fry as before directed. These cakes may be cut in rings, stars, baskets, or any other fancy shapes.

PIES AND PASTRY.

Directions for Baking and Making Pies, Tarts, &c.

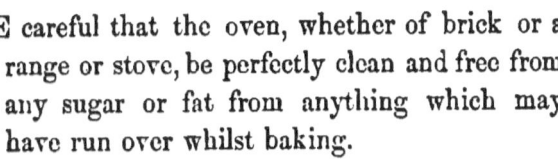

BE careful that the oven, whether of brick or a range or stove, be perfectly clean and free from any sugar or fat from anything which may have run over whilst baking.

The delicacy of pastry depends as much upon the baking as the making, therefore strict attention should be paid to the following directions:

Puff paste requires a quick oven heat; a hot oven would curl the paste and scorch it.

Tart paste or short paste requires a degree less of heat.

For raised or light crust, the oven may be heated as for puff paste.

A brick oven must be thoroughly heated, that is, have a body of heat, else it will render pastry or cakes heavy; this must be attended to before beginning to bake; there may be sufficient heat to raise, and yet not enough to finish baking.

When baking with coal, if the fire is not brisk enough, do not put on more coal, but add a stick or two of hard wood, or if nearly done, put in a stick of pine wood.

COMMON PUFF PASTE, *for Pies.*—Put one pound of sifted wheat flour on the slab, or into an earthen basin; make a hollow in the centre, work into it quarter of a pound of lard, and a teaspoonful of salt; when it is mixed through the flour, add as much cold water as will bind it together; then strew a little flour over the paste-board, or table; flour the rolling-pin, and roll out the paste to half an inch thickness; divide half a pound of butter in three parts; spread one evenly over the paste; fold it up, dredge a little flour over it, and the paste-slab, or table; roll it out again, spread another portion of the butter over, and fold, and roll again; so continue until all the butter is used; roll it out to quarter of an inch thickness for pies.

Green Currant Pie.

Currants will make good and wholesome pies at nearly all stages of their growth. They only require to be stewed, and sweetened according to their degree of acidity, and baked between two crusts in the ordinary manner. The addition of a little dried or green apple gives a fine flavor.

Gooseberry Pie.

This is made in the same way as the preceding, but requires a larger proportion of sugar. The berries should be nearly or quite full grown. A little apple may be used if preferred.

Rhubarb Pie.

Take the tender stalks of the rhubarb, strip off the skin, and cut the stalks into thin slices. Line deep plates with pie crust, then put in the rhubarb, with a thick layer of sugar to each layer of rhubarb—a little grated lemon peel improves the pie. Cover the pies with a thick crust—press it down tight round the edge of the plate, and prick the crust with a fork, so that the crust will not burst while baking, and let out the juices of the pie. Rhubarb pies should be baked about an hour, in a slow oven—it will not do to bake them quick. Some cooks stew the rhubarb before making it into pies, but it is not so good as when used without stewing.

Tomato Pie.

Take green tomatoes, turn boiling water on them, and let them remain in it a few minutes—then strip off the skin, cut the tomatoes in slices, and put them in deep pie plates. Sprinkle sugar over each layer, and a little ginger. Grated lemon peel, and the juice of a lemon improve the pie. Cover the pies with a thick crust, and bake them slowly for about an hour.

Lemon Pie.

For one pie, take a couple of good sized fresh lemons, squeeze out the juice, and mix it with half a pint of molasses, or sufficient sugar to make the juice sweet. Chop the peel fine, line a deep pie plate with your pastry, then sprinkle on a layer of your chopped lemon peel, turn in part of the mixed sugar or molasses, and juice, then cover the whole with pie crust, rolled very thin—put in another layer of peel, sweetened juice, and crust, and so on, till all the lemon is used. Cover the whole with a thick crust, and bake the pie about half an hour.

Cherry and Blackberry Pie.

Cherries and blackberries for pies should be ripe. Bake them in deep pie plates, sweeten them with sugar, and put in cloves or cinnamon to the taste. Bake them about half an hour.

Grape Pie.

Grapes make the best pies when very tender and green. If not very small, they should be stewed and strained, to get out the seeds, before they are made into pies—sweeten them to the taste when stewed. They do not require any spice.

If made into a pie without stewing, put to each layer of grapes a thick layer of sugar, and a tablespoonful of water.

Currant and Gooseberry Pie.

Currants and gooseberries are the best for pies when of a full growth, just before they begin to turn red—they are tolerably good when ripe. Currants mixed with ripe raspberries or mulberries, make very nice pies. Green currants and gooseberries for pies are not apt to be sweet enough without the sugar is scalded in before they are baked, as the juice of the currants is apt to run out while they are baking, and leave the fruit dry. Stew them on a moderate fire, with a teacup of water to a couple of quarts of currants—as soon as they begin to break, add the sugar, and let it scald in a few minutes. When baked without stewing, put to each layer of fruit a thick layer of sugar. There should be as much as a quarter of a pound of sugar to a pint of currants, to make them sufficiently sweet. Green currant pies are good sweetened with molasses and sugar mixed.

Prune Pie.

Prunes that are too dry to eat without stewing, can be made into good pies. Turn enough boiling water on the prunes to cover them, set them on a few coals, and let them remain till swelled out plump. If there is not water sufficient to make a nice syrup for the pies, add more, and season them with cinnamon or cloves. The juice and grated peel of a lemon gives them a fine flavor. Add sugar to the taste, and bake them in deep pie plates.

Whortleberry Pie.

Put a quart of picked huckleberries into a basin of water, take off whatever floats, take up the berries by the handful, pick out all the stems and unripe berries, and put them into a dish; line a buttered pie dish with a pie paste, put in the berries half an inch deep, and to a quart of berries put a teacup of brown sugar, and half a teacup of water; dredge a teaspoonful of flour over, strew a saltspoonful of salt, and half a nutmeg grated over; cover the pie, cut a slit in the centre, or make several small incisions on either side of it, press the two crusts together around the edge, trim it off neatly with a sharp knife, and bake in a quick oven for three-quarters of an hour.

Peach Pie.

Take juicy and mellow peaches; peel, stone, and slice them; then put them in a deep pie plate lined with the under crust; sprinkle through them a sufficient quantity of sugar, equally distributed; put in about a tablespoonful of water; dust a little flour over the top; cover with a rather thick crust, and bake nearly an hour.

Peach Pot-pie.

Put your crust into a pot, fill with peaches and cover them with sugar-house molasses, put a crust on the top, and let it boil until the peaches are done. Plums, apples, and berries of all kinds, may be made the same way.

Dried Peach Pie.

Select clean and medium tart peaches; stew until soft; sweeten with sugar, and flavor with cinnamon. Place the peaches half an inch thick between the crusts, and bake a nice brown.

Green Apple Pie.

Peel and core moderately tart and ripe apples—pippins, russets, and greenings are excellent; cut them into very thin slices; fill the under crust; then sprinkle over them brown sugar, or pour over molasses to sweeten sufficiently; lay over the upper crust; and bake them in a moderate oven about forty minutes.

Dried Apple Pie.

Select clean and rich flavored fruit, and that which is not very sour; stew until soft; sweeten with brown sugar or molasses; place the apples half an inch thick between the crusts, and bake them about half an hour.

Scotch Apple Pie.

Take a dozen good baking apples; peel, core, and cut them up small; put an edge of crust to a pie dish; throw in some sugar at the bottom, then put in your apples, and lay half a pot of Scotch marmalade on the top; cover with a lid of crust, and bake for an hour.

Pumpkin Pie.

Peel your pumpkin, take away the seeds, then cut it into small pieces, and put it into a saucepan with a tablespoonful of water or cider at the bottom; when tender, mash it very smooth, and while warm, stir in a quarter of a pound of fresh butter, the yolks of eight eggs well beaten, some nutmeg, half an ounce of grated ginger, sugar to taste, and enough cream to lighten it. Bake it in a dish lined with a paste, and cover it with a top crust. An hour and a half will do it.

Plum Pie.

Make a rich crust, put in one pound of sugar to two pounds of plums, and a little molasses—it must be well baked.

Cherry Pie.

A rich crust. The cherries must be well sweetened, and the pie well baked.

Apple and Quince Pie.

Peel twelve apples and two quinces, stew and sweeten them; bake in a rich crust.

Orange or Lemon Pie.

Rub six oranges or lemons with salt, and put them into water, with a handful of salt, for two days. Put every day fresh water without salt for a fortnight. Boil them tender, cut them in half quarters, corner ways, quite thin; boil six pippins, pared, cored, and quartered, in a pint of water till they break, then put the liquor to the oranges or lemons, with half the pulp of the pippins well broken, and a pound of sugar; boil them a quarter of an hour, then put them into a pot and squeeze in two spoonsful of the juice of either orange or lemon, according to the kind of tart; put puff paste, very thin, into shallow patty-pans. Take a brush, and rub them over with melted butter, sift double refined sugar over them, which will form a pretty icing, and bake them,

Codlin Pie.

Put some small codlins into a glazed saucepan, lay vine-leaves over them, and add enough water to cover them: place them by the side of a very slow fire; keep the steam from escaping, and when they are nicely greened, take them out, arrange them in a dish with plenty of powdered loaf sugar; put a rim of paste round the dish and a top of light crust. Bake for an hour. Either serve with a custard apart, or when done, lift the crust and pour a custard over the fruit.

Mince Pie.

Rub and pick clean seven pounds of currants, and three pounds and a-half of beef suet chopped fine, three pounds and a-half of the lean of a sirloin of beef minced raw, three pounds and a-half of apples, chopped fine (which should be the pippin), half a pound of citron cut in small pieces, half a pound of lemon peel, half a pound of orange peel, two pounds of fine moist sugar, one ounce of spice (such as cloves, mace, nutmegs, and cinnamon, pounded together, and sifted), the rind of four lemons, and four Seville oranges; rub all this together till well mixed, then put it into a deep pan; mix one bottle of brandy, and the juice of the lemons and oranges that have been grated, together in a basin; pour half over, and press it down tight with your hand, then add the other half, and let it remain at the top to soak in by degrees; cover up close. It should be made six weeks before wanted; the pans must be sheeted with puff paste, and covered with the same. About ten minutes will bake them.

Lent Minced Pie.

Take the yolks and whites of four hard-boiled eggs; shred them fine; add to them three or four apples pared, cored, and chopped small, half a pound each of dried currants and raisins stoned and cut up, two ounces of sugar, a quarter of a pound of mixed candied-peel, and the juice of two Seville oranges. Stir the whole well together; line a dish with a puff paste, lay in your mince, cover it with a top-crust, and bake for three-quarters of an hour in a gentle oven. If preferred, you can make it into small pies, and bake them for twenty minutes.

Lemon Mince Pie.

Squeeze a lemon, boil the outside till tender enough to beat to a mash, add to it three apples chopped, four ounces of suet, half a pound or currants, four ounces of sugar; put the juice of a lemon, and candied fruit, as for other pies. Make a short crust and fill the patty-pans.

Yankee Mince Pie.

Two pounds of meat, one pound of suet, half a peck of apples, one pound raisins, one pound currants, four ounces citron, two nutmegs, four spoonsful ground cinnamon, two dozen ground cloves, the juice of two lemons, the rinds of two grated, a little ground allspice, sugar to the taste, moisten with yankee rum, enough to suit the taste.

Raisin Pie.

For six good sized pies take one pound of seedless raisins, stew until soft, sweeten with about half a pound of sugar, thicken with a little flour and place between rich crusts, and bake half an hour.

Cheese Cakes.

TIME, FIFTEEN TO TWENTY MINUTES.

Beat half a pint of good curd with four eggs, three spoonsful of rich cream, a quarter of a nutmeg grated, a spoonful of ratafia, and a quarter of a pound of currants washed and dried. Mix all well together, and bake in patty-pans lined with a good puff paste.

Apple Cheese Cakes.

TIME, FIFTEEN TO TWENTY MINUTES.

Pare and core twelve large apples, and boil them as for apple sauce, with a small quantity of water. Mash them very smooth, and stir in the juice of two lemons and the peel grated, the yolks of five or six eggs, and four ounces of butter beaten to a cream, sweeten to your taste with pounded loaf sugar, and bake them in patty-pans lined with a rich puff paste.

Lemon Cheese Cakes.

TIME, FIFTEEN TO TWENTY MINUTES.

A quarter of a pound of warmed butter; peel of two lemons, juice of one; a quarter of a pound of loaf sugar; a few almonds; puff paste.

Just warm the butter; stir into it the sugar pounded fine, and when dissolved, mix with it the peel of two lemons grated, and the juice of one strained. Mix all well together, and pour it into patty-pans, lined with puff paste. Put a few blanched almonds on the top of each.

Almond Cheese Cakes.

TIME, FIFTEEN TO TWENTY MINUTES.

A quarter of a pound of sweet almonds; six bitter almonds; one spoonful of water; a quarter of a pound of loaf sugar; one spoonful of cream; whites of two eggs; puff paste.

Blanch and pound the sweet and bitter almonds with a spoonful of water; then add a quarter of a pound of sugar pounded, a spoonful of cream, and the whites of two eggs, well beaten. Mix all as quick as possible, put it into very small patty-pans lined with puff paste, and bake in a warm oven nearly twenty minutes.

Cream Puffs.

Two ounces of finely pounded sweet almonds, the same of clarified butter and sifted sugar, two spoonsful of flour, the yolks of two eggs, half a pint of cream, and a very little orange jelly; beat all well together; butter the pans, fill them only half full, and bake for half an hour in a slow oven.

French Puffs.

Roll out puff paste of nearly half an inch thick, cut it into pieces of five inches wide, to have when doubled the form of squares or triangles; place some raspberry jam on each, then double them up and pinch them close to the edges, and bake them.

Rich Custards.

Boil a pint of milk with lemon peel and cinnamon; mix a pint of cream, and the yolks of five eggs well beaten; when the milk tastes of the seasoning, sweeten it enough for the whole; pour it into the cream, stirring it well; then give the custard a simmer till of a proper thickness. Do not let it boil; stir the whole time one way; season as above. If to be extremely rich, put no milk, but a quart of cream to the eggs.

Baked Custard.

Boil one pint of cream and half a pint of milk, with mace, cinnamon, and lemon peel, a little of each. When cold, mix the yolks of three eggs; sweeten and make your cups or paste nearly full. Bake them ten minutes.

Lemon Custards.

Beat the yolks of eight eggs till they are as white as milk; then put to them a pint of boiling water, the rinds of two lemons grated, and the juice sweetened to your taste. Stir it on the fire till thick enough; then add a large glass of rich wine, and half a glass of brandy; give the whole one scald, and put in the cups, to be eaten cold.

Mottled Custards.

Stir into a quart of milk, while boiling, the beaten yolks of six eggs. Beat the whites of the eggs with three tablespoonsful of powdered white sugar, if the custards are liked very sweet—if not, a less quantity will answer. Stir in the whites of the eggs a minute after the yolks have set, so as to be thick. Season the custard with essence of lemon or rosewater—stir it till it becomes thick and lumpy, then turn it into cups.

Cream Custards.

Sweeten a pint of cream with powdered white sugar—set it on a few coals. When hot, stir in white wine until it curdles—add rosewater or essence of lemon to the taste, and turn it into cups. Another way of making them, which is very nice, is to mix a pint of cream with one of milk, five beaten eggs, a tablespoonful of flour, and three of sugar. Add nutmeg to the taste, and bake the custards in cups or pie plates in a quick oven.

Almond Custards.

Blanch and pound fine, with a tablespoonful of rosewater, four ounces of almonds. Boil them four or five minutes in a quart of milk, with sufficient white sugar to sweeten the milk. Take it from the fire, and when lukewarm, stir in the beaten yolks of eight, and the whites of four eggs. Set the whole on the fire, and stir it constantly until it thickens—then take it up, stir it till partly cooled, and turn it into cups. If you wish to have the custards cool quick, set the cups into a pan of cold water—as fast as it gets warm, change it. Just before the custards are to be eaten, beat the reserved whites of the eggs to a froth, and cover the top of the custards with them.

French Raspberry Tart.

Choose a pint of very fine ripe raspberries, either red or white; stem them, and throw them into a boiling syrup, made with a quarter of a pound of loaf-sugar and a tablespoonful of water; withdraw them immediately from the fire; line a tart-dish with a puff paste rolled as thinly as possible; lay in the fruit and syrup, observing to keep the raspberries as whole as possible; put it into a quick oven for twenty minutes; strew more sugar over it, and glaze it; or, if to be served cold, pour raw cream over it.

Strawberry Tart.

Stew the fruit until soft; sweeten with brown sugar, about six ounces to a pound of the fruit, and bake moderately on a single crust.

Cranberry Tart.

Wash the berries in a pan of water, rejecting all the bad ones; simmer them until they become soft and burst open; sweeten with half a pound of sugar to a pound of the fruit; place it again over the fire till it comes to the boiling point; then place it on a thick under crust, and bake in a moderate oven.

Black Currant Tart.

Lightly stem and top the currants, being careful not to bruise them; put them into a tart-dish with a rim of paste, and, as they are considered to be too rich by themselves, it is advisable to add a little white currant juice or cider to dilute their flavor; throw in a good deal of sugar, cover them with a top crust, and bake rather more than an hour.

Apple Tart.

Peel and slice some nice tart apples and stew them with a small teacup of water, and the same of sugar, to a quart of sliced apples; add half a nutmeg grated, a saltspoonful of salt, and a little grated lemon peel or lemon extract, or half a teaspoonful of ground cinnamon, set them to become cold; line some small pie-plates with rich pie paste or light puff paste, put in the stewed apples, half an inch deep, roll out some of the paste, wet it over slightly with the yolk of an egg beaten with a little milk and a teaspoonful of sugar, cut it in strips the width of a finger, and lay it in bars or diamonds across the tart, lay another strip around the edge, trim off the outside neatly with a sharp knife, and bake in a quick oven until the paste loosens from the dish.

Plum Tart.

Three-quarters of a pound of good short crust, one and a half pints of plums, one-quarter pound of moist sugar.

Line the edge of a deep tart-dish with crust; fill the dish with plums, and place a small cup or jar, upside down, in the midst of them. Put in the sugar, cover the pie with crust, ornament the edges, and bake in a good oven from a half to three-quarters of an hour.

Floating Island.

Put four quarts of cream or milk in your glass, sweeten and add rosewater and grated lemon peel, to your taste, beat the whites of twenty eggs until stiff, color it with currant or quince jelly, beating all the time, until it will stand alone, then put it with a tablespoon on top of the milk. To be eaten immediately.

Meat and Vegetable Pie.

Take either cold beef, veal, or mutton, mince it very fine, and mix it with some bread crumbs; have a dish covered with paste, put some mince at the bottom, then put in a few bearded oysters, next the limbs of chicken, turkey, or rabbit boned;

then put a layer of peas or spinach, some force-meat balls, and a few small mushrooms, pour in some rich gravy, thicken with cream and flour; strew it over thickly with bread crumbs, and at the top an egg beat well; then bake in the oven.

Rabbit or Hare Pie.

Cut into pieces, season with pepper, salt, nutmeg, and mace; put it into a jug, with half a pound of butter, close it up, set it in a copper of boiling water, and make a force-meat, with a quarter of a pound of scraped bacon, two onions, a glass of red wine, crumbs of bread, winter savory, the liver cut small, and nutmeg. Season high with pepper and salt; mix it well up with the yolks of three eggs, raise the pie, and lay the force-meat in the bottom of the dish. Then put in the rabbit or hare, with the gravy that came out of it; lay on the lid, and send it to the oven. An hour and a half will bake it.

Pigeon or Game Pie.

Line the sides of a dish with paste, and put at the bottom either a beef steak or veal cutlet, dredge with flour; clean six young pigeons very nicely, pound a little of the white part of chicken, veal, or turkey very fine; mix four hard boiled yolks of eggs with it, and a little butter; roll the force-meat in flour and stuff the pigeons with it; place them in the dish with their breasts down.

Oyster Pie.

Line a tin plate with plain paste, and then put in two dozen oysters, sprinkle with a little pepper, salt, and grate on a little nutmeg. Strew in a little butter, and cover with a rich paste. Bake twenty minutes, and serve immediately. 'Chicken or game cut up and mixed in will improve this pie greatly.

Turkey Patties.

Mince some of the white part of cold turkey, mix with it a little salt and a very little cream or butter; have pattypans covered with light paste, fill them and bake them. The meat of cold fowl or game may be used in the same way.

To Glaze Pastry.

To glaze pastry, which is the usual method adopted for meat or raised pies, break an egg, separate the yolk from the white, and beat the former for a short time. Then, when the pastry is nearly baked, take it out of the oven, brush it over with this beaten yolk of egg, and put it back in the oven to set the glaze.

Oxford Dumplings.

Take eight ounces of biscuit or crackers that is pounded fine, and soak it in just sufficient milk to cover it. When soft, stir in three beaten eggs, a tablespoonful of flour, and a quarter of a pound of currants. Grate in half a nutmeg, and do up the mixture into balls of the size of an egg—fry them till a light brown.

Apple Dumplings.

Pare tart, mellow apples—take out the cores with a small knife, and fill the holes with sugar. Make good pie crust—roll it out about two-thirds of an inch thick, put it into pieces just large enough to enclose one apple. Lay the apples on them, and close the crust tight over them—tie them up in small pieces of thick cloth, that has been well floured—put the dumplings in a pot of boiling water, and boil them an hour without any intermission—if allowed to stop boiling, they will be heavy. Serve them up with pudding sauce, or butter and sugar.

Baked Apple Dumplings.

One pound of flour, four ounces of chopped suet, half a pint of water, a pinch of salt, eight or ten large apples peeled. With the above ingredients prepare some suet paste; divide the paste into about eight equal parts, first make these into balls with the hand, and then roll them out with a rolling-pin to the size of a large saucer, envelope an apple in each flat of paste, and, wetting the edges with water, gather them round in a purse-like form, and twist the ends tightly together to fasten them securely. The dumplings, thus formed, must be placed on the twisted end, at equal distances of three inches apart from each other, upon a tin baking-dish, and baked in the oven for about three-quarters of an hour.

Peach Dumplings.

Pare and stone some fine large peaches, and follow directions the same as for apple dumplings.

Raspberry Dumplings.

Make a good cold paste, roll it a quarter of an inch thick, and spread over it raspberry jam to your own liking, roll it up, and boil it in a cloth one hour at least, take it up and cut it in five slices, and lay one in the middle and the other four round it, pour a little good melted butter in the dish, and grate fine sugar round the edge of the dish.

PUDDINGS.

HOUSEWIVES generally vie with each other in the production of puddings. I therefore offer for their assistance a selection of the very best American, English, and French receipts that can be obtained.

Plum Pudding.
TIME, THREE HOURS.

Six ounces of raisins; six ounces of currants; six ounces of bread crumbs; six ounces of suet; half a nutmeg; a little lemon peel; five eggs; half a wineglass of brandy.

Mix these ingredients together, and put the pudding into a mold and boil it.

Fruit Pudding.
CAN BE MADE WITH ANY KIND OF FRUIT.

This pudding may either be made of apples pared and cut in pieces, green unripe gooseberries, currants, cherries, damsons, or blackberries. The paste generally used for this pudding is made with beef suet finely chopped, and flour, in the proportion of four ounces of suet to a pound of flour; mix it into a dough with water and a little salt, then knead it and roll it out; place the fruit in it, gather up the edges and tie it in a cloth, or put it in a mold with paste at the top, and tie it in a cloth and boil it.

Victoria Batter Pudding.

Six eggs; six tablespoonsful of flour; one quart of milk.

Beat six eggs with the flour until very light, then stir it into a quart of milk, beat them well together; butter a dish and put in the mixture; bake it an hour in a hot or quick oven. Serve with brandy or sweet sauce, or, instead of brandy or wine, lemon juice may be used.

This pudding may be tied in a cloth or put into a basin, and boiled two hours.

Ragon's Cream Custard Pudding.
TIME, THREE-QUARTERS OF AN HOUR.

Six eggs; one quart of cream; half a nutmeg; sugar to your taste; a teaspoonful of vanilla.

Beat the eggs very light, stir them into the cream, sweeten it to your taste, and add the nutmeg and vanilla. Bake it one hour in a quick oven in a dish, with or without a bottom crust.

Cup Puddings.
TIME TO BAKE, TWENTY MINUTES.

Three ounces of flour; three ounces of butter; two ounces of sugar; half a pint of milk.

Beat the butter to a cream, add to it the sugar pounded, stir in the flour, and mix it with a pint of milk. Put the mixture into buttered cups, and bake them.

A Yorkshire Pudding.

Four ounces of grated bread, four ounces of currants, four ounces of apples, two ounces of sugar, three eggs, a few drops of essence of lemon, a little grated nutmeg.

Pare, core, and mince the apples very finely, sufficient, when minced, to make four ounces; add to these the currants, which should be well washed, the grated bread, and sugar; whisk the eggs, beat these up with the remaining ingredients, and, when all is thorougly mixed, put the pudding into a buttered basin, tie it down with a cloth, and boil for three hours.

Bread Pudding.

TIME, ONE HOUR, OR MORE.

Take a pint of bread crumbs; put them into a stew-pan with as much milk as will cover them; add the peel of a lemon grated, and a little nutmeg and cinnamon. Boil it for ten minutes, and then sweeten it to your taste. Take out the cinnamon, and stir in the well-beaten eggs. Beat all well together, and bake it for one hour. If boiled, it will require rather more than the hour.

Plain Rice Pudding.

TIME, ONE HOUR.

Beat three eggs light, and stir them into a quart of milk, with a little salt, and a wineglass of rice well washed; put to it two tablespoonsful of sugar, half a nutmeg grated, and a tablespoonful of butter. Bake one hour in a quick oven.

American Christmas Pudding.

Two pounds each of stoned raisins and cleaned currants, one pound each of chopped apple and French prunes, one pound each of bread crumbs and moist sugar, two pounds of suet, some beaten nutmeg, mace, and cloves, a little salt, the juice of three lemons, eight beaten eggs, and sufficient white wine to make it a very stiff batter. Boil in a cloth for eight hours.

Plain Suet Pudding.

TIME, TWO HOURS AND A HALF TO THREE HOURS.

One pound of flour; four ounces of beef suet; a pinch or two of salt; half a pint of water.

Chop the suet very fine, and mix it with the flour, and a pinch or two of salt, and work the whole into a smooth paste with about half a pint of water. Tie the pudding in a cloth, the shape of a bolster, and when done, cut it in slices and put butter between each slice. Or boil it in a buttered basin, turn it out when done, and serve it whole and without butter.

One or two beaten eggs added to the above, with a less quantity of water may be used.

Tapioca Pudding.

TIME, ONE HOUR TO BAKE.

One quart of new milk; three ounces of tapioca; an ounce and a half of butter; four eggs; grated lemon peel, or any other flavoring; three ounces of sugar; puff paste.

Put the tapioca into a stewpan with a quart of milk, and let it simmer by the side of the fire for nearly twenty minutes, stirring it frequently to prevent its burning, turn it out to cool, and then stir into it the sugar, the flavoring, and the eggs well-beaten. Bake it in a well buttered pie-dish with a puff paste round the edge, or without, as you may prefer. One hour will bake it in a moderate oven.

Cocoanut Pudding.

Grate a small fresh cocoanut; work together a quarter of a pound of powdered loaf sugar and butter until they froth; gradually stir into a pint of cream six beaten eggs; mix all the ingredients together; bake the pudding with or without the addition of a light crust in the dish; sift powdered sugar over it when served.

Baked Apple Pudding.

Pare and quarter four large apples; boil them tender, with the rind of a lemon, in so little water that, when done, none may remain; beat them quite fine in a mortar, and add the crumb of a small roll, four ounces of butter melted, the yolks of five and whites of three eggs, juice of half a lemon, and sugar to taste; beat all together, and lay it in a dish with paste to turn out.

Winter Pudding.

Take the crust of a baker's loaf of bread, and fill it with plums; boil it in milk and water.

A Swiss Pudding.

Put layers of bread crumbs and sliced apples, with sugar, till the dish is filled; let the last layer be of crumbs; pour some melted butter over it, and bake it.

JELLIES AND JAMS.

Strawberry, Raspberry, and Blackberry Jelly.

JELLIES of these fruits are all made in the following manner: Take the berries when ripe, and in their prime, mash them, and let them drain through a flannel bag, without squeezing it. To each pint of juice, put a pound of white sugar, and the beaten white of an egg to three pounds of the sugar. Set it on the fire—when it boils up well, take it from the fire and skim it clear. Set it back on the fire—if any more scum rises, take it from the fire and skim it off. Boil it till it becomes a jelly, which is ascertained by taking a little of it up into a tumbler of cold water. If it falls to the bottom in a solid mass, it is sufficiently boiled.

Cranberry, Grape, and Currant Jelly.

They are all made in the same manner. Take the fruit in its prime, wash and drain it till nearly dry, then put it in an earthen jar, or pot, and set the pot in a kettle of hot water. Set the kettle where the water will boil, taking care that none of it gets into the jar. When the fruit breaks, turn it into a flannel bag, and let it drain slowly through, into a deep dish, without squeezing. When the juice has all passed through the bag, put to each pint of it a pound and a half of white sugar. Put to each quart of the syrup the beaten white of an egg. Set the syrup where it will boil gently—as fast as any scum rises, take the syrup from the fire, and skim it clear. When the jelly has boiled fifteen or twenty minutes, try a little of it in a tumbler of cold water—if it sinks to the bottom of the tumbler in a solid lump, it is sufficiently boiled. Jellies are improved by being put in the sun for several days—care must be taken that the dew does not fall on them.

Green Gage or other Plum Jelly

Slightly bruise the ripe fruit and place it in an earthenware colander; set this over a basin, in which you have put twelve ounces of loaf sugar to each quart of plums; stand it in a slack oven, and when the juice has pretty well left the fruit, boil the syrup until it is thick enough. Keep it in small glasses or ornamental molds, covered closely from the air.

Claret Jelly.

Dissolve an ounce and a quarter of isinglass and half a pound of loaf sugar in half a pint of water; add a pint of good claret, a wineglassful of brandy, and half that quantity of maraschino; strain through a jelly-bag and put into a mold.

Orange Jelly.

Squeeze the juice from some sweet oranges, strain it through a fine hair sieve, and to every pint of juice put a full pound of good loaf sugar, and a quarter of an ounce of dissolved isinglass; let it boil for twenty minutes.

Calves Feet Jelly.

Boil four calves-feet or cow-heels in two gallons of water until it is reduced to two quarts; strain it, and when cold skim off the fat; then put the jelly to boil, with a pint of sherry, a glass of good brandy, the peel and juice of three lemons, enough loaf sugar to sweeten it, and the whites and *shells* of six eggs, well-beaten. Stir all together till it comes to a boil; let it boil quickly for a few minutes, then strain it through a flannel jelly-bag until it is quite clear. A very little saffron boiled with it gives a rich color.

Confectioner's Jelly.

Isinglass dissolved in water by boiling, and evaporated until it jellies on cooling. In order to render it perfectly transparent, it should be clarified with white of egg. Spices, wine, and milk, may be added to suit the taste. Three ounces of good isinglass should make at least a quart of very strong jelly.

Iceland Moss Jelly.

Take one ounce of Iceland moss, wash it well, then break it up, and put it to stand all night in water just tepid when the moss is put in. Next morning take it out, and boil it in a quart of water till the quantity is reduced one half. Then strain it off into a basin.

This jelly is a slight tonic, rather bitter; and may be taken either plain or with milk or wine.

Quince Jelly.

Halve the quinces, and take out the cores. Boil the quinces till very soft, in clear water, mash them, and let them drain through a flannel bag, without squeezing them. Put to the quince liquor, when drained through the bag, white sugar, in the proportion of a pound to a pint of the liquor. Add the whites of eggs, and clarify it. When clear, boil it on a moderate fire, till it becomes a thick jelly. Fill glasses with the jelly, and cover them tight. The quince pulp that remains in the jelly-bag can be made into marmalade.

Apple Jelly.
(AN AMERICAN RECEIPT.)

Take any quantity of sound common apples, those with red skins make the brightest colored jelly; wash carefully, but do not peel them; fill a preserving-pan with the apples, and just cover them with water; boil till they are all in a pulp, then strain it through a hair sieve. To every pint of juice add one pound of white sugar, and a little essence of lemon; boil the whole till it is perfectly clear, and jellies when cold; it ought to turn out of a shape quite stiff and clear. The Americans make it of wild crab apples, and the bright red of their skins makes the jelly a most beautiful color.

Raspberry and Blackberry Jam.

For each pound of berries allow a pound of sugar. . Put a layer of each alternately in a preserving dish. Let them remain half an hour—then boil them slowly, stirring them frequently, to keep them from burning. When they have boiled half an hour, take a little up in a cup, and set it in a dish of cold water, if it appears of the consistency of thick jelly take the whole from the fire, if not, boil it until it becomes so.

Strawberry Jam.

Put an equal weight of good ripe scarlet strawberries and broken loaf sugar into a preserving-pan; let them boil very slowly until the sugar is all dissolved. The fruit should be kept as much unbroken as possible, therefore stir very carefully; remove the scum as it rises; the addition of half a pint of white currant juice to every four pounds of fruit is a great improvement, strawberry jam being rather a luscious preserve.

Boil from forty minutes to an hour, until the fruit looks clear. Gooseberry jam may be made in the same way.

Currant Jam.

Strip the currants from the stalks, and put them into the preserving-pan, with three-quarters of a pound of sugar to each pound of fruit; add the sugar after the fruit has boiled a few minutes; boil together, mashing the fruit with a wooden spoon, and taking off all the scum; boil all gently for half an hour, then fill the jars. Red, white or black currants may be used in this receipt.

Codlin Jam.

Pare and core two dozen full-grown codlins; put them into an enamelled saucepan, with only enough water to cover them. Boil them to a pulp, mash them with a spoon until they are smooth, and to every pound of fruit put half a pound of white sugar; boil it again for an hour, skimming it when necessary. As soon as sufficiently cold, put it into your preserving pots.

Cherry Jam.

Stone either May-duke, or Kentish cherries when they are perfectly ripe; break about half of the stones, blanch the kernels and add them to the fruit. Put all into a preserving-pan with half the weight of refined sugar; simmer gently till tolerably thickened; turn it into pots and cover them with brandied paper and skin. The stones may be pushed out by a skewer, as the fruit loses its color if a knife is used for the purpose.

Orange Jam.

Take sweet oranges, squeeze them, pass as much of the pulp as will go through a sieve; to every quart of fruit put a pound of white sugar, and boil it twenty minutes.

Peach Marmelade.

Weigh two pounds of sugar and three pounds and a half of sound ripe peaches; take the stones from the latter; place the fruit in a hair sieve, and press out the pulp; place this in a preserving-pan with the above quantity of sugar. Do it gently for fifteen minutes; blanch and slice the kernels, add them to the marmelade, give a boil up altogether, and put the preserve into pots, molds, or glasses.

PRESERVES AND SWEETMEATS.

SWEETMEATS should be kept in a cool, dry place; they should be properly boiled, and then they will not be likely to ferment; but they should be well looked to the first two months, and if not likely to keep, set the jar in the oven after the bread comes out, or on a hot hearth.

As soon as preserved fruit is entirely cold, it should be covered with either a carmel cover, or white paper cut the exact size of the pot or jar, that the fruit may be covered; then dip the paper in a liquid, one part pepper-sauce, two parts brandy. Then an entire white paper tied down over the top, pricked full of holes, and the article mentioned that the pot contains, and the year made, &c. Jellies should be covered in the same way.

A pan should be kept for preserving, of double block tin. A bow handle opposite the straight one for safety will do well; skimmers, sieves, and spoons, should be kept on purpose for sweet things. If brass is ever used, it must be kept free from verdigris.

To Clarify Sugar.

Take half a pint of water to one pound of loaf sugar, set it over the fire to dissolve; to twelve pounds of sugar thus prepared, beat up an egg very well, put in when cold, and, as it boils up, check it with a little cold water. The second time boiling, set it away to cool. In a quarter of an hour skim the top, and turn the syrup off quickly, leaving the sediment which will collect at the bottom.

To Preserve Peaches.

Take ripe free-stone peaches, pare, stone, and quarter them. To six pounds of the cut peaches allow three pounds of the best brown sugar. Strew the sugar among the peaches, and set them away in a covered vessel. Next morning put the whole into a preserving kettle, and boil it slowly about an hour and three-quarters, or two hours, skimming it well.

To Preserve Raspberries.

Choose raspberries not too ripe, take the weight of them in sugar, wet the sugar with a little water, and put in the berries, boil them softly, take care not to break them; when clear take them up, boil the syrup until it be thick enough, then put them in again: do not put them away until cold.

To Preserve Tomatoes.

One pound of sugar to every pound of tomatoes; and a quarter of a pint of water to each pound; two lemons.

Take the small plum-shaped yellow or red tomatoes, pour boiling water over them, and peel off the skins. Make the syrup of an equal weight of sugar and a quarter of a pint of water to each pound; set it over the fire. When the sugar is dissolved and boiling hot, put in the tomatoes, let them boil very gently, and stir in two lemons boiled in water until the peels are tender, and cut into very thin slices; let it boil until the fruit is clear throughout, and the syrup rich. Then place the tomatoes on flat dishes, and set them to become cold. Boil the syrup until very rich and thick, and then set it to cool and settle. Put the tomatoes into jars or pots, pour the syrup over them free from any sediment, or strain it through muslin. Cover them over as directed, and keep them in a dry place.

To Preserve Quinces.

Pare and core your quinces, put them into a kettle, cover them with the parings and cores, fill up with spring water, and let them boil until they are a pink color; take out the quinces, strain the liquor through a bag, and set it away for quince jelly; make a syrup of loaf sugar, pound for pound, boil the quinces in it two hours, slowly, frequently putting them under the liquor; after taking them out let the liquor boil until it is reduced to a syrup.

To Preserve Plums.

TIME, THREE-QUARTERS OF AN HOUR.

To every pound of fruit allow three-quarters of a pound of sugar.

Divide the plums, take out the stones, and put the fruit on a dish with pounded sugar strewed over; the next day put them in a preserving pan, and let them simmer gently by the side of the fire for about thirty minutes, then boil them quickly, removing the scum as it rises, and keep them constantly stirred, or the jam will stick to the bottom of the pan. Crack the stones and add the kernels to the preserve when it boils.

To Preserve Pears.

TIME, SIX OR SEVEN HOURS.

Three-quarters of a pound of loaf sugar to each pound of pears; peel of a lemon.

Weigh the pears when pared, and put three-quarters of a pound of loaf sugar to a pound of fruit; add the peel of a small lemon cut very thin, and just water enough at the bottom of the stew-pan to prevent the fruit burning; stew it *gently* for six or seven hours, and it will keep good for three months.

A few drops of cochineal may be added, which will improve the color, and the pears may be served in a glass dish or to garnish rice.

To Preserve Green Gages.

Choose the largest, when they begin to soften; split them without paring, and strew a part of the sugar of which you have previously weighed an equal quantity. Blanch the kernels with a small sharp knife. Next day pour the syrup from the fruit, and boil it with the other sugar, six or eight minutes, but very gently; skim, and add the plums and kernels. Simmer till clear, taking off any scum that rises: put the fruit singly into small pots, and pour the syrup and kernels to it. If you would candy it, do not add the syrup; some may be done each way:

To Preserve Strawberries.

Get the largest strawberries before they are too ripe; have the best loaf sugar, one pound to each of strawberries—stew them very gently, taking them out to cool frequently, that they may not be mashed; when they look clear, they are done enough.

To Preserve Cherries.

One pound of sugar to every pound of cherries; and three tablespoonsful of red currant juice.

Lay some pounded sugar at the bottom of the preserving pan, and place some cherries on it, then another layer of sugar, then of cherries, repeating this until all are in, leaving out a little of the sugar to strew in as they boil; add three spoonsful of currant juice to each pound of fruit, and set it over a clear fire. Boil them quickly, *shaking* them round frequently to prevent their burning, but do not stir them. Take off the scum as it rises, and when the syrup is thick and they look clear, put them into pots, and when cold cover them over.

To Preserve Whole or Half Quinces.

Into two quarts of boiling water put a quantity of the fairest golden pippins, in slices not very thin, and not pared, but wiped clean. Boil them very quick, close covered, till the water becomes a thick jelly; then scald the quinces. To every pint of pippin jelly put a pound of the finest sugar; boil it, and skim it clear. Put those quinces that are to be done whole into the syrup at once, and let it boil very fast; and those that are to be in halves by themselves; skim it, and when the fruit are clear, put some of the syrup into a glass to try whether it jellies before taking off the fire. The quantity of quinces is to be a pound to a pound of sugar, and a pound of jelly already boiled with the sugar.

To Preserve Crab Apples.

Siberian crabs need only be wiped. French crabs should be pared. Make a syrup by boiling two pounds of loaf sugar with a pint of good cider; prick the apples with a needle, place them in the syrup, and simmer as slowly as possible until you think the crabs are done; place them carefully in jars or glasses; reduce and skim the syrup until it is thick enough, and pour it upon the fruit; cover with wetted skins.

To Preserve Rhubarb and Orange.

Six oranges; one quart of rhubarb; one pound and a half of loaf sugar.

Peel the oranges carefully, take away the white rind and the pips, slice the pulps into a stew-pan, with the peel cut very small, add one quart of rhubarb cut very fine, and from a pound to a pound and a half of loaf sugar. Boil the whole down in the way usual with all preserves.

To Preserve Grapes in Brandy for Winter Dessert.

Grapes; white sugar-candy; brandy.

Take some fine close bunches of grapes, prick each twice with a fine needle, and lay them carefully in jars, cover the grapes thickly over with pounded sugar-candy, and then fill up the jars with good brandy. Tie the jars tightly over with a bladder, and set them in a cool dry place.

PICKLES.

To Pickle Peaches.

TIME, EIGHT OR TEN DAYS.

PEACHES; one gallon of vinegar; four pounds of brown sugar; five or six cloves into each peach.

Take some sound cling-stone peaches, remove the down with a brush; make the vinegar hot, add to it the sugar, boil and skim it well, stick five or six cloves into each peach, then pour the vinegar boiling hot over them, cover them over, and set them in a cold place for eight or ten days; then drain off the vinegar, make it hot, skim it, and again pour it over the peaches, let them become cold, then put them into glass jars, and secure them as for preserves.

To Pickle Plums like Olives.

TIME, TWENTY-FOUR HOURS.

Green plums; vinegar; mustard seed, and salt.

Make a pickle of vinegar, mustard seed, and salt, make it boiling hot, then pour it over green plums, gathered before they begin to turn, or before the stone is formed; let them stand all night, then drain off the vinegar, make it hot again, and pour it over the plums. When cold, cover them closely over.

To Pickle Barberries.

Take a quantity of barberries not over ripe, pick off the leaves and dead stalks, put them into jars with a large quantity of strong salt and water, and tie them down with a bladder. When you see a scum rise on the barberries put them into fresh salt and water, cover them close and set them by for use.

To Pickle Asparagus.

Pour boiling salt and water on, and cover them close—next day, take them out, dry them, and after standing in vinegar, put them with the yellow pickle.

To Pickle Tomatoes.

Cut a peck of green tomatoes in slices, and lay in a stone jar; cover with one pint of molasses. Skim when it ferments, and your pickles are made. This is *good*.

To Pickle Onions.

Onions; vinegar; ginger and whole pepper.

Take some nice onions, peel and throw them into a stew-pan of boiling water, set them over the fire, and let them remain until quite clear, then take them out quickly, and lay them between two cloths to dry. Boil some vinegar with the ginger and whole pepper, and when cold, pour it over the onions in glass jars, and tie them closely over.

To Pickle Red Cabbage.

To one quart of vinegar, one ounce of whole pepper.

Remove the coarse leaves from some red cabbage, and wipe them very clean; cut them in long thin slices or shreds, and put them on a large sieve, well covering them with salt, and let them drain all night; then put them into stone jars, and pour over them some boiling vinegar and whole peppers; cover them over, and set them by for use.

To Pickle French Beans and Radish Pods.

Gather them while quite small and tender. Keep them in salt and water, till you get through collecting them—changing the water as often as once in four or five days. Then scald them with hot salt and water, let them lie in it till cool, then turn on hot vinegar spiced with pepper-corns, mace and allspice. The radish top, if pickled in small bunches, are a pretty garnish for other pickles.

To Make Green Pickles.

Put the articles you intend to pickle, in a pot—and cover them with boiling salt and water; put a thick cloth on the top, and then a plate that will fit it—let it stand till the next morning, then pour off the salt and water, boil it again, and cover them as before; do this until your pickles are a good green—then put them in plain cold vinegar, and at the end of a fortnight, put them up, as you do the yellow pickle.

Spiced Peaches.

Take nine pounds of good ripe peaches, rub them with a coarse towel and halve them. Put four pounds of sugar and a pint of good vinegar in a preserving kettle with cloves, cinnamon, and mace; when the syrup is formed, throw in the peaches a few at a time, so as to keep them as whole as possible. When clean take them out and put in more. Boil the syrup until quite rich, and then pour over the peaches. Pears, quinces, apples, and cherries may be spiced in the same manner.

SAUCES.

Wine Sauce.

TAKE half a pint of good melted butter, sweeten it with about two ounces of sifted sugar, and then add to it very gradually two small wine-glasses of sherry and a little grated lemon or nutmeg. Keep stirring the sauce over the fire till it nearly boils, when either pour it over the pudding, or serve in a tureen.

Red Wine Sauce.

Simmer half a pint of red wine, and a quarter of a pound of loaf sugar, until the quantity is greatly reduced. Claret or home-made wine will do for this sauce.

Sauce Au Vin.

Pour half a pint of wine upon the yolks of three eggs; beat it together for ten minutes; add sugar, grated lemon-peel, and cinnamon to your taste. Warm it, but do not let it come to a boil.

Plum Pudding Sauce.

To four ounces of melted butter, or of thick arrow-root, add one ounce and a half of sherry, the same of brandy, and the same of curacoa (the latter may be omitted); sweeten to palate, and add a little grated lemon peel and nutmeg.

Apple Sauce.

TIME, TWENTY MINUTES.

Pare, core, and cut into slices eight good boiling apples; put them into a sauce-pan with sufficient water to moisten and prevent them from burning, boil them until sufficiently tender to pulp. Then beat them up smoothly with a piece of butter, and put sugar to your taste.

Cranberry Sauce.

A quart of cranberries are washed and stewed with sufficient water to cover them; when they burst mix with them a pound of brown sugar and stir them well. Before you take them from the fire, all the berries should have burst. They will be jellied when cold.

Lobster Sauce.

TIME, TEN MINUTES.

One hen lobster with coral; two-thirds of its weight of good cream; one-third of fresh butter.

Cut the flesh in small pieces, mix it up with two-thirds of good cream and one-third of fresh butter.

No stock, fish-sauces, anchovies, or essences to be used.

Oyster Sauce.

TIME, FIVE MINUTES.

One dozen of oysters; half a teacupful of good gravy; half a pint of melted butter.

Stew the beards of the oysters in their own juice with half a teacupful of good clear gravy; strain it off, add it to the melted butter—which should be ready—put in the oysters, and let them simmer gently for three minutes.

Maitre d'Hotel Sauce.

TIME, ONE MINUTE TO SIMMER.

Half a pint of melted butter; one teaspoonful of chopped parsley; one lemon; Cayenne and salt to taste.

Melt the butter, add to it the strained juice of a lemon, the parsley and seasoning, and let it just boil.

Mint Sauce for Roast Lamb.

Two tablespoonsful of green mint; one tablespoonful of pounded sugar, and a quarter of a pint of vinegar.

Pick and wash the green mint very clean, chop it fine, mix the sugar and vinegar in a sauce tureen, put in the mint, and let it stand.

Caper Sauce

Is made by mixing a sufficient quantity of capers, and adding them to the melted butter, with a little of the liquor from the capers; where capers cannot be obtained, pickled nasturtiums make a very good substitute, or even green pickle minced and put with the butter.

SALADS.

French Chicken Salad.

THE remains of cold roast or boiled chicken, two lettuces, a little endive, one cucumber, a few slices of boiled beet-root.

Trim neatly the remains of the chicken; wash, dry, and slice the lettuces, and place in the middle of a dish; put the pieces of fowl on the top, and pour the salad dressing over them. Garnish the edge of the salad with hard boiled egg cut in rings, sliced cucumber, and boiled beet-root cut in slices. Instead of cutting the eggs in rings, the yolks may be rubbed through a hair sieve, and the whites chopped very finely, and arranged on the salad in small bunches, yellow and white alternately. This should not be made long before it is wanted for table.

American Chicken Salad.

Take a fine white bunch of celery (four or five heads,) scrape and wash it white, reserve the delicate green leaves; shred the white part like straws, lay this in a glass or white china dish, in the form of a nest. Mince all the white meat of a boiled or white stewed fowl, without the skin, and put it in the nest.

Make a salad dressing thus: rub the yolks of two hard boiled eggs to a smooth paste, with a dessertspoonful of salad oil or melted butter; add to it two teaspoonsful of made mustard, and a small teaspoonful of fine white sugar, and put to it gradually (stirring it in), a large cup of strong vinegar.

Lobster Salad.

Break up a lobster, obtaining as much of the flesh as possible, which cut into slices, have likewise two hard boiled eggs also in slices, two anchovies filleted, and two cabbage lettuces, or any other salad cut up small; mix the whole well together in a basin, season with half a teaspoonful of chopped parsley, a little pepper and salt, six spoonsful of salad oil and two of vinegar; when well mixed, turn the whole into a salad bowl and serve. Crab may be dressed the same.

Salade de Bœuf.

Thinly slice some lean boiled salt beef, cut it into small but long shaped pieces; mix with it an equal quantity of cold boiled carrot sliced in rounds, and sauce it with a good remolade mixture. Garnish it with tufts of scraped horseradish and finely-shred shallot or onion. If you have one or two pickled capsicums, they are an improvement.

SOUPS.

ANY of the things from the following list will, with the proper addition of herbs, roots, and seasoning, make a tureen of good soup for a small family:—

One pound of lean meat.
A wood-pigeon.
A small rabbit.
A sheep's or lamb's head.
A chicken or old fowl.
Two pounds of raw bones.
A tame pigeon.
A set of giblets.

The reduced liquor in which has been boiled a calf's head, fowl, turkey, rabbit, joint of meat, etc., etc.

The three kinds of stock mostly employed as a foundation for soups are either composed of fish, vegetables, or butchers' meat.

Soup a la Cardinal.

Boil a fowl in water; add to it half a pound of blanched rice, four ounces of butter, and some carrots cut in slices; season it with salt, let it boil two hours, mix well with it two ounces of butter; then skim it carefully, and serve it with the best parts of the fowl in it.

Oyster Soup.

Beard oysters enough for the purpose you require; make a fish stock, properly seasoned and strained; when this is boiling hot, put in the oysters, and thicken the soup with some beaten yolks of eggs; or the oysters may, together with the eggs, be beaten in a mortar until they form a paste; stir them into the soup, and add a little cream, or essence of anchovy, if approved of. Some epicures introduce a little macaroni, first stewed in stock.

Clam Soup.

Boil for three hours a knuckle of veal, with a goodly portion of water and one onion. Strain and add the liquor of fifty clams. Thicken with a tablespoonful of flour, well rubbed with butter, the size of a small egg. Have your clams cut in three pieces, with the hard rind removed. Beat the yolks of two eggs very light, and put into your tureen with chopped parsley and one-half pint milk. Just before serving, drop the clams into boiling soup, letting them boil up once. Pour into tureen, stirring well its contents while doing so.

Common Vegetable Soup.

Three potatoes, three turnips, three parsnips, and three carrots, boiled in a gallon of water, with a handful of green peas, until reduced to nearly half the quantity; add a little salt, and some weak stock, if thought requisite.

White Soup Maigre.
A FRENCH RECEIPT.

Boil a cupful of vermicelli, with a little mace and some salt, in a quart of water, till the vermicelli is very soft; whisk up the yolks of three eggs in the soup tureen; pour the vermicelli and water on the eggs, and mix them all well together.

Pea Soup.

Soak the peas over night; next morning boil them an hour, adding a little saleratus; then change the water and add a pound of salt pork; boil until perfectly soft.

Maccaroni Soup.

To a rich beef or other soup, in which there is no seasoning other than pepper or salt, take half a pound of small pipe maccaroni, boil it in clear water until it is tender, then drain it and cut in pieces of an inch length, boil it for fifteen minutes in the soup and serve.

Noodle Soup.

Take two eggs and a little fine flour, and make a thick, consistent dough, knead it well and roll it out thin, let it remain a few minutes to get dry, and then cut it into fine strips. Cut the strips of proper length and put them in boiling soup, allow them to cook sufficiently, and then serve.

Beef Tea.

This is the simplest of all soups, being but a pound or two of shin of beef cut in small pieces, and gently stewed, with a little salt, in a pint of cold water to each pound of meat, without either vegetables or spice, for three hours. It is generally served in a basin, with toasted bread.

Ox Tail Soup.

Two tails, if properly stewed, will make soup without any addition of meat; they must be cleaned and cut into pieces, and boiled very quietly for several hours in water; put in a crust of bread and a little salt. When tender the liquor must be strained and the fat removed; thicken it with a little cream, and put in two tablespoonsful of ketchup; serve up with the tails cut in pieces. Calves' tails can be used instead of ox tails.

Veal Broth.

Stew a small knuckle, with two ounces of rice, a blade of mace, and some salt, in three quarts of water, until reduced one-half.

Pepper-Pot.

This is composed of equal parts of fish, flesh, and fowl. Cut small some lean beef or mutton, the flesh of a fowl, and the meat from a lobster; and what vegetables you fancy, and a small quantity of rice, or pulse of any kind. Pour in sufficient water, and do very slowly, keeping it well skimmed. When the meat, etc., is tender, season with Cayenne pepper and salt. Very small dumplings may be served in the tureen with it.

Tripe may be used instead of fish, flesh, and fowl.

Chicken Broth.

TIME, ONE HOUR.

Cut up a chicken, put to it the cold water, or weak broth, a tablespoonful of salt, half a teacupful of barley (or rice if preferred); cover it close and let it simmer for an hour, skim it clear, and add pepper to your taste. The chicken may be placed on a dish with pieces of butter over it, a dust of pepper, and served with mashed potatoes.

Rice or Barley Soup.

Put the rice into plenty of cold water; when it boils throw in some salt, let it simmer ten minutes, drain it, throw it into the boiling soup, and simmer it gently for a few minutes longer.

Green Turtle Soup.

Cut the head off the turtle the day before you dress it, and place the body so as to drain it well from blood; then cut up in the following manner: divide the back, belly, head, and fins, from the intestines and lean parts; take care to cut the gall clean out without breaking; scald in boiling water the first named parts so as to take off the skin and shell; cut them in neat square pieces and throw them into cold water; boil the back and belly in a little water long enough to extract the bones easily, then make good stock of a leg of veal, a slice of ham, and the flesh of the inside of the turtle; let it do away until it is browned, then fill it up with water, and the liquor and bones of the boiled turtle. Season with sliced lemon, whole pepper, a bunch of parsley, a leek sliced, and salt to taste. Let it boil slowly for four hours, then strain it to the pieces of the back, belly, head, and fins of the turtle (take the bones from the fins); add to it half a pint of Madeira wine and quarter of a pound of fresh sweet butter, with a tablespoonful of flour worked into it, and a lemon sliced thin; let it boil gently for two hours, then serve.

In cutting up the turtle, the fat should be taken great care of; it should be separated and cut in neat pieces, and stewed tender in a little of the soup, and put into the tureen when ready to serve.

Mock Turtle Soup.

A fine calf's head, cut the meat clean from the bones, then boil the bones in water; season with Cayenne, nutmeg, and mace; pour into the gravy a pint of Madeira wine, with a little parsley and thyme.

VEGETABLES.

ALL vegetables ought to be carefully washed and picked, and laid in cold water before being cooked. When boiled they should have plenty of water. Care should be taken not to overdo them, as it spoils their color, and deprives them of their crispness. They ought to be put into boiling water with a handful of salt in it, and when they begin to sink it is a sign that they are sufficiently done; if the water has not been allowed to slacken in the boiling, they should, when taken up, be drained immediately, or they will lose their color. Hard water destroys the color of those vegetables that should look green. A piece of soda, about the size of a bean, put into a pot holding two gallons of water, in which the vegetables are to be boiled, will keep them of a beautiful green color. The lid of the pot should be left off while boiling.

To Broil Potatoes.

Parboil, then slice and boil them. Or parboil, and then set them whole on the gridiron over a very slow fire, and when thoroughly done send them up with their skins on. This last way is practised in many Irish families.

To Roast Potatoes.

Half boil, take off the thin peel, and roast them of a beautiful brown.

To Fry Potatoes.

Take the skin off raw potatoes, slice and fry them, either in butter or thin batter.

Saratoga Potato Chips.

Wash and pare off the skins of two or three or more large potatoes, and when you have done this, go on paring them, cutting them as thin and as evenly as possible in ribbons nearly an inch wide; throw these into boiling fat, let them take a nice light color, drain them well before the fire, and serve immediately (or they lose their crispness), piled high on a napkin. They may be sent in with game in the third course.

To Mash Potatoes.

Boil the potatoes, peel them, and break them to paste; then to two pounds of them add a quarter of a pint of milk, a little salt, and two ounces of butter, and stir it all well over the fire. Either serve them in this manner, or place them on the dish in a form, and then brown the top with a salamander, or in scallops.

Puree of Potatoes.

Mash the potatoes, and mix them while quite hot with some fine white veal gravy, and thicken with butter or cream. The purée should be about the consistency of apple sauce.

Potato Balls.

Mash the potatoes very nicely, make them into balls, rub them over with the yolk of an egg, and put them into the oven or before the fire to brown. These balls may be varied by the introduction of a third part of grated meat.

Potatoes with Bacon.

Cook the potatoes well, peel them, cut them into small pieces and fry them a light brown; meantime, cut a small piece of tender cooked bacon into small pieces, and mix with the potatoes; fry a short time longer and serve.

Potatoes Mashed with Onions.

Prepare some onions by putting them through a sieve, and mix them with potatoes; in proportioning the onions to the potatoes, you will be guided by your wish to have more or less of their flavor.

Oyster Potato Balls.

This is a very palatable dish for suppers, and its production being so very simple, it only requires to be pointed out to become popular.

Beard a dozen (more or less, according to the number you provide for) small plump oysters, cover them singly with the plain mashed potato paste, roll them with flour, or beaten-up egg and bread-crumbs, into balls, and fry them in butter or dripping.

Put into each ball when you make it up a teaspoonful of the oyster liquor.

Sweet Potatoes Stewed.

Wash and wipe them, and if they be large, cut them in two lengths; put them at the bottom of a stew-pan, lay over some slices of boiled ham; and on that, one or two chickens cut up with pepper, salt, and a bundle of herbs; pour in some water, and stew them till done, then take out the herbs, serve the stew in a deep dish—thicken the gravy, and pour over it.

Baked Sweet or White Potatoes.

Clean, scrub, and *dry* carefully some large ones, and bake them in the oven of your range, or in what I have heard called the "American Dutch," before the fire; if very large, they may be parboiled before being put in the oven. With a pat of fresh butter, and a little salt and pepper, they are worthy their great popularity.

Spinach with Gravy.

Prepare the spinach nicely, put it into boiling water, and when sufficiently tender to be squeezed, strain it in a cullender, put it into cold water for a few minutes; then put a small quantity in a towel and press it, so as to form balls; lay these upon the board, chop them very fine, fry them with butter, and then add some strong gravy, and boil.

Beignets of Spinach.

Take some washed and picked spinach; mix the yolks of four eggs, some butter, and four ounces of sugar, with some bread-crumbs; add this to the chopped spinach, form it into round cakes, and fry them in butter.

Carrots a la Maitre d'Hotel.

Boil the carrots tender, put a piece of butter into a stew-pan with a little flour; when it is browned add a little gravy; then put in the carrots and let them stew a little. Turnips can be done the same way, only they do not require so much gravy.

Carrots—American Style,

Require a good deal of boiling. When young, wipe off the skin after they are boiled; when old, boil them with the salt meat, and scrape them first.

Cauliflowers.

Cut off the stalks, boil the cauliflower in milk and water until it is tender, make a drawn butter and serve over it, or put bits of butter over, strew pepper over and serve hot.

Cauliflower in White Sauce.

Half boil it; then cut it into handsome pieces and lay them in a stew-pan, with a little broth seasoned with salt, let them simmer half an hour; have mixed some cream, butter and flour, which add to it.

Artichokes.

Soak them in cold water, wash them well, then put them into plenty of boiling water, with a handful of salt, and let them boil gently till they are tender, which will take an hour and a half or two hours; the surest way to know when they are done enough, is to draw out a leaf; trim them, and drain them on a sieve, and send up melted butter with them.

Fricassee of Parsnips.

Boil a few parsnips in milk until they are soft; then cut them lengthwise into bits two or three inches long, and simmer in a white sauce, made of two spoonsful of broth and half a cupful of cream, a bit of butter, some flour and salt.

Mashed Parsnips.

Boil them tender, scrape, then mash them in a stew-pan with a little cream, a good piece of butter, and some salt.

Fried Parsnips.

TIME, ONE HOUR TO ONE HOUR AND A HALF.

Parsnips, butter and pepper.

Boil the parsnips until they are tender, then skin them, and cut them in slices lengthwise of a quarter of an inch in thickness; fry them in boiling butter or beef dripping. When one side is brown, turn them over to brown the other; then put them on a dish and dredge them with a little pepper. Serve them with fried or roast meat.

Turnips and Rutabagas.

White turnips require about as much boiling as potatoes. When tender, take them up, peel and mash them—season them with a little salt and butter. Yellow turnips require about two hours boiling—if very large, split them in two. The tops of white turnips make a good salad.

White Turnips.

Peel off half an inch of the stringy outside—full grown turnips will take about an hour and a half gentle boiling; try them with a fork, and when tender, take them up, and lay them on a sieve till the water is thoroughly drained from them; send them up whole; to very young turnips, leave about two inches of green top; the old ones are better when the water is changed as directed for cabbage.

Peas.

Peas should be put into boiling water, with salt and saleratus, in the proportion of a quarter of a teaspoonful of saleratus to a half a peck of peas. Boil them from fifteen to thirty minutes, according to their age and kind. When boiled tender, take them out of the water with a skimmer, salt and butter them to the taste. Peas to be good should be fresh gathered, and not shelled till just before they are cooked.

Green Peas.
VOLIERIES' RECEIPT.

Stew the peas in butter, they will produce a juice of themselves; after stewing a little, dredge a little fine meal, and moisten with rich broth; add sugar and salt to your taste, and let the whole stew well. Before serving, add a little milk, and let it cook for an instant. They are usually served with roast fowls.

Peapods Stewed.

Take the sugar-pea when young, pare off the outer edges of the pods, carefully removing the strings; then put them into good gravy, and thicken with a little butter and flour; and let them stew gently until quite tender.

To Dress Beans.

Boil tender with a bunch of parsley, which must be chopped to serve with them. Bacon or pickled pork must be served to eat with, but not boiled with them.

French Beans.

String and cut them into four or eight; the last looks best. Lay them in salt and water; and when the sauce-pan boils, put them in with some salt. As soon as they are done, serve them immediately, to preserve the green color.

Shelled Beans.

Wash in several waters, and put them in a basin with boiling water. Boil one hour. Do not drain them very dry. Season with butter and salt.

Fricasseed Beans.

When grown large, but not mealy, boil, blanch, and lay them in a white sauce, ready hot; just heat them through in it, and serve. If they are not of a fine green, do not use them for the dish.

Kidney Beans Boiled.

String them, slit them down the middle, and cut them across; let them stand some time in salt and water; boil them and when tender they are done. Serve with melted butter.

Lima Beans.

Lay a quart of shelled Lima beans in cold water for one hour, then put them into a stew-pan and pour boiling water over to cover them, cover the stew-pan and let it boil fast for half an hour; then take one between your finger and thumb, if it will mash easily, it is done; drain off nearly all the water, add a small teacup of butter, a teaspoonful of salt, and a little pepper; cover them for a few minutes over the fire, then serve hot.

Egg Plant.

Cut an egg plant in thin slices, pare off the purple rind, then strew each slice with salt, and lay them together on a plate, placed slanting that the liquor which exudes may run off, after an hour rinse the slices, wipe them dry, dip each slice in batter or flour, and fry a nice brown, turning them that each side may be a nice brown, fry in seasoned fat or lard, or sweet butter.

Baked Tomatoes—American.

TIME, NEARLY ONE HOUR.

Five or six tomatoes; a saltspoonful of salt; half as much of pepper; a piece of butter the size of a nutmeg.

Wash five or six smooth tomatoes; cut a small piece from the stem end, and put a little salt, pepper, and a piece of butter the size of a nutmeg in each, place them in a dish, and bake them in a moderate oven for nearly an hour. Serve them up hot.

To Stew Tomatoes.

Take off the skin, and put them in a pan with salt, pepper, and a large piece of butter; stew them till sufficiently dry.

To Scollop Tomatoes.

Peel off the skin from large, full, ripe tomatoes—put a layer in the bottom of a deep dish, cover it well with bread grated fine; sprinkle on pepper and salt, and lay some bits of butter over them—put another layer of each, till the dish is full—let the top be covered with crumbs and butter—bake it a nice brown.

Boiled Green Corn.

Trim off the husks and silk; throw it into hot water, and let it boil half or three-quarters of an hour, according to the size of the ear. The sweet or sugar corn is the best for this purpose. It should never be boiled in salted water, as this makes it harder and comparatively indigestible.

Roasted Green Corn.

Remove the husks and lay the ears over red-hot coals on a gridiron. It is "not bad" roasted by laying the ears directly on burning coals, care being taken to turn them before they are burned injuriously.

Succotash.

This is usually made of green corn and garden beans, although string beans are sometimes added. Cut the kernels of corn from the cob; and stew them and the beans, closely covered, in water or milk, for about three-quarters of an hour. If a richer dish is wanted, stir in a little cream, and let the whole simmer for ten minutes longer.

Some persons string the beans, and then cut them into small pieces, before mixing and stewing—a plan only to be recommended to those who have abundance of time for "small things."

Beets.

Wash clean, but do not scrape; if you do they will look white when cooked. When young they will cook in two hours; but old ones will require four or five hours. When done, plunge them into cold water, and the skin will peel off easily. Cut in thin slices, and lay in a flat dish. Serve with butter, pepper, and salt to taste.

Pickled Beets.

Cut the beets that are left from dinner into thin slices, and lay them in an earthen vessel, and cover with cold vinegar and a few whole cloves. Keep in a cold place.

Asparagus.

Cut off the white part, wash and tie in small bunches, and put into a sauce-pan with boiling water enough to cover it, and a handful of salt. When young it will boil in twenty minutes; if not tender, boil thirty. Dish on toast, and season with a little butter.

To Stew Red Cabbage.

Slice a small, or half a large, red cabbage; wash and put it into a sauce-pan with pepper, salt, no water but what hangs about it, and a piece of butter. Stew it till quite tender, and when going to serve, add two or three spoonsful of vinegar, and give one boil over the fire. Serve it for cold meat, or with sausages on it.

Cabbage with Onions.

Boil them separately, and mix them in the proportions you like; add butter, pepper, and salt, and either stew them, or fry them in a cake.

To Boil Sprouts and Greens.

Cabbage sprouts, young beet-tops, and the green leaves of young turnips, are boiled with salt meats, or in clear water, with a little salt.

Onions.

Peel and put them in boiling milk, (water will do, but it is not as good). When boiled tender, take them up, salt them and turn a little melted butter over them.

To Stew Onions.

Peel six large onions, fry gently of a fine brown, but do not blacken them; then put them into a small stew-pan, with a little weak gravy, pepper and salt; cover and stew two hours gently. They should be lightly floured at first.

Stewed Mushrooms.

Take some middling sized mushrooms, stew them well in a little clear brown gravy; when done add a little ketchup to them.

Lettuce or Salad.

Break the leaves apart one by one from the stalk and throw them into a pan of cold water, rinse them well, lay them into a salad bowl or a deep dish, lay the largest leaves first, put the next size upon them, then lay on the finest white leaves, cut hard boiled eggs in slices or quarters and lay them at equal distances around the edge and over the salad; serve with vinegar, oil, and made mustard in the castor.

To Stew Celery.

Wash six heads; strip off the outer leaves; cut into lengths of four inches; put into a stew-pan, with a little broth or weak gravy; stew till tender, then add cream, flour and butter; season with pepper, salt, and nutmeg, and simmer all together.

To Stew Cucumbers.

First slice them thick, then cut in half or divide them into two lengths; stew some salt and pepper, and sliced onions, add a little broth, or a bit of butter. Simmer very slowly; and before serving, if no butter was in before, put some, and a little flour, or if there was butter in, only a little flour.

To Stew and Dress Squash.

Cut the squash small, take off the outside skin, and the inside strings and seeds; then put it into a stew-pan, with hot water to cover it, cover the stew-pan for half an hour or longer until they are tender, take them into a cullender with a skimmer, press out the water, then take them into a dish and mash them perfectly smooth, add a good bit of butter, and pepper and salt to taste; make it in a neat form the same as mashed turnips or potatoes; but do not brown it; put pepper over in spots, and garnish with sprigs of parsley, or celery leaves, if you wish it ornamental.

Salsify, or Oyster Plant.

Scrape and wash the roots, put them into boiling water with salt; when done, drain them, and place them in the dish without cutting them up. They are a very excellent vegetable, but require nicety in cooking; exposure to the air, either in scraping or after boiling, will make them black.

Excellent Sour Crout.

Cut your cabbage heads in half, put them in a tub of clean fresh water for fifteen minutes, for the purpose of perfectly cleansing them from any flies or snails that may be sticking to them; then cut in a large cutter, not too fine; then place in your barrel with a sprinkling of salt; then stamp each layer until the juice rises to the top. Cover with clean cabbage leaves; cover with boards and place heavy weights thereon, and let it remain two or three weeks before using.

FISH AND SHELL FISH.

HERE are general rules for choosing fish of most sorts.

If the gills are red and full, and the whole fish firm and stiff, it is good.

If, on the contrary, the gills are brownish, the eyes sunk, and the flesh flabby, they are stale.

Fresh shad, haddock. and whiting are considered by some persons better for salting a night before cooking.

Fresh water fish have often a muddy taste and smell, which may be got rid of by soaking in strong salt and water.

Great care must be taken to see that the fish be properly cleaned before dressing; that is, they must be perfectly free from scales, and every particle of the inside scraped from the backbone; but not washed beyond what is really necessary, as that diminishes the flavor of most fish.

Great care and punctuality is necessary in cooking fish. If not done sufficiently, or if done too much, they are not good. They should be eaten as soon as cooked. For a garnish to the fish use parsley, a lemon, or eggs boiled hard, and cut in slices.

Roasted Salmon.

Take a large piece of fine fresh salmon, cut from the middle of the fish, well cleaned and carefully scaled. Wipe it dry in a clean coarse cloth. Then dredge it with flour, put it on the spit, and place it before a clear bright fire. Baste it with fresh butter, and roast it well. Serve it up plain; garnishing the dish with slices of lemon, as many persons like a little lemon-juice with salmon.

Broiled Salmon.

Cut slices an inch thick, and season with pepper and salt; lay each slice in half a sheet of white paper well buttered, twist the ends of the paper, and broil the slices over a slow fire six or eight minutes. Serve in the paper with anchovy-sauce.

Potted Salmon.

Take a large piece, scale and wipe, but do not wash it; salt very well, let it lie till the salt is melted and drained from it, then season with beaten mace, cloves and whole pepper; lay in a few bay-leaves, put it close into a pan, cover it over with butter, and bake it; when well done, drain it from the gravy, put it into the pots to keep, and when cold cover it with clarified butter.

In this manner you may do any firm fish.

Fried Salmon.

Cut into steaks about an inch thick; roll in a batter of eggs and flour, or cracker dust, and fry in lard or butter as may be preferred.

Boiled Salmon.

Boil the same as halibut, and serve with drawn butter.

Boiled Halibut.

Take a piece weighing four or five pounds, scrape the skin clean, dredge flour over it, and boil according to its weight—

ten minutes to a pound. Serve with plain boiled potatoes, and drawn butter, or egg, or parsley sauce. Cold boiled halibut may be served the same as codfish; any of the sauce which may remain may be put with the cold fish.

Fried Halibut.

Take a slice of halibut, sprinkle with salt, and dredge with flour. Fry four slices of salt pork, add to the pork fat one spoonful of lard. When boiling hot put in the halibut. Fry a light brown on one side, then turn and fry the same on the other. Serve the pork with it.

Broiled Halibut.

Grease the gridiron with a little butter, place the halibut upon it, sprinkle a little salt over it, and place over clear coals. Cook one side ten minutes, then turn and cook upon the other side ten more. Have the dish warm; put the fish upon it, season with pepper and butter and send to the table.

Smoked Halibut.

Broiled the same as the fresh, omitting the pepper and salt. Smoked salmon cooked in the same way.

Boiled Haddock.

TIME, A QUARTER TO HALF AN HOUR, ACCORDING TO SIZE.

Two haddocks; enough water to cover them; a quarter of a pound of salt to each gallon of water.

Clean the fish, and wash them thoroughly, they will require scraping first, then put them in the fish-kettle; simmer them gently Serve with a garnish of sliced lemon and parsley.

Sauce melted butter, or anchovy.

Fried Haddock.

TIME, A QUARTER OF AN HOUR, OR EIGHTEEN MINUTES.

Haddock; egg; bread crumbs; a sprig of parsley; a little lemon thyme; a few chives; pepper and salt.

Haddocks of medium size are very nice cut open, covered with egg, bread crumbs, chives, parsley, and a little lemon thyme minced very fine, salt and pepper, and fried.

Baked Haddock.

TIME, FROM HALF AN HOUR TO AN HOUR.

Thoroughly clean and dry the haddock, fill the inside with veal stuffing, sew it up, and curl the tail into its mouth. Brush it over with egg, and strew bread crumbs over it. Set it in a warm oven to bake for about half an hour. Serve it on a dish without a napkin, with any sauce you please, anchovy, melted butter, etc.

Broiled Haddock.

TIME, FIFTEEN MINUTES.

Thoroughly clean and dry them in a cloth, rub them over with a little vinegar, and dredge them with flour. Rub some grease on the bars of the gridiron, put it over a clear fire, and when it is *hot*, place your fish on it; turn them two or three times, and broil them a nice brown color. Serve them with shrimp sauce, or plain melted butter.

Boiled Perch.

TIME, HALF AN HOUR, IF LARGE.

In season from September to November.

Cut off the spines from the back, scrape off the scales with an oyster knife, and thoroughly clean and wash them. Then boil them in cold water very carefully, as they are a most delicate fish.

Fried Perch.

TIME, TWELVE MINUTES.

Some bread crumbs and egg.

Thoroughly clean and scale the perch, brush them over with a well beaten egg, dip them into bread crumbs, and fry them a nice brown in boiling fat. Serve them with anchovy sauce or melted butter.

White Perch a la Daub.

Boil as many large white perch as will be sufficient for the dish; do not take off their heads, and be careful not to break their skins; when cold, place them in the dish, and cover them with savory jelly broken. A nice piece of rock-fish is excellent done in the same way.

Boiled Trout.

TIME, TWENTY TO THIRTY MINUTES.

The fish; one wineglassful of vinegar, water, salt, and a piece of horseradish.

Rub and wipe the fish very dry, put them into a fish-kettle of boiling water with a wineglassful of vinegar, two tablespoonsful of salt, and a piece of horseradish. Boil them slowly for twenty minutes or half an hour, taking care that the skin is not broken, and serve them on a napkin with anchovy sauce or plain melted butter.

Fried Trout.

TIME, TWENTY MINUTES.

One or two trout; one egg; bread crumbs; one lemon.

Thoroughly clean and remove the gills, brush them over with the yolk of a well beaten egg, dip them into bread crumbs and fry them in hot fat until of a fine brown. Serve with anchovy sauce, and garnish with sliced lemon.

Broiled Trout.

TIME, FIFTEEN MINUTES.

The trout; a quarter of a pound of butter; some salt; one anchovy; one tablespoonful of capers; half a spoonful of vinegar; pepper, salt, nutmeg, and a little flour.

When you have thoroughly cleaned your fish, wipe it dry in a cloth, and tie it round with thread to preserve its shape entire. Then melt the butter with one tablespoonful of salt, and pour it over the trout till it is perfectly covered; let it remain for two or three minutes, take it out, and put it on a gridiron over a clear fire, that it may do gradually. When done, lay it on a dish, and pour over it the sauce previously made, with an anchovy washed, boned, and cut up very small, a large spoonful of chopped capers, a little pepper, salt, and nutmeg, half a spoonful of vinegar, and some melted butter. Boil it up for a few minutes and pour it over your fish.

To Boil a Shad.

Get a nice fat shad, fresh from the water, that the skin may not crack in boiling, put it in cold water on a slice, in a kettle of proper length, with a wineglass of pale vinegar, salt, a little garlic, and a bundle of parsley; when it is done, drain all the water from the fish, lay it in the dish, and garnish with scraped horseradish; have a sauce boat of nice melted butter, to mix with the different ketchups, as taste shall direct.

To Roast a Shad.

Fill the cavity with good forcemeat, sew it up, and tie it on a board of proper size, cover it with bread crumbs, with some salt and pepper, set it before the fire to roast; when done on one side, turn it, tie it again, and when sufficiently done, pull out the thread, and serve it up with butter and parsley poured over it.

To Broil a Shad.

Separate one side from the back-bone, so that it will lie open without being split in two; wash it clean, dry it with a cloth, sprinkle some salt and pepper on it, and let it stand till you are ready to broil it; have the gridiron hot and well greased, broil it nicely, and pour over it melted butter.

To Bake Shad.

Lay the fish in a deep pan, putting its tail to its mouth; bake two hours, pour the gravy round it, and send it to the table; any fish may be baked in this way; the fish should be stuffed with forcemeat made of bread crumbs, butter, chopped parsley, pepper and salt.

To Smoke Herrings.
TIME, TWENTY-FOUR HOURS.

Clean and lay some fresh herrings in salt and a little saltpetre for *one* night; then run a stick through their eyes, and hang them in a row. Put some saw-dust into an old cask, and in the midst of it a *heater red hot*; hang the stick on which you have threaded the fish over the smoke, and let them remain for twenty-four hours.

Fried Herrings.
TIME, SIX OR EIGHT MINUTES.

Clean and scale the fish, and dry them thoroughly in a cloth. When they are quite dry, fry them to a bright color. The herring, being so rich a fish, should be fried with less butter than fish of most kinds, and well drained and dried afterwards. A nice sauce to eat with herrings is sugar, mustard, and a little salt and vinegar. Some serve melted butter, but herrings are too rich to eat with a rich sauce. Crisp parsley may be used as a garnish.

Broiled Herrings.
TIME, SIX OR EIGHT MINUTES.

Herrings; a spoonful of flour; a quarter of a pint of table beer or ale; a slice of onion; six ounces of whole peppers; one ounce of butter; a spoonful of mustard.

Clean and dry the fish, cut off their heads, flour them and broil them. Break up the heads and boil them for a quarter of an hour in a little table beer or ale, with a little whole pepper and a slice of onion; strain off the liquor, thicken it with butter and flour, beat mustard up with it, and serve it in a tureen to eat with the herrings.

Broiled Mackerel.

Split down the back and clean. Be careful to scrape all the thin black skin from the inside. Wipe dry and lay on the gridiron; broil on one side a nice brown, then turn and brown the other side; it will not take so long to brown the side on which the skin is. (All fish should have the side on which the skin is turned to the fire last, as the skin burns easily, and coals are not so hot after you have used them ten minutes.) Season with butter, pepper and salt.

Fried Mackerel.

Fry brown six good-sized slices of pork. Prepare your mackerel as for broiling. Take out your pork, sprinkle a little salt over the mackerel, then fry a nice brown. Serve the fried pork with it.

Mackerel a la Maitre d'Hotel.

Clean your mackerel, split it, soak it for an hour or more in oil seasoned with salt, grill it, brush it over with the oil, and serve very hot.

To Dress Fresh Sturgeon.

Cut slices, rub egg over them, then sprinkle with crumbs of bread, parsley, pepper, salt; fold them in paper, and broil gently.

Sauce: butter, anchovy and soy.

To Roast Sturgeon.

Put it on a lark-spit, then tie it on a large spit; baste it constantly with butter; and serve with good gravy, an anchovy, a squeeze of Seville orange or lemon, and a glass of sherry.

To Boil Sturgeon

Soak the fish in salt and water four hours, remove it, let it drain an hour, then put it into boiling water, let it be well covered, add three onions, a faggot of sweet herbs, and a small quantity of bay-salt. When it is boiled so tender that the bones will separate readily, remove it from the fire, take away bones and skin, cut it into slices, dredge it with flour, brown it before the fire, and serve with a gravy, the same as given above for roasting.

Sturgeon Broiled.

Cut a fine piece of the fish, and skinning it, divide it into slices. Beat up three eggs, and dip each of the slices into them; powder fine bread crumbs mixed with finely-chopped parsley, pepper and salt over them, fold them in paper, and broil them, being careful that the fire is clear. Send them to table with essence of anchovies and soy, accompanied by cold butter.

Cod.

Some people boil the cod whole; but a large head and shoulders contain all the fish that is proper to help, the thinner parts being overdone and tasteless, before the thick are ready. But the whole fish may be purchased at times more reasonably; and the lower half, if sprinkled and hung up, will be in high perfection in one or two days. Or it may be made salter, and served with egg-sauce, potatoes, and parsnips.

Cod when small is usually very cheap. If boiled quite fresh it is watery; but eats excellently if salted and hung up for a day to give it firmness, then stuffed and broiled, or boiled.

A good sauce for cod may be made thus: Boil four eggs hard, first half chop the whites, then put in the yolks, and chop them both together, but not very small; put them into half a pound of good melted butter, and let it boil up—then pour it on the fish.

To Dress Cod Sounds.

Steep your sounds as you do the salt cod, and boil them in a large quantity of milk and water; when they are very tender and white, take them up, and drain the water out and skin them; then pour the egg sauce boiling hot over them. and serve them up.

To Boil Salt Cod.

Clean and soak over night in water, with a glass of vinegar; boil it well and break into flakes; pour over a consistency of cream, thickened with flour and butter, and serve with egg sauce.

To Make a Currie of Cod.

It should be made of sliced cod, that has either been crimped or sprinkled a day, to make it firm. Fry it of a fine brown with onion; and stew it with a good white gravy, a little currie-powder, a bit of butter and flour, three or four spoonsful of rich cream, salt, and Cayenne, if the powder be not hot enough.

To Make Codfish Cakes.

First boil soaked cod, then chop it fine, put to it an equal quantity of potatoes boiled and mashed; moisten it with beaten eggs or milk, and a bit of butter and a little pepper; form it in small round cakes; flour the outside, and fry in hot lard or beef drippings until they are a delicate brown: like fish, these must be fried gently, the lard being boiling hot when they are put in.

To Boil Rock Fish.

The best part of the rock is the head and shoulders—clean it nicely, put it into the fish kettle with cold water and salt, boil it gently and skim it well; when done, drain off the water, lay it in the dish, and garnish with scraped horseradish; have two boats of butter nicely melted with chopped parsley, or for a change you may have anchovy butter; the roe and liver should be fried and served in separate dishes.

Stewed Flounders.

Procure four or six flounders, cut each in halves, put half a pint of water in a sauce-pan, with a little scraped horseradish, a little pepper, salt, sugar and fresh parsley; place over the fire, boil a minute, then add the flounders, stew ten minutes, take them out and place in a dish, reduce the liquor they were stewed in a little, pour over and serve.

Fried Flounders.

Let them be rubbed with salt inside and out, and lie two hours to give them some firmness. Dip them into egg; cover with crumbs and fry them.

Eels, a la Creme.

After cleaning the fish carefully, remove the cartilage which runs down the back, and season with a small quantity of cloves, mace, nutmeg, pepper, and allspice; put it into a small stew-pot, with very strong beef-gravy, port, and an equal quantity of Madeira or sherry.

It must be covered close; stew till tender, then take out the lampreys and keep hot, while you boil up the liquor with two or three anchovies chopped, and some flour and butter; strain the gravy through a sieve and add lemon-juice and some made-mustard. Serve with sippits of bread and horseradish.

Baked Eels.

Prepare as for frying; then put into a baking-pan, with a little water, flour, pepper, and salt. Bake twenty minutes. Make a gravy of the liquor in which they were baked, adding a little butter.

Fried Eels.

Skin them; then turn on boiling water, and let them stand in it a few moments; then cut them into pieces about three inches long. Fry a nice brown and serve.

Fried Catfish.

Skin your fish; cut off the heads; roll in flour or cracker dust, or in a batter of eggs and flour. Place in your frying-pan, in hot lard, season with pepper and salt, and fry a nice light brown.

To Fry Black Fish.

Scale the fish, and scrape the inside clean to the back bone, wash it in water, with a little vinegar; wipe it dry with a clean towel; then dip it in wheat flour, or rolled crackers. Have in a thick bottomed frying-pan plenty of lard salted, (a large tablespoon of salt to a pound of lard,) let it become boiling hot; then lay in the fish and fry it gently.

Sea Bass with Tomatoes.

Take three large fine sea bass or black fish. Cut off their heads and tails, and fry the fish in plenty of lard till about half done. Have ready a pint of tomatoes, that have been pickled cold in vinegar flavored with a muslin bag of mixed spices. Drain the tomatoes well from the vinegar; skin them, and mash them in a pan; dredging them with about as much flour as would fill a large tablespoon heaped up. Pour the mixture over the fish while in the frying-pan; and continue frying till they are thoroughly done.

To Fry Soles.

Skin them and cut off the fins, roll them in a cloth, dredge them with flour, rub them over with the yolk of an egg, shake bread crumbs over them, and fry them in boiling fat.

A Fricassee of Soles.

Fry them a nice brown, drain them, and make a few balls with a small sole boned and chopped, a little grated bread and lemon peel, parsley chopped, pepper, salt, nutmeg, yolk of egg, a piece of butter; fry these; thicken some good gravy (and some port wine, not too much) with a little flour, boil it up; add Cayenne ketchup and lemon juice; lay in the fish and balls, simmer them a few minutes, garnish with lemon.

Baked Pike.

Prepare the fish, let them dry for an hour, brush them over with an egg, cover one-half with butter, the other with bread crumbs, and bake them in hot butter. Perch can be done the same way, and so can many other fish.

To Fry Smelts.

They should not be washed more than is necessary to clean them. Dry them in a cloth; then lightly flour them, but shake it off. Dip them into plenty of egg, then into bread crumbs, grated fine, and plunge them into a good pan of *boiling* lard; let them continue gently boiling, and a few minutes will make them a bright yellow-brown. Take care not to take off the light roughness of the crumbs, or their beauty will be lost.

Red Mullet.

It is called the Sea-Woodcock. Clean, but leave the inside, fold in oiled paper, and gently bake in a small dish. Make a sauce of the liquor that comes from the fish, with a piece of butter, a little flour, a little essence of anchovy, and a glass of sherry. Give it a boil; and serve in a boat, and the fish in the paper cases.

Thornback and Skate

Should be hung one day at least before they are dressed; and may be served either boiled, or fried in crumbs, being first dipped in egg.

Crimp Skate.

Boil and send up in a napkin; or fry as above.

Maids.

Should likewise be hung one day at least. They may be boiled or fried; or, if of a tolerable size, the middle may be boiled and the fins fried. They should be dipped in egg, and covered with crumbs.

Boiled Carp.

Serve in a napkin, and with the sauce which you will find directed for it under the article Stewed Carp.

Stewed Carp.

Scald and clean, take care of the roe, etc., lay the fish in a stew-pan, with a rich beef gravy, an onion, eight cloves, a dessertspoonful of Jamaica pepper, the same of black, a fourth part of the quantity of gravy or port (cider may do); simmer close covered: when nearly done add two anchovies chopped fine, a dessertspoonful of made mustard, and some fine walnut ketchup, a bit of butter rolled in flour; shake it, and let the gravy boil a few minutes. Serve with sippets of fried bread, the roe fried, and a good deal of horseradish and lemon.

SHELL FISH.

How to Choose.

LOBSTERS and crabs when they are light, they are poor and watery. They should be solid and heavy when good. This can be easily ascertained by comparison.

Oysters and clams have the shells firmly closed. If they are in the slightest degree open, they are unfit for use. If opened and the liquor found to be stiff and slimy they are stale; but if perfectly good and sweet the liquor will be short and drip off quickly from the shell or spoon.

To Dress Lobsters.

When the lobster is boiled, rub it over with a little salad-oil, which wipe off again; separate the body from the tail, break off the great claws, and crack them at the joints, without injuring the meat; split the tail in halves, and arrange all neatly in a dish, with the body upright in the middle, and garnish with parsley.

Lobster Patties.

Minced lobster, four tablespoonsful of béchamel, six drops of anchovy sauce, lemon juice, Cayenne to taste.

Line the patty-pans with puff paste, and put into each a small piece of bread; cover with paste; brush over with egg, and bake of a light color. Take as much lobster as is required, mince the meat very fine, and add the above ingredients; stir it over the fire for five minutes; remove the lids of the patty-cases, take out the bread, fill with the mixture, and replace the covers.

Lobster Sauce.

The lobster being boiled, extract the meat from the shell, and beat it in a mortar. Rub it through a cullender or sieve, and put it into a sauce-pan with a spoonful of veloute (or velvet essence), if you have it, and one of broth. Mix it well, and add a piece of butter, some salt, and Cayenne pepper. Stew it ten minutes, and serve it up, with boiled fresh fish.

Lobster Cutlets.

One large lobster, one ounce fresh butter, half a saltspoonful of salt, pounded mace, grated nutmeg, Cayenne and white pepper to taste, egg, and bread crumbs.

Buttered Lobster.

Boil a lobster, then take the meat from the shell, and mince or chop it small; put the coral and green inside if liked, (leave out what is called the lady,) to a wineglassful of vinegar or hot water, and a quarter of a pound fresh butter; add a saltspoonful of Cayenne pepper, and made mustard, if liked; and put it with the lobster in a stew-pan over a gentle fire; stir it until it is thoroughly heated throughout. Serve hot; serve with lettuce in a salad-bowl; garnish with hard boiled egg: serve rolls with it.—For supper or a second course dinner dish.

To Stew Lobsters.
TIME, TWENTY MINUTES.

Pick the meat from one large, or two small hen lobsters in large pieces; boil the shells in a pint of water with a blade of mace and some whole pepper corns; when all the strength is extracted from the shells and spice, strain the liquor, mix the coral and the rich part of the lobster with a few spoonsful of melted butter, a wineglass of white wine, and the juice of half a lemon strained. Put in the picked lobster, boil it up and serve.

Scalloped Lobster.
TIME, FIFTEEN MINUTES.

Pick out all the meat from one large; or two middling-sized lobsters, and pound it in a mortar with a little pepper, salt, Cayenne, and a spoonful or more of white sauce, or thin melted butter, sufficient to moisten it. Split the empty shells of the tails and the bodies, and fill each of them neatly with the pounded lobster, cover them with grated bread, and put them into an oven. Serve on a folded napkin with fried parsley. Six or seven divided shells will be sufficient for a dish.

Broiled Lobsters.—An American Receipt.
TIME, FIFTEEN OR TWENTY MINUTES.

After having boiled the lobster, split it from head to tail. Take out the uneatable part called the "lady," lay it open, put pieces of butter over the meat, sprinkle it with pepper, and set the shells on a gridiron over bright coals until nicely heated through. Serve in the shells.

Crabs a la Russe.

Boil them from half to an hour, with a little salt; when done wipe dry, and take off the shell; take out the blue veins, and what is called the lady-fingers, as they are unwholesome; send to the table cold, garnish with melted butter.

Devilled Crabs.

Remove the meat from the shell, mix it with bread crumbs—about one-fourth will be sufficient; add white pepper, salt, a little Cayenne, grated nutmeg, and half a dozen small lumps of butter, each about the size of a nut; this last ingredient should be added to the fish after it has been returned to the shell. Squeeze lemon juice over it, lay a thick coat of bread crumbs over all, and bake.

Cold Dressed Crab.

Empty the shells and mix the flesh with oil, vinegar, salt, and a little white pepper and Cayenne; then put the mixture into the large shell, and serve. Very little oil is necessary.

Clam Soup.

Take fifty large, or one hundred small sand clams, and their liquor from the shells; strain the liquor; add to it a quart of milk and water each; if the clams are large, cut each in two and put them into it; set them over a moderate fire until the clams are tender, (about one hour,) skim it clear; put to it half a pound of soda crackers broken small, or half a pound of butter crackers rolled fine; cover the pot for ten minutes, then add quarter of a pound of sweet butter and serve hot.

To Fry Soft Shell Clams.

Get them from the shell, as they are very troublesome to clean. Wash them in plenty of water, and lay them on a thickly folded napkin to dry out the water; then roll a few at a time into wheat flour, until they will take up no more. Have a thick bottomed frying-pan, one-third full of boiling hot lard, and salted; (in proportion, a tablespoonful of salt to a pound of lard,) lay the clams in with a fork, one at a time; lay them close together and fry gently, until one side is a delicate brown, then turn carefully and brown the other; then take them off on a hot dish. When fried properly, these clams are very excellent.

To Stew Soft Shell Clams.

Get fifty clams taken from their shells, and freed from the black skin; wash them well in clear water and put them in a stew-pan with very little water; cover and set it over a gentle fire for half an hour; then add to them a bit of butter the size of a large egg or larger; dredge in a tablespoonful of flour, and salt and pepper to taste; stir it in them; cover the stew-pan for ten minutes, then serve hot. Many persons like the addition of a wineglass of vinegar.

Boiled Clams.—Boston Style.

Wash them clean, put them in a cooking vessel, with a little water, boil until the shells open; then remove the shells, cook in the same water, adding salt, pepper, and a good quantity of butter; when done, lay in a tureen, and eover with a few slices of toast bread.

To Fry Oysters—Washington Style.

Take a quarter of a hundred of large oysters, wash them and roll them in grated bread, with pepper and salt, and fry them a light brown; if you choose, you may add a little parsley, shred fine. They are a proper garnish for calves' head, or most made dishes.

To Make Oyster Loaves.

Take little round loaves, cut off the tops, scrape out all the crumbs, then put the oysters into a stew-pan with the crumbs that came out of the loaves, a little water, and a good lump of butter; stew them together ten or fifteen minutes, then put in a spoonful of good cream, fill your loaves, lay the bit of crust carefully on again, set them in the oven to crisp. Three are enough for a side dish.

To Fry Oysters.

Make a batter, wipe the oysters dry, dip them in the batter and roll them in crumbs of bread finely powdered, and fry in butter.

To Stew Oysters.

When you open them preserve the liquor and strain it; wash the oysters from the grit, simmer them very gently in their liquor; add pepper, cream, flour and butter, and serve with crackers or bits of bread.

To Stew Oysters—New York Style.

After carefully opening them, lay them in a stew-pan, and pour their own liquor (strained), on them, and heat slowly. When just commencing to simmer, lift them out with a slice and take off the beards; add to the liquor some good cream, a seasoning of pounded mace and Cayenne, and a little salt, and when it boils stir in some butter mixed with flour. Continue to stir the sauce until these last are blended with it, then put in the oysters, and let them remain by the side of the fire until they are very hot. Serve them garnished with pale fried sippets.

A little lemon-juice may be stirred quickly into the stew just as it is taken from the fire.

Oysters and Chestnuts.

Dip some oysters into a savory batter; bread crumb them, and fry them brown. In the same manner treat a similar number of blanched Spanish chestnuts. Make a sauce with the oyster liquor, a piece of butter rubbed in flour, and two glasses of white wine. Stew the chestnuts in this, add some yolk of egg to thicken, and pour it upon the oysters.

Oysters and Macaroni.

Lay some stewed macaroni in a deep dish; put upon it a thick layer of oysters, bearded, and seasoned with Cayenne pepper and grated lemon-rind. Add a small teacupful of cream; strew bread crumbs over the top, and brown it in a pretty quick oven. Serve hot, with a piquante sauce.

Scalloped Oysters.

Beard the oysters, wash in their own liquor, steep bread crumbs in the latter, put them with the oysters into scallop shells, with a bit of butter, and seasoning of salt, pepper, and a little grated nutmeg; make a paste with bread crumbs, crumbs and butter; cover, and roast them before the fire, or in an oven.

Oyster Fritters.

Beard, dip them into an omelette, sprinkle well with crumbs of bread, and fry them brown.

Oyster Pancakes.

Mix equal quantities of milk and oyster juice together. To a pint of the liquor when mixed, put a pint of wheat flour, a few oysters, a couple of eggs, and a little salt. Drop by the large spoonful into hot lard.

Philadelphia Roast.

Large oysters not opened, a few minutes before they are wanted, put them on a gridiron over a moderate fire. When done they will open, do not lose the liquor that is in the shell with the oysters; serve them hot upon a napkin.

Oyster Sauce.

Take a dozen oysters; blanch them by putting them in cold water, and boiling them for ten minutes. Make a nice melted butter, thus:—Take a pint of milk, let it boil; add a little flour for thickening; put in two ounces of butter, well-stirring it to keep it from burning. Then put in the oysters, with a pinch of Cayenne pepper, a little salt, and a tablespoonful of mushroom ketchup.

Milk Oyster Stew.

Take a pint of fine oysters, put them with their own liquor, and a gill of milk into a stew-pan, and if liked, a blade of mace; set it over the fire, take off any scum which may rise; when they are plump and white turn them into a deep plate; add a bit of butter, and pepper to taste.

Oyster Patties.

Beard some oysters, let them stew a minute or two in cream, have patty-pans covered with a light paste, place a bit of bread in each, put in two or three oysters on the top, sprinkle some sifted bread, and bake them in a quick oven.

Oysters—Vol-au-Vent.

Quarter sweet-breads after they have been soaked and blanched, put them into a stew-pan with a very little veal gravy, and the liquor strained off two dozen oysters, adding a very little salt; then put two ounces of butter into a stewpan, stir it, and thicken it with flour, and when the sweetbreads are sufficiently stewed add them with the gravy; after a few minutes put in the oysters, let them stew until the oysters are heated through: just before serving add a wineglassful of cream. A delicious stew may be made of oysters and tripe in this manner, simply omitting the veal gravy.

Panned Oysters.

Take a dozen large sized oysters; put first the liquor in the stew-pan, let it come to a boil, then put in your oysters with a lump of butter; season with pepper and salt to taste, and stew about two minutes. Can be served with toast.

To Feed Oysters.

Wash them perfectly clean in a pan of water, then lay them bottom downwards in a deep pan, and pour over them water with a large quantity of salt. Change the water every day. The salt should be previously dissolved in the water, allowing about five or six ounces to each gallon of water. You may fatten them by putting oatmeal into the water every day.

Prawns or Shrimps.

Take them out of the shells and warm them with a little good gravy, a bit of butter and flour, a scrape of nutmeg, salt and pepper; simmer a minute or two, and serve with sippets, or with a cream-sauce instead of brown.

To Pot Shrimps.

When boiled, take them out of the skins, and season them with salt, white pepper, and a very little mace and cloves. Press them into a pot, set it in the oven ten minutes, and when cold put butter.

Shrimp Sauce.

Pick half a pint of shrimps, and mix them in a sauce-pan with as much melted butter (brought to the thickness of cream) as you may require, and a teaspoonful of essence of anchovies.

For a family sauce, the heads and skins should be boiled up in a separate sauce-pan, and the liquor which is strained from them mixed with the butter; but as it is apt to give too strong a flavor, if you wish to make a delicate sauce you had better not use it.

MEATS, POULTRY, GAME, &c.

Beef.

HOW TO CHOOSE.

THIS is one of the most important branches of household affairs. There is not one person in fifty who is capable of selecting good meats, if his butcher chooses to impose upon him; and as for cooking, I suppose every one will admit there is room enough for reform in this department, all the world over. I have therefore taken pains to prepare a complete system of rules and observations by which any person of ordinary prudence and sagacity can not only purchase good meats, but have them cooked properly. The first thing in order then is to give the following hints in the selection of beef.

True well-fed ox-beef may be known by the texture and color; the lean will exhibit an open grain of deep coral red, and the fat will appear of a healthy, oily smoothness, rather inclining to white than yellow; the suet firm and white. Yellow fat is a test of meat of an inferior quality. Heifer-beef is but little inferior to ox-beef; the lean is of a closer grain, the red paler and the fat whiter. Cow-beef may be detected by the same signs, save that the older the beast the closer the texture of the meat will appear, and the flesh coarser to the sight, as well as harder to the touch.

The following receipts for the different modes of cooking beef have been selected with the greatest care possible, and each one of them has been fairly tested in the principal hotels in the different cities of the United States and Europe.

Roast Beef—American.

The tender loin and first and second cuts off the rack are the best roasting pieces—the third and fourth cuts are good. When the meat is put to the fire a little salt should be sprinkled on it, and the bony side turned towards the fire first. When the bones get well heated through, turn the meat, and keep a brisk fire—baste it frequently while roasting. There should be a little water put into the dripping pan when the meat is put down to roast. If it is a thick piece, allow fifteen minutes to each pound to roast it in—if thin, less time will be required.

Roast Sirloin of Beef—English.

Choose a nice sirloin of beef. Spit it or hook it on to the jack firmly, dredge it slightly with flour, and place it near the fire at first. Then draw it to a distance, and keep continually basting until the meat is done. Sprinkle a small quantity of salt over it, empty the dripping-pan of all the dripping, pour in some boiling water slightly salted, stir it about, and *strain* over the meat. Garnish with tufts of horseradish, and send horseradish sauce and Yorkshire pudding to table with it.

Beef a-la-Daube.

Get a round of beef, lard it well, and put it in an oven; cut the meat from a shin of beef, or any coarse piece in thin slices, put round the sides and over the top some slices of bacon, salt, pepper, onion, thyme, parsley, cellery tops, or seed pounded, and some carrots cut small, strew the pieces of beef over, cover it with water, let it stew very gently till perfectly done, take out the round, strain the gravy, let it stand to be cold, take off the grease carefully, beat the whites of four eggs, mix a little water with them, put them to the gravy, let it boil till it looks clear, strain it, and when cold put it over the beef.

Beef Stewed with Carrots.

Take a small piece of juicy beef, cut some carrots in thin slices, add a spoonful of flour and four ounces of butter, let them stew well with the beef, put in some salt and some stock, if necessary, serve with the carrots over the beef.

Beef Stewed with Raisins.

Boil two pounds of meat in a little good beef tea, cut the meat in pieces, then add half a pound of raisins, four ounces of butter, some browned flour, a quarter of a pound of sweet almonds cut in pieces, and allow all to stew some time.

Beefsteaks and Oysters Stewed.

TIME, ONE HOUR AND TWENTY MINUTES.

Put into a stew-pan a pound and a half of beefsteak, with two ounces of butter and a little water; when the meat is a nice brown, pour in half a pint of water, a little pepper and salt, and the liquor strained from the oysters. Set the pan over a moderate fire, and let the meat stew gently; then add five dessertspoonsful of port wine, a piece of butter, rolled in flour, and the oysters. Stew it all together till the oysters are done, and serve it up very hot.

Fricassee of Beef.

Cut some cold roast beef in thin slices, take off all the fat and skin, beat it up in a sauce made of some good broth thickened with flour and butter, add a little ketchup.

Broiled Beef.

Cut some slices of cold beef, broil them over a clear fire, and serve them with fried eggs or scalloped potatoes and brown sauce.

Broiled Beefsteak Rare.

When beef is desired very rare, have a good bed of live coals ready, lay the beef on the gridiron and put it on the coals. It should be ready to turn in three minutes. When it is turned, take it up carefully with two forks; roll it up so as to save the juice of the meat which has collected in cooking; do not squeeze the steak, but merely drain off the juice on the dish; put it back as quickly as possible, so that it may lose no heat in turning; add to the juice of the meat pepper, salt, and considerable butter, and set the dish over a kettle of boiling water. In three minutes, if the fire is right, it will be done.

Beef a-la-Mode.

Take the bone from a round of beef, fill the space with a forcemeat made of the crumbs of a stale loaf, four ounces of marrow, two heads of garlic chopped with thyme and parsley, some nutmeg, cloves, pepper and salt, mix it to a paste with the yolks of four eggs beaten, stuff the lean part of the round with it, and make balls of the remainder; sew a fillet of strong linen wide enough to keep it round and compact, put it in a vessel just sufficiently large to hold it, add a pint of red wine, cover it with sheets of tin or iron, set it in a brick oven properly heated, and bake it three hours; when done, skim the fat from the gravy, thicken it with brown flour, add some mushroom and walnut ketchup, and serve it up garnished with forcemeat balls fried. It is still better when eaten cold with salad.

Beefsteaks with Onions.

Take four pounds of the best sirloin steaks, cut thin. Season them with black pepper, and a very little salt. Put four tablespoonsful of butter into a frying-pan, and set it over the fire. When it is quite hot, put in the steaks and let them brown. Have ready your onions seasoned with a little pepper and salt, and thickened slightly with a good dredging of flour. Pour them over the steaks in the frying-pan, and then let them cook till thoroughly done.

Venison steaks will be found excellent dressed in this manner, but the venison must be fresh.

Boiled Beef.

The round is the best boiling piece. Put the meat in the pot with water enough to cover it; let it boil very slow at first, this is the great secret of making it tender; from two to three hours, according to size, is the rule for boiling.

Beefsteak Dumpling.

Take a nice juicy piece of beef, cut it in neat bits, which sprinkle some salt on and roll up tight, flour them a little, have a basin lined with plain suet paste, fill it with the rolls of beef, pour in a little ketchup, cover up the meat with paste, tie up the basin in a floured cloth, and boil it three hours.

Beef Tongue—London.

Boil a fresh tongue in beef broth, skin it, then add a quarter of a pint of stewed apples, and some small raisins; let them stew with the tongue a little, and if the sauce gets too thick add some more stock.

Beef Tongue—American.

Take a fresh tongue, divide it longways, boil it tender, dip it in flour, and bake it in butter to a nice bright brown; then stew it in a thick brown sauce, and serve it with red currant jelly.

French Roast Tongue.

TIME, TO BOIL, TWO HOURS AND A HALF; TO ROAST, HALF AN HOUR.

The tongue; twenty-four cloves; a quarter of a pound of butter; about six ounces of bread crumbs; two eggs.

Soak the tongue till it has thoroughly disgorged in lukewarm water, for about ten or twelve hours. Trim and scrape it, stick it over with the cloves, and boil it slowly for two or (if large) three hours. Then take it up and brush it over with the yolks of the eggs, sprinkle it with bread crumbs. Run a long iron skewer through it and roast it of a nice brown, basting it constantly with butter. Put it on a hot dish, and pour round it half a pint of good gravy, with a glass of wine. Serve it with red currant jelly.

Corned Beef.

The lean pieces are to be chosen for boiling; the "round" is one of the best. It should be but *slightly* corned—not allowed to remain in brine over two or three days, and boiled till the fibres are cut easily.

Potted Beef.

Take some cold boiled beef (the lean half of the round is the best), remove all the skinny parts, mince fine, and then pound in a mortar with some fresh butter till quite smooth. Season with a little nutmeg, a little black pepper, some Cayenne, a little mace, and salt if necessary. Press it very firmly into flat pots; clarify some fresh butter, and pour over the top of each pot, and when cold, paper it over, and keep in a cold place.

Spiced Beef.

TIME, ACCORDING TO WEIGHT.

The thin part of the ribs of beef; half an ounce of cloves; half an ounce of mace; half an ounce of black pepper; half an ounce of Jamaica pepper, and some chopped parsley.

Take the thin part of a piece of beef, after the rib piece (called the flap) has been cut off, if any of the ends of the bones are left, take them out. Rub it well with salt, and let it lay in pickle two days; then take the above quantities of spice and a little chopped parsley, and spread the whole equally over the beef; roll it up neatly and tie it very tight. Set in a stew-pan over a moderate fire, and let it stew slowly till quite tender. Then press it well, and when cold it will be fit to serve. The spices are to be laid on whole..

Cold Beef Hashed.

Slice the beef in very thin pieces, and shake a little flour over it. Chop a middle-sized onion, and put it into a stew-pan with a tablespoonful of sauce, and an equal quantity of ketchup; boil these together for two minutes, and then add half a pint of stock or gravy; boil this down to half its quantity, throw in the beef, set the hash to boil for five minutes longer, and then serve with sippets of bread round it.

Beef Sausages.

Take six pounds of beef quite free from skin, gristle, and fat; chop it very fine. Three pounds of fat shred very fine;

season it with two ounces of white pepper, a quarter of a pound of salt, half-quartern of the crumb of bread soaked in water; mix well together, put it into skins well cleaned, or press it into jars. When to be used, roll it up about the usual size of sausages. A little allspice is a great improvement.

Nice Patties from Under-done Beef.

Cut the meat into small dice, season with pepper, salt, and a little chopped onion. Make a plain paste, and roll it out thin; fill it with the mince, close up, and fry or bake to a light brown.

Stewed Beef Kidney.
TIME, HALF AN HOUR.

Cut the kidney into slices, and season it highly with pepper and salt, and fry it a light brown; then pour a little warm water into the pan, dredge in some flour, put in the slices of kidney, and let it stew very gently.

Kidney Toast.

Take a cold veal kidney, with a part of the fat, cut it into very small pieces, and pound the fat in a mortar with a little salt, bind altogether with the beaten whites of eggs; heap it upon toast, cover the whole with yolks beaten, dredge with bread crumbs, and bake in the oven.

To Fry Tripe.

Cut it into squares of about three inches. Make a nice batter; dip the pieces in, and then fry them in boiling fat. Peel twelve large onions, and boil them gently for an hour; then strain the water from them; dip them in the batter and fry them; then place a bit of tripe and onion alternately round the dish, the tripe resting on the onions; serve perfectly plain, or with a little fried parsley.

Fricaseed Tripe.

Cut a pound of tripe in narrow strips, put a small cup of water or milk to it, add a bit of butter the size of an egg, dredge in a large teaspoonful of flour, or work it with the butter; season with pepper and salt, let it simmer gently for half an hour, serve hot. A bunch of parsley cut small and put with it is an improvement.

To Dress a Bullock's Heart.
TIME, TWO HOURS.

Soak a bullock's heart for three hours in warm water; remove the lobes, and stuff the inside with veal forcemeat; sew it securely in; fasten some white paper over the heart, and roast it for two hours before a strong fire, keeping it basted *frequently*. Just before serving, remove the paper, baste, and froth it up, and serve with a rich gravy poured round it, and currant jelly separately.

Fried Liver.

Cut beef liver into slices about half an inch thick, and pour boiling water over them, in which let them stand twenty minutes; then drain, and dredge with flour, salt, and pepper. Fry in fat fifteen minutes.

Broiled Liver.

Prepare as for frying, and broil fifteen minutes over clear coals. Season with butter, salt, and pepper. When for dinner, serve boiled or baked potatoes, squash, and macaroni; the latter only if desired.

Beef Marrow Bones.

Cut them in short pieces, stop up the holes with a bit of bread or dough; boil them some hours, and serve the marrow bones, each enveloped in a napkin, with dry toast.

Beef Palates.

Simmer them in water several hours, till they will peel; then cut the palates into slices, or leave them whole, as you choose, and stew them in a rich gravy, till as tender as possible; before being served, season with a little salt and ketchup.

Veal.
HOW TO CHOOSE.

The flesh of a bull-calf is firmer than that of a cow, but then it is seldom so white; the fillet of a cow-calf is generally preferred, on account of the udder; if the head is fresh, the eyes are plump, but if stale, they are sunk and wrinkled. If a shoulder is stale, the vein is not of a bright red; if there are any green or yellow spots in it it is very bad. The breast and neck to be good should be white and dry; if they are clammy, and look green or yellow at the upper end, they are stale. The loin is apt to taint under the kidney; if it is stale it will be soft and slimy. A leg should be firm and white; if it is limp and the flesh flabby, with green or yellow spots, it is not good.

A loin of veal must always be roasted; the fillet or leg may be dressed in various ways, the knuckle or knee is proper for soup or for boiling; these are the pieces that compose the hind quarter. In the fore-quarter, the breast and rack admit variety in cooking; the shoulder and neck are only fit for soup.

To Roast Veal

Will take a quarter of an hour to a pound. Paper the fat of the loin and fillet; stuff the fillet and shoulder with the following ingredients—A quarter of a pound of suet, chopped fine, parsley and sweet herbs, chopped, grated bread and lemon peel, pepper, salt, nutmeg, and yolk of an egg; butter may supply the want of suet; roast the breast with the caul on till it is almost done, then take it off, flour it, and baste it; veal requires to be more done than beef. For sauce, salad, pickles, potatoes, brocoli, cucumbers, raw or stewed, French beans, peas, cauliflower, celery, raw or stewed

To Stew a Breast of Veal.

Cut it into pieces about three inches in size, fry it nicely; mix a little flour with some beef broth, an onion, two or three cloves; stew this some time, strain it, add three pints or two quarts of peas, or some heads of asparagus cut like peas; put in the meat, let it stew gently; add pepper and salt.

To Stew a Neck of Veal.

Take the best end of the neck, put it into a stew-pan with some boiling water, some salt, whole pepper, and cloves tied in a bit of muslin, an onion, a piece of lemon-peel; stew this till tender; take out spice and peel, put in a little milk and flour mixed, some celery ready boiled and cut into lengths; boil it up, then serve.

Veal Cutlets, a-la Maitre d'Hotel.

Fry three or four slices of pork until brown—take them up, then put in slices of veal, about an inch thick, cut from the leg. When brown on both sides, take them up—stir half a pint of water into the gravy, then mix two or three teaspoonsful of flour with a little water, and stir it in—soak a couple of slices of toasted bread in the gravy, lay them on the bottom of the platter, place the meat and pork over it, then turn on the gravy. A very nice way to cook the cutlets, is to make a batter with half a pint of milk, an egg beaten to a froth, and flour enough to render it thick. When the veal is fried brown, dip it into the batter, then put it back into the fat, and fry it until brown again.

Baked Fillet of Veal.

Take the bone out of the fillet, wrap the flap around and sew it, make a forcemeat of bread crumbs, the fat of bacon, a little onion chopped, parsley, pepper, salt, and a nutmeg pounded, wet it with the yolks of eggs, fill the place from which the bone was taken, make holes around it with a knife and fill them also, and lard the top; put it in a Dutch oven with a pint of water, bake it sufficiently, thicken the gravy with butter and brown flour, add a gill of wine and one of mushroom ketchup, and serve it garnished with forcemeat balls fried.

Scotch Collops of Veal.

They may be made of the nice part of the rack, or cut from the fillet, rub a little salt and pepper on them, and fry them a light brown; have a rich gravy seasoned with wine, and any kind of ketchup you choose, with a few cloves of garlic, and some pounded mace, thicken it, put the collops in and stew them a short time, take them out, strain the gravy over, and garnish with bunches of parsley fried crisp, and thin slices of middling of bacon, curled around a skewer and boiled.

Veal Olives.

Take the bone out of the fillet, and cut thin slices the size of the leg, beat them flat, rub them with the yolk of an egg beaten, lay on each piece a thin slice of boiled ham, sprinkle salt, pepper, grated nutmeg, chopped parsley, and bread crumbs over all, roll them up tight, and secure them with skewers, rub them with egg and roll them in bread crumbs, lay them on a tin dripping-pan, and set them in an oven; when brown on one side, turn them, and when sufficiently done, lay them in a rich highly seasoned gravy made of proper thickness, stew them till tender, garnish with forcemeat balls and green pickles sliced.

Ragout of Breast of Veal.

Separate the joints of the brisket, and saw off the sharp ends of the ribs, trim it neatly, and half roast it; put it in a stew-pan with a quart of good gravy seasoned with wine, walnut and mushroom ketchup, a teaspoonful of curry powder, and a few cloves of garlic; stew it till tender, thicken the gravy, and garnish with sweetbreads nicely broiled.

Fricando of Veal.

Cut slices from the fillet an inch thick and six inches long, lard them with slips of lean middling of bacon, bake them a light brown, stew them in well seasoned gravy, made as thick as rich cream, serve them up hot, and lay round the dish sorrel stewed with butter, pepper and salt, till quite dry.

To Stuff and Roast a Calf's Liver.

Take a fresh calf's liver, and having made a hole in it with a large knife run in lengthways, but not quite through, have ready a forcemeat, or stuffing made of part of the liver parboiled, fat of bacon minced very fine, and sweet herbs powdered; add to these some grated bread and spice finely powdered, with pepper and salt. With this stuffing fill the hole in the liver, which must be larded with fat bacon, and then roasted, flouring it well, and basting with butter till it is enough. This is to be served up hot, with gravy sauce having a little wine in it.

To Broil Calf's Liver.

Cut it in slices, put over it salt and pepper; broil it nicely, and pour on some melted butter with chopped parsley after it is dished.

To Fry Calf's Feet.

Prepare them as for the fricassee, dredge them well with flour and fry them a light brown, pour parsley and butter over, and garnish with fried parsley.

To Stew Calf's Feet.

Take a calf's foot, divide it into four pieces, put it to stew with half a pint of water; pare a potato, take a middling onion peeled and sliced thin, some pepper, and salt; put these ingredients to the calf's foot, and let them simmer very softly for two hours. It is very good.

To Bake a Calf's Head.

Divide the calf's head, wash it clean, and having the yolks of two eggs well beaten, wash the outside of the head all over with them, and on that strew raspings of bread sifted, pepper, salt, nutmeg and mace powdered; also, the brains cut in pieces and dipped in thick batter, then cover the head with bits of butter, pour into the pan some white wine and water, with as much gravy, and cover it close. Let it be baked in a quick oven, and when it is served up, pour on some strong gravy, and garnish with slices of lemon, red beet root pickled, fried oysters and dried bread.

To Boil Calf's Head.

Tie it up in a cloth, and boil it for two and a half hours in plenty of water. Tie the brains in a bit of cloth, with a little parsley and a leaf or two of sage. Boil them one hour; chop them small; warm them up in a sauce-pan, with a bit of butter and a little pepper and salt; lay the tongue, boiled the same time, peeled, in the middle of a small dish; place the brains round it; have in another dish bacon or pickled pork.

To Roast Calf's Heart.

TIME, FROM HALF AN HOUR TO AN HOUR, DEPENDING ON THE SIZE.

Put the heart to disgorge in lukewarm water for an hour nearly; then wipe it dry, stuff it with a nice and highly seasoned veal stuffing or forcemeat. Cover it with buttered paper, and set it down to roast at a good fire. Serve it with good gravy, or any sharp sauce.

Send it up as hot as possible to table.

To Fry Sweetbreads.

Cut them in long slices, beat up the yolk of an egg, and rub it over them with a feather; make a seasoning of pepper, salt, and grated bread; dip them into it, and fry them in butter. For sauce—ketchup and butter, with stock-gravy or lemon sauce; garnish with small slices of toasted bacon and crisped parsley.

To Fry Calf's Brains.

Take the brains, being very careful not to break them, season them with pepper and salt to taste. Roll them in cracker dust or in a batter of egg and flour, fry them in hot lard, until a light brown, same as fried oysters, and serve.

To Hash Veal.

When sliced, flour it, put it into a little gravy, with grated lemon-peel, pepper, salt, ketchup, boil it up, add a little juice of lemon; serve round it toasted sippets.

To Dress a Calf's Pluck.

Boil the lights and part of the liver; roast the heart, stuffed with suet, sweet herbs and a little parsley all chopped small, a few crumbs of bread, some pepper, salt, nutmeg, and a little lemon-peel; mix it up with the yolk of an egg.

To Pot Veal.

Take a part of a knuckle or fillet of veal, that has been stewed, or bake it on purpose for potting; beat it to a paste, with butter, salt, white pepper, and mace, pounded; press it down in pots, and pour over it clarified butter.

Directions for Cleaning Calf's Head and Feet.

FOR THOSE WHO LIVE IN THE COUNTRY AND BUTCHER THEIR OWN MEATS.

As soon as the animal is killed, have the head and feet taken off, wash them clean, sprinkle some pounded rosin all over the hairs, then dip them in boiling water, take them instantly out; the rosin will dry immediately, and they may be scraped clean with ease; the feet should be soaked in water three or four days, changing it daily; this will make them very white.

Mutton.

TO CHOOSE MUTTON.

Good mutton is firm and close in the grain, the color is red, and the fat white and firm. Wether mutton is better than that of the ewe.

Mutton is in the highest perfection from August until Christmas, when it begins to decline in quality.

Mutton for roasting or steaks should hang as long as it will keep without tainting. Let it hang in the air in a cool, dry place. Pepper will keep flies from it. The chine or rib bones should be wiped every day. The bloody part of the neck should be cut off. In the breast the brisket changes first. In the hind-quarter, the part under and about the kidneys is first to taint.

Mutton for stewing or broiling should not be so long kept. It will not be so fine a color if it is.

Saddle of Mutton.

TIME, A QUARTER OF AN HOUR TO A POUND.

Take off the skin, cover the fat with a sheet of well-greased paper, and roast it a nice brown, just before it is finished cooking remove the paper, sprinkle the joint with salt, dredge it well over with flour, and drop warm butter over it. Serve it with good gravy, or empty the contents of a dripping-pan into a basin, from which remove the fat, add a little warm water and use this natural gravy. Red currant jelly as sauce.

Roast Shoulder of Mutton.

TIME, A QUARTER OF AN HOUR TO EACH POUND.

A shoulder of mutton should not be basted in roasting, but simply rubbed with a little butter.

Put the spit in close to the shank bone, and run it along to the blade bone. Roast this joint at a sharp, brisk fire. It should be well hung; and served with onion sauce. It may be filled with bread, butter, salt, pepper, and sage; or, if preferred, potato stuffing may be used.

Broiled Mutton with Tomato Sauce.

Cold boiled leg of mutton, if not too much boiled, is very good cut in rather thick slices, sprinkled with pepper and salt and broiled. To be served very hot, with a thick sauce flavored strongly with fresh tomatoes or tomato sauce.

Broiled Mutton Chops.

Cut the rack as for the harrico, broil them, and when dished pour over them a gravy made with two large spoonsful of boiling water, one of mushroom ketchup, a small spoonful of butter and some salt, stir it till the butter is melted, and garnish with horseradish scraped.

Breast of Mutton in Ragout.

Prepare the breast as for boiling, brown it nicely in the oven, have a rich gravy well seasoned and thickened with brown flour, stew the mutton in it till sufficiently done, and garnish with forcemeat balls fried.

Stewed Mutton.

Stew the chops in a little water till very tender; then dredge a little flour in the water.

Boiled Leg of Mutton.

Wash a leg of mutton, dredge it well with flour, and wrap it in a cloth, then put it in a pot of hot water, and boil according to its weight. Serve with drawn butter or parsley sauce, with boiled vegetables and pickles.

Boiled Breast of Mutton.

Separate the joints of the brisket, and saw off the sharp ends of the ribs, dredge it with flour, and boil it; serve it up covered with onions—see onion sauce.

Minced Mutton, and Mashed Potatoes.

Mince the mutton finely, and stew it in a little gravy, to which add a dessertspoonful of mushroom or walnut ketchup, and a little butter. Stew till hot; thicken with a little flour, and serve on a dish surrounded by mashed potatoes.

Lamb.
HOW TO CHOOSE.

The vein in the neck of a fore-quarter of lamb will be a fine blue if it is fresh; if it is of a green or yellowish color it is stale.

The hind-quarter first becomes tainted under the kidney.

A fore-quarter includes the shoulder, neck and breast.

A hind-quarter is the leg and loin.

The pluck is sold with the head, liver, heart and lights. The melt is not used with us.

The fry contains the sweet-breads, skirts, and some of the liver.

Lamb may be hashed, stewed, roasted, fried, broiled, or made in a pie, the same as veal.

Lamb Cutlets and Green Peas, a-la-Royal.
TIME, EIGHT OR TEN MINUTES.

Take the cutlets from the best end of the neck; chop off the thick part of the chine bone, and trim the cutlets neatly by taking off the skin and the greater part of the fat, scraping the upper part of the bones perfectly clean. Brush each cutlet over with well-beaten yolk of egg, and then sprinkle them with fine bread crumbs, seasoned with pepper and salt. After this dip them separately into a little clarified butter. Sprinkle more crumbs over them and fry them, turning them occasionally. Have ready half a peck of green peas, nicely boiled, and arranged in a pyramid or raised form in the centre of a hot dish. Lay the cutlets before the fire to drain, and then place them round the green peas.

Roast Leg of Lamb.
TIME, ONE HOUR AND THREE-QUARTERS FOR SIX POUNDS.

Procure a fine fresh leg of lamb, and place it some distance from the fire, basting it frequently a short time before it is done, move it nearer, dredge it with flour and a little salt, and baste it with dissolved butter, to give it a nice frothy appearance. Then empty the dripping-pan of its contents, pour in a cupful of *hot* water, stir it well round, and pour the gravy over the meat, through a fine sieve. Serve with mint sauce and a salad.

Roast Shoulder of Lamb.
TIME, ONE HOUR AND A QUARTER.

Place the joint at a moderate distance from a nice clear fire, and keep it constantly basted, to prevent the skin from becoming burnt. When done, dish it up; and serve it with gravy made in the dripping-pan and poured round it. Send up mint sauce in a tureen.

Lamb Chops.
TIME, EIGHT TO TEN MINUTES.

Chops from the loin; pepper and salt; a mold of mashed potatoes.

Cut the chops from a loin of lamb; let them be about three-quarters of an inch thick. Broil them over a clear fire. When they are done, season them with pepper and salt. Have ready a mold of nicely mashed potatoes in a hot dish; place the chops leaning against them, and serve very hot. Or they may be served garnished only with fried parsley.

Lamb's Fry.

The heart and sweet bread are nice fried plainly, or dipped into a beaten egg and fine bread crumbs. They should be fried in lard.

Stewed Lamb.

Take half a shoulder of lamb and boil it in two quarts of water for two hours. Then put in potatoes, onions, turnips cut in quarters, salt and pepper to taste. Ten minutes before serving put in the dumplings.

Boned Quarter of Lamb.

TIME, A QUARTER OF AN HOUR TO EACH POUND.

One pound of forcemeat; melted butter.

Bone a quarter of lamb, fill it with forcemeat, roll it round, and tie it with a piece of string, cover it with a buttered paper, and roast it. Serve it with melted butter.

Pork, Hams, &c.

HOW TO CHOOSE.

Pork, if it is measley, is very dangerous to eat; it may be easily seen, the fat being full of little kernels; if it is young, the lean will break if pinched, and the skin will dent by nipping it with the fingers; the fat will be soft and pulpy, like lard; if the rind is thick, rough, and cannot be nipped with the fingers, it is old; if the flesh is cool and smooth, it is fresh; if it is clammy, it is tainted; it will be worse at the knuckle than at any other part.

Very great care should be used in purchasing pork, as of late years pigs have been subject to much disease, and the flesh of the animal then becomes perfectly poisonous. If possible, learn where and how the pork you eat is fattened.

A pig should only be six months old for boiling or roasting, larger and older, of course, for salting. A pig should be short-legged and thick-necked, and have a small head.

Hams with short shanks are best. Put a knife under the bone, if it comes out clean and smells well, it is good; but if it is daubed and smeared, and has a disagreeable smell, it is bad.

To Roast Leg of Pork with Stuffing.

TIME, TWENTY MINUTES FOR EACH POUND.

Cut a slit in the knuckle, raise the skin, put under it some nice sage and onion stuffing, and fasten it in with a small skewer; put it at some distance from the fire, and baste it frequently. Just before it is done, moisten the skin all over with a little butter, dredge it with flour, and place it near the fire to brown and crisp. When done, put it on a hot dish, pour a litttc gravy made in the dripping-pan round it, and serve with apple sauce.

To Roast a Sparerib of Pork.
TIME, ONE HOUR AND THREE-QUARTERS FOR SIX POUNDS.

Score the skin, put the joint down to a bright fire to roast, rub a little flour over it. If the rind is kept on, roast it without a buttered paper over it, but if the skin and fat are removed, cover it with a buttered paper. Keep it frequently basted. About ten minutes before taking it up, strew over it some powdered sage; froth it with a little butter, and serve with gravy strained over it, and apple sauce in a tureen.

Baked or Roast Pig.

A pig for roasting or baking should be small and fat. Take out the inwards, and cut off the first joint of the feet, and boil them till tender, then chop them. Prepare a dressing of bread soaked soft, the water squeezed out, and the bread mashed fine, season it with salt, pepper, and sweet herbs, add a little butter, and fill the pig with the dressing. Rub a little butter on the outside of the pig, to prevent its blistering. Bake or roast it from two hours and a half, to three hours. The pan that the pig is baked in should have a little water put in it. When cooked, take out a little of the dressing and gravy from the pan, mix it with the chopped inwards and feet, put in a little butter, pepper and salt, and use this for a sauce.

Pork Olives.

Cut slices from a fillet or leg of cold·fresh pork. Make a forcemeat in the usual manner, only substituting for sweet herbs some sage leaves chopped fine. When the slices are covered with the forcemeat, and rolled up and tied round, stew them slowly either in cold gravy left of the pork, or in fresh lard. Drain them well before they go to table. Serve them up on a bed of mashed turnips or potatoes, or of mashed sweet potatoes, if in season.

Pork Chops.

Take a loin of pork and divide it into chops, strew some parsley and thyme, cut small, some pepper, salt, and grated bread over them; boil them a fine brown; have ready some good gravy, a spoonful of ready-made mustard, two eschalots shred small; boil these together over the fire, thickened with a piece of butter rolled in flour, and a little vinegar, if agreeable. Put the chops into a hot dish, and pour the sauce over them.

To Toast a Ham.

Boil it well, take off the skin, and cover the top thickly with bread crumbs, put it in an oven to brown, and serve it up.

To Stuff a Ham.

Take a well smoked ham, wash it very clean, make incisions all over the top two inches deep, stuff them quite full with parsley chopped small and some pepper, boil the ham sufficiently; do not take off the skin. It must be eaten cold.

To Boil a Ham

Steep it all night in soft water; a large one should simmer three hours, and boil gently two; a small one should simmer two hours and boil about one and a half; pull off the skin, rub it over with yolk of egg; strew on bread crumbs, set it before the fire till of a nice light brown.

Genuine Country Sausage.

Three parts of pork to one of beef; four ounces of salt and one of pepper to every ten pounds of sausage meat.

Chop the pork and the beef nicely together, and mix it well up with the seasoning, and either press it into pots and roll it when it is used, or put it into skins.

Holland Pudding.

Boil a belly-piece of pork till tender; cut it into dice; put to it some hog's blood, some rice flour, or other flour, to thicken it; season it well with pepper, what salt is necessary, and pounded cloves; put this into the great skins, which fill about half full; boil them; when enough they will swim; the pork is best to be out of the pickle for hours.

To Roast a Pig's Head.
TIME, TO ROAST, HALF AN HOUR.

Half an ounce of sage; one tablespoonful of salt; one dessertspoonful of pepper.

Boil it till tender enough to take the bones out. Then chop some sage fine, mix it with the pepper and salt, and rub it over the head. Hang it on the spit, and roast it at a good fire. Baste it well. Make a good gravy and pour over it. Apple sauce is eaten with it.

Pig's Head Boiled.
TIME, ONE HOUR AND A HALF.

This is the more profitable dish, though not so pleasant to the palate; it should first be salted, which is usually done by the pork butcher; it should be boiled gently; serve with vegetables.

Pig's Cheek.
TIME, THREE-QUARTER'S OF AN HOUR.

Pig's cheek; one ounce of bread crumbs. Boil and trim in the shape of ham, and, if very fat, carve it as a cockle-shell; glaze it well, or put over it bread crumbs and brown them.

Pig's Kidneys.
TIME, FIFTEEN MINUTES.

Pig's kidneys are prepared exactly as sheep's kidneys are; they are nearly divided, fastened flat open with a tiny skewer, and broiled over a clear fire. They are served quite plain, or with maitre d'hotel sauce, if preferred.

Pig's Feet and Ears.
TIME, TO BOIL, ONE HOUR AND A HALF; TO BROIL, TEN MINUTES.

Two onions; one teaspoonful of made mustard; two ounces of butter; one teaspoonful of flour.

When you have cleaned and prepared the feet and ears, boil them; then split the feet in halves, egg and bread crumb them, and broil them. Cut the ears into fillets, put them into a stewpan with two sliced onions, two ounces of butter, and a teaspoonful of flour. When they are browned, take them up, add a teaspoonful of made mustard to the *puree*, and lay them on a hot dish. Put the feet on the top of them, and serve.

Hog's Head Cheese.

Boil a pig's head until the bones will drop out. When cold, chop fine and season with pepper, salt, and sage; then put it into a kettle, and to every quart of meat add half a pint of the liquor in which it was boiled. Simmer slowly for half an hour, turn it into deep earthen dishes, and on top place a plate with a weight upon it. When cold cut in slices.

American Pork Pudding.

Take the refuse parts of pork after killing, such as lights, liver, head, and all the offal of bones. Put in a kettle of boiling water; let the whole remain until the meat falls from the bones. Chop fine, season, and flavor as you would sausage, then place it in skins loose. Boil again for about twenty minutes, then remove and cool them off with cold water, and hang them up to dry, when they will be ready for use. The meat may be potted instead of pressing into skins.

Bologna Sausage.

TIME TO BOIL, ONE HOUR.

Take a pound of bacon, fat and lean together, the same each of beef, pork, and veal, chop all very fine, and mix it with three-quarters of a pound of finely-chopped beef suet, sage leaves, and sweet herbs; season it highly with pepper and salt. Then fill a large skin, and put it into a sauce-pan of boiling water, pricking the skin for fear of its bursting; let it boil slowly for an hour, then place it on straw to dry.

Pig's Feet Soused.

TIME, ONE HOUR AND A HALF.

Scald the feet and scrape them clean; if the covering of the toes will not come off without, singe them in hot embers, until they are loose; then take them off. Some persons put the feet in weak lime-water to whiten them. Having scraped them clean and white, wash them and put them into a pot of warm, but not boiling water, with a little salt. Let them boil gently till by turning a fork in the flesh it will easily break and the bones are all loosened. Take off the scum as it rises. When they are done, take them out of the water and lay them in vinegar enough to cover them, adding to it a quarter of a pint of the water in which they were boiled. Add whole pepper and spice with cloves and mace. Put them in a jar, and cover them closely.

Soused Feet in Ragout.

Split the feet in two, dredge them with flour and fry them a nice brown; have some well seasoned gravy thickened with brown flour and butter; stew the feet in it a few minutes.

To Pickle Pork.

Rub each piece with common salt, lay them on a slanting board, that the brine may run off; the next day rub each piece with pounded saltpetre; dry some salt, and put a layer at the bottom of the pan, then a layer of pork, and so on till the pan is full; fill all the hollow places with salt, and lay salt on the top; cover the pan. Half a pound of saltpetre is enough for a middle-sized pig.

To Keep Smoked Hams.

Make sacks of coarse cotton cloth, large enough to hold one ham, and fill in with chopped hay all around, about two inches thick. The hay prevents the grease from coming in contact with the cloth, and keeps all insects from the meat. Hang in the smoke-house, or other dry, cool place, and they will keep a long time.

Fried Sausages.

Lay them in the pan and pour boiling water over them; let them boil two minutes, then turn off the water and prick the sausages with a fork, or they will burst open when they begin to fry. Put a little butter in the pan with them, and fry twenty minutes. Turn them often that they may be brown on all sides. Cut stale bread to fry in the sausage fat, and garnish the dish with it. Bread is delicious fried in this way. Serve plain boiled potatoes, squash, mashed turnips, and apple-sauce.

Pig's Tongues.

Partially boil the tongues in order to remove the skin. Pickle them as you do hams (according to previous receipts); lay them one on the top of each other under a heavy weight. Cover the pan in which you place them, and let them remain for a week, then dry them, and put them into sausage skins. Fasten them up at the ends, and smoke them.

POULTRY AND GAME.

How to Choose.

VENISON.—If the fat be clear, bright, and thick, and the cleft part close and smooth, it is young; but if the cleft is wide and tough, it is old.

TURKEYS.—In old birds the legs are rough and reddish; in young birds they are smooth and black. When fresh killed the eyes are clear and full, and the feet moist.

FOWLS.—If a cock, choose one with short spurs, observing that they have not been pared or cut; if a hen, her comb and legs must be smooth; feel whether the breast-bone is well covered; if not, they have probably died from disease.

GEESE.—When old the bills and feet are red; when young they are yellow. When fresh killed the feet are pliable; when too long kept they are stiff.

DUCKS.—Those with pliable feet and plump breasts are the best.

PIGEONS.—They have supple feet when young.

PARTRIDGES.—If young birds, the bills are dark colored, and the legs yellow.

PHEASANTS.—The cock bird is accounted best, except when the hen is with egg. If young, he has short blunt or round spurs; but if old, they are long and sharp.

SNIPE AND WOODCOCK.—The feet are thick and hard when the birds are old; if soft and tender they are young and recently killed.

PLOVERS.—When young, they are limber-footed; when fat, they feel hard at the vent; when lean, they feel thin in the vent; when stale, they are dry-footed.

HARES AND RABBITS.—When old, the haunches are thick, and the ears dry and tough. The ears of a young hare tear very easily.

To Roast Venison.

Put over it a sheet of paper, then a paste of flour and water, over that a sheet of thick paper, well tied on; a haunch, if it be large, will take four hours; just before it is sent to table, take off the papers and paste; flour, and baste it with butter. For sauce, gravy and sweet sauce in separate boats.

To Hash Venison.

Cut nice slices from the venison you may have left cold, not forgetting to put plenty of fat with it, flour it, place it in a sauce-pan; pour over it three half-pints of stock gravy, a gill of port wine, a little currant jelly, and two tablespoonsful of ketchup; let it simmer gently, it must not boil, or it will make the venison hard; as soon as it is thoroughly hot, add a little salt and Cayenne paper; serve with sippets round the dish. There should be currant jelly on the table.

To Mince Venison.

Mince some cold venison finely, season with salt, make it up into balls, with sufficient gravy to make them stick, dip them in batter, roll them in bread crumbs, and broil them; serve with brown sauce.

To Stew Venison.

Cut some slices of cold venison, stew it in some of its own gravy, dredge some flour over it, and add a mixture of butter, ketchup, and red currant jelly; serve with square pieces of fried bread on it.

Roast Turkey with Chestnuts.

Fifty chestnuts; marrow from marrow bones; a little butter, flour, and salt.

Truss a turkey for roasting. Boil half a hundred of chestnuts till tender; remove the shell; chop them very fine. Take the marrow of two marrow bones, cut into pieces, stuff the turkey with the marrow and chestnuts. Fix a buttered paper over the breast; put it down to a good fire, and baste it constantly while roasting. Then take off the paper, baste the turkey well with butter, sprinkle a little salt over it, and dredge it with flour to froth it. When done, take it up, pour over it a little chestnut sauce, and serve it with brown gravy separately.

Sauce: bread sauce.

To Roast Turkey—American.

Make the stuffing of bread, crumbled fine, one pound of butter, salt, pepper, and two onions chopped fine, stuff it, sprinkle it with salt, pepper and flour. Two hours and a half will cook it, unless very large. Baste it frequently.

The giblets must be boiled tender for gravy, with salt and pepper, and a little onion, thickened with flour and butter.

Fricasseed Turkey.

Cut up a small young turkey, rinse it in cold water, put it in a stew-pan, with water to cover it, cover the stew-pan and set it over a gentle fire; take off the scum as it rises, add a large teaspoonful of salt when it is tender and white; add a small teaspoonful of pepper, work a tablespoonful of flour with quarter of a pound of sweet butter, stir it into the fricassee by the spoonful. Dip a bunch of parsley in hot water, chop it small, and put it in the stew-pan; cover it and let it simmer gently, for fifteen or twenty minutes, then serve with boiled rice or mashed potatoes.

To Bone Turkey.

Have a tender turkey; and after drawn, and washed, and wiped dry, lay it on a table, and take a sharp knife, with a narrow blade and point. Begin at the neck; then go round to the shoulders and wings, and separate the flesh from the bone, scraping it down as you proceed. Loosen the flesh from the breast, and back, and body, and from the thighs. The knife should always penetrate quite to the bone; scraping loose the flesh rather than cutting it. When all the flesh has been completely loosened, take the turkey by the neck, give it a pull, and the whole skeleton will come out entire from the flesh. The flesh will then fall down, a flat and shapeless mass. Sew up any holes that have accidentally been torn in the skin. Then fill with forcemeat, when it will be ready for roasting.

Devilled Turkeys and Fowls.

Take the first and second joints of a roast turkey and cut deep gashes in them, and into these gashes put a little mixed mustard, a little salt and Cayenne pepper; lay on the gridiron until heated through; then place on a very hot dish, and spread with butter. Serve immediately.

To Roast Chickens or Fowls.

Leave out the livers, gizzards, and hearts, to be chopped and put into the gravy. Fill the crops and bodies of the fowls with a forcemeat, put them before a clear fire, and roast them an hour, basting them with butter, or with clarified dripping.

Having stewed the necks, gizzards, livers, and hearts in a very little water, strain it, and mix it hot, with the gravy that has dripped from the fowls, which must be first skimmed. Thicken it with a little browned flour, add to it the livers, hearts, and gizzards chopped small.

Fried Fowl.

Beat up two yolks of eggs, with butter; cut cold fowl into neat pieces, dip them in the egg and butter, then in bread crumbs, and fry them; put them on a dish with some chopped spinach or peas round them.

Boiled Chickens and Tongue.

TIME, HALF AN HOUR.

Draw and dress a couple of young chickens. Have a tongue trimmed and glazed, place it in the centre of the dish, and a chicken on each side. Garnish with brocoli. Pour over the *chickens* and the *brocoli*, but not the tongue, a little white sauce; and serve them up hot.

Stewed Fowl.

Take an old fowl, boil it for three hours in two quarts of water; then add a quarter of a pound of rice, a little salt; take out the fowl, put it on a dish, and arrange the rice round it; pour on it some thick white sauce made from cream.

Croquettes of Fowl.

Pound the white part of a fowl or some cold veal in a mortar, add a little salt; beat up an egg, with a little flour and milk, into batter, and mix the pounded meat with it; roll it into balls the size and shape of eggs, and fry them.

To Roast Capons.
TIME, THREE-QUARTERS OF AN HOUR TO ONE HOUR.

A capon must be drawn and trussed, then placed on a spit, and roasted before a fine brisk fire for about three-quarters of an hour, but if *very* large, a longer time. When done, put it on a hot dish, pour some good gravy round it, and serve with bread sauce.

Broiled Chicken.

After cleaning nicely, split the backs; pepper and salt them, and broil them a nice brown. Pour over them sweet butter melted, and serve as hot as possible. A sauce to be eaten with this may be made of mushrooms, tomatoes, oysters, or green peas.

To Roast a Goose or Duck.

Cut six onions very fine, season them highly with salt, pepper, and sage. (Some add bread and butter, or mashed potatoes.) Put it into the fowl, sprinkle salt and pepper over it; baste frequently, and be careful to dish it before the breast falls; two hours is sufficient for a tolerably large goose; one for ducks. The giblets must be boiled with salt, pepper, and onions, for gravy, three hours.

To Stew a Duck.

Choose a fine fat duck, put it into a stew-pan, with a few leaves of sage and mint cut small, pepper, and salt, and a small bit of onion shred as fine as possible; add a quart of green peas, put in a piece of butter and a little flour. Give it one boil, and serve in one dish.

To Dress Wild Ducks.

Stuff the ducks, cut the roots off small onions, blanch them in scalding water, then pick and put them into a stew-pan with a little gravy, set them over a gentle fire, and let them simmer; when they are done, thicken them with cream and flour, and when the ducks are roasted, dish them, pour the ragout of onions over, and serve them up hot.

To Stew Wild Ducks.

Having prepared the fowls, rub the insides with salt, pepper, and a little powdered cloves; put a shallot or two, with a lump of butter in the body of each, then lay them in a pan, putting butter under and over them, with vinegar and water, and add pepper, salt, lemon-peel, and a bunch of sweet herbs; then cover the pan close, and let them stew till done, and serve them up hot, with a garnish of lemon sliced, and raspings of bread fried.

To Broil Pigeons.

After cleaning, split the backs, pepper and salt them and broil them very nicely; pour over them either stewed or pickled mushrooms in melted butter, and serve as hot as possible.

To Roast Pigeons.

Should be stuffed with parsley, either cut or whole; and seasoned within. Serve with parsley and butter. Peals or asparagus should be dressed to eat with them.

To Stew Pigeons with Macaroni.

Stew the pigeons either whole or cut in pieces, in a good gravy seasoned with salt, and a very little ketchup: when half done, put in some macaroni, and let it stew gently in a closed pan, till quite tender. Fowls may be done in the same way.

To Roast Woodcocks or Snipes.

Pluck them, but do not draw them, put them on a small spit, dust and baste them well with butter; toast a few slices of bread, put them on a clean plate, and set it under the birds while they are roasting; if the fire be good, they will take about ten minutes' roasting; when you draw them upon the toasts on the dish, pour melted butter round them, and serve them up.

To Truss Teal.

Pick the bird carefully; twist each leg at the knuckle; rest the claws on each side of the breast, and secure them by passing a skewer through the thighs and pinions of the wings.

To Roast Teal.
TIME, TEN TO FIFTEEN MINUTES.

Teal should not be eaten till after the first frost, and should be plump and fat. Roast them before a bright hot fire, and baste them very frequently with butter. Serve with orange sauce. Garnish with watercresses. Send up a cut lemon on a plate with them, and a tureen of sauce or brown gravy.

To Roast Pheasants and Partridges.

Roast them as turkey; and serve with a fine gravy (into which put a small bit of garlic), and bread sauce. When cold they may be made into excellent patties, but their flavor should not be overpowered by lemon.

Reed Birds.

TIME, TEN MINUTES TO A QUARTER OF AN HOUR.

Put them on a bird spit, tie them on another, and put them before a clear fire to broil; place a round of toast under them, sprinkle a little salt over them, and baste them well with butter. When done, cut the toast into four pieces, put it into a hot dish with a little gravy and butter over it, place the birds on the toast, and serve them up hot.

To Roast Grouse.

TIME, HALF AN HOUR.

Grouse; slices of fat bacon; vine leaves; melted butter.

Hang the grouse for some time; pick and truss them like a fowl for roasting, laying over them thin slices of bacon and vine leaves, which tie on with a thin thread. Roast them for half or three-quarters of an hour, and when done, serve them on a slice of toasted bread, and pour some good melted butter over them.

To Dress Plovers.

Roast the green ones in the same way as wood-cocks and quails, without drawing, and serve on a toast. Gray Plovers may be either roasted, or stewed, with gravy, herbs, and spice.

Stewed Rabbit.

Take a nice fat rabbit, skin it and prepare it properly; then cut it in pieces, and stew it in milk, thickened with flour and a little flour of rice; season it with salt, when sufficiently done; serve it with a wall of mashed potatoes.

Ragout of Rabbit.

TIME, THIRTY-FIVE MINUTES.

One rabbit; a quarter of a pound of bacon; two onions; half a lemon; a piece of butter the size of an egg; one tablespoonful of flour; and seasoning to taste.

To Roast Hare or Rabbit.

After it is skinned let it be well washed, and then soaked an hour or two in water. Put a relishing stuffing into the belly, and then sew it up. Baste it well with milk till half done, and afterwards with butter. If the blood has settled in the neck, soak the part in warm water. The hare should be kept at a distance from the fire at first. Serve with a fine froth, rich gravy, melted butter, and currant-jelly sauce. For stuffing use the liver, an anchovy, some fat bacon, a little suet, herbs, pepper, salt, nutmeg, a little onion crumbs of bread, and an egg to bind it all.

THE ART OF CARVING;

OR,

THE ETIQUETTE OF THE DINING TABLE.

Without a perfect knowledge of the Art of Carving, it is impossible to perform the honors of the table with propriety; and nothing can be more disagreeable to one of a sensitive disposition, than to behold a person at the head of a well-furnished board, hacking the finest joints, and giving them the appearance of having been gnawed by wolves.

It also merits attention in an economical point of view—a bad carver mangles joints so as not to be able to fill half a dozen plates from a sirloin of beef, or a large turkey; which, besides creating a great difference in the daily consumption in families, often occasions disgust in delicate persons, causing them to loathe the provisions, however good, which are set before them, if helped in a clumsy manner.

I cannot, therefore, too strongly urge the study of this useful branch of domestic economy; and I doubt not that whoever pays due attention to the following instructions, will, after a little practice, without which all precept is unavailing, speedily acquire the reputation of being a good carver.

Ladies ought especially to make carving a study; at their own houses they grace the table, and should be enabled to perform the task allotted to them with sufficient skill to prevent remark, or the calling forth of eager proffers of assistance from good-natured visitors near, who probably would not present any better claim to a neat performance.

In carving, your knife should not be too heavy, but of a sufficient size, and keen edge. Be sure to put the guard upon your fork, to prevent accident from the slipping of your knife.

The dish should be sufficiently near to enable the carver to reach it without rising, and the seat should be elevated so as to give command over the joint. No great personal strength is required, as constant practice will render it an easy task to carve the most difficult articles, more depending on address than force. Show no partiality in serving, but let each person at table have a share of such articles as are considered best, for, however you conciliate the one you favor, you must bear in mind that you make enemies of the other guests.

To Carve a Sirloin of Beef.

There are two modes of carving this joint. The better way is to carve long, thin slices, lengthwise. The other way is by cutting it across, which, however, spoils it, and very much disfigures the grain of the meat. If the pieces should prove too long by cutting the former way, they may be divided in two to give them a more elegant cut. The most tender and prime part is next to the loin. There will also be found some delicate fat, part of which should be served with each piece of the meat. It would prevent much trouble if the joints of the loin, neck and breast, were cut through by the butcher, previous to the cooking, so that when sent to table, they may be easily severed. Should the whole of the meat belonging to each bone be too thick, one or more slices may be taken off between every two bones.

In some boiled joints, round and aitch-bone of beef for instance, the water renders the outsides vapid, and of course unfit to be eaten; you will therefore be particular to cut off and lay aside a thick slice from the top, before you begin to serve.

To Carve Chuck—Ribs of Beef.

This joint is very nice to stand cold for breakfast or supper. If the outside cut is preferred by any one, cut it thin off the top of the joint; if it is not required, cut a thick slice off. By so doing, you come to the underdone at once; and as most people like roast beef with the gravy in it, you will thereby be enabled to give satisfaction to the persons whom you are carving for. Cut the slices thin, and do not give too much gravy, unless asked for. Do not help to too much at a time, as it is easy for the persons whom you are carving for to send their plates again. You will find by doing this, that there will not be so much left on the plates to waste.

To Carve the Aitch Bone of Beef.

Cut off and lay aside a thick slice from the entire surface, then help. There are two kinds of fat attached to this joint, and as tastes differ, it is necessary to learn which is preferred; the fat must be cut horizontally; the softer, which resembles marrow, at the back of the bone.

A silver skewer should be substituted for the one which keeps the meat properly together while boiling, and it may be withdrawn when you cut down to it.

To Carve a Tongue.

Cut nearly through the middle, and take thin slices from each side. The fat is situated underneath, at the root of the tongue.

To Carve a Loin of Veal.

The piece should be jointed previous to being sent to the table, when each division may be easily cut through with a knife. The fat surrounds the kidney, and portions of each should be given with the other parts.

To Carve a Breast of Veal.

Separate the ribs from the brisket. The brisket is the thickest part, and a gristly substance. Carve each, and help according to preference.

To Carve a Fillet of Veal.

A Fillet resembles a round of beef, and should be carved similar to it, in thin and very smooth slices, off the top. Cut deep into the flap for the stuffing, and help a portion of it to each person.

Slices of lemon are always served with this dish.

To Carve a Calf's Head.

Cut the slices from the nose to the back of the head to the bone. Should the eye be requested, extract with the point of the knife, and help to a portion. The palate, a delicate morsel, lies under the head. The sweet-tooth, too, not an inferior delicacy, lies back of all the rest, and, in a young calf, is easily extracted with the knife. On removing the jaw-bone, fine lean will appear. Help to each of these.

To Carve a Leg of Mutton.

The nicest part lies at midway between the knuckle and the other end. Thence, cut thin slices each way, quite deep. The outside being seldom very fat, some favorite pieces may be sliced off the broad end. The knuckle is tender, but the other parts more juicy, some good slices may be cut lengthwise, from the broad end of the back of the leg. The cramp-bone is much thought of by some; to get it cut down to the bone.

To Carve a Shoulder of Mutton.

Cut into the bone, commencing a short distance from the shank, and help thin slices of lean from each side of the incision; the prime part of the fat lies at the outer edge.

Should more meat be required than can be got from that part, cut from the thick or fleshy part, which represents the blade bone, and some good and delicate slices may be procured. By cutting horizontally from the under side, many "nice bits" will be obtained.

To Carve a Loin of Mutton.

The loin of mutton, if small, should be carved in chops, beginning with the outer chop; if large, carve slices the whole length. A neat way is to run the knife along the chine bone and under the meat along the ribs; it may then be cut in slices, as the saddle of mutton; and by this process fat and lean are served together; your knife should be very sharp, and it should be done cleverly.

To Carve a Saddle of Mutton.

The tail end is divided, and the kidneys skewered under each division; this is a matter of taste, and is not always done. Carve in thin slices, help fat from the vertebræ on both sides of the loin, and then carve crosswise, which gives you fat and lean; help a slice of kidney to those who desire it.

To Carve a Fore-Quarter of Lamb.

First divide the shoulder from the scoven, which consists of the breast and ribs, by passing the knife under the knuckle, and cutting so as to leave a fair portion of meat on the ribs; lay it on a separate dish; the other part, which, after being sprinkled over with pepper and salt, should be divided so as to separate the ribs from the gristly part, and you may help from either, as may be chosen.

To Carve a Leg, Loin, or Shoulder of Lamb.

As these parts are so like those of mutton, the same directions should be followed in the carving.

To Carve a Pig.

First split in the centre, from head to tail, along the loin; separate a shoulder from the body, and then the leg; divide the ribs into convenient portions, and send around with a sufficiency of the stuffing and gravy. Many prefer the neck and between the shoulders, although the ribs are considered the finest part; but as this all depends on taste, the question should be put. The ear is reckoned a delicacy.

Should the head not be divided, it must be done, and the brains taken out, and mixed with the gravy and stuffing.

To Carve a Loin of Pork.

This may be carved and served in the same manner as a loin of mutton.

To Carve a Leg of Pork.

Commence carving about midway, between the knuckle and farther end, and cut thin deep slices from either side. For the seasoning in a roast leg, lift it up, and it will be found under the skin at the large end.

To Carve a Ham.

The usual mode of carving this joint, is by long delicate slices, through the thick fat, laying open the bone at each cut, which brings you to the prime part at once. A more saving way is to commence at the knuckle and proceed onwards.

To Carve a Haunch of Venison.

First let out the gravy, by cutting in to the bone across the joint; then turn the broad end towards you, make as deep an incision as you can in the fleshy part, and help thin slices from each side. The greater part of the fat, which is much esteemed, will be found on the left side; and those who carve must take care to proportion both it and the gravy to the number of the company

To Carve a Fowl.

It will be more convenient carving this to take it on your plate, replacing the joints, as separated, neatly on the dish. Place the fork in the middle of the breast, and remove the wing, separating the joint, and lifting up the pinion with the fork, and drawing the entire wing towards the leg. This drawing will separate the fleshy part more naturally than cutting. Cut between the leg and the body, to the joint. By giving the blade a sudden turn, the joint will break. Repeat the same operation for the other wing and leg. Next take off the merry-thought by drawing the knife across the breast, and turning the joint back; and then remove the two neck bones. Divide the breast from the back, by cutting through all the ribs, close to the breast. Turn the back up; half way between the extreme ends press the point of the knife, and on raising the rump end the bone will part. Take off the sidesmen, having turned the rump from you:—and done.

The wings should be made as handsome as possible. These, with the breast, are the most delicate parts of the fowl; the legs are more juicy,

To Carve a Turkey.

To carve, without withdrawing the fork, place your fork firmly in the lower part of the breast, so as to have the turkey at perfect command. It is not difficult to complete the entire carving of this fowl without extracting the fork till done—the whole back, of course, making one joint. Proceed to remove the wing; the leg; another wing and leg. (This may be done either before or after slicing the breast.) Next, remove the merry-thought, the neck bones, the neck itself; then, cutting through the ribs, the job is done.

To Carve a Goose or Duck.

With the neck end toward you, to take off the wing, put the fork into the small end of the pinion, and press it close to the body, dividing the joint, and carrying the knife alone. Take off the leg by an incision, and separate the drumstick. Part the wing and leg from the other side, cut long slices from each side of the breast. The apron must be removed by cutting, to get at the stuffing. The merry-thought being removed, the neck bones and all other parts are to be divided as in a fowl.

A *Duck* may be carved in a similar manner.

To Carve Partridges and Pigeons.

Partridges are carved like fowls, but the breast and wings are not often divided, the bird being small. The wing is the prime bit, particularly the tip; the other choice parts are the breast and merry-thought. Pigeons may be cut in two, either from one end to the other of the bird, or across.

To Carve Woodcock, Grouse, &c.

These birds are carved like fowls, when large. When small, they must be cut into quarters. The same directions may be applied to all small birds.

To Carve a Hare or Rabbit.

Take off the legs, by cutting through the joints, which you must endeavor to hit. You will then be able to cut a few slices from each side of the back. Next dissever the shoulders, which are called the sportsman's joints and are preferred by many. The back may then be carved into convenient portions, and the pieces laid neatly on a dish, and served with stuffing and gravy to each person.

To Carve Fish.

Fish requires very little carving. It should be carefully helped with a fish-slice, which, not being sharp, prevents the flakes from being broken; and in salmon and cod these are large, and add much to their beauty. A portion of the roe, milt, or liver should be given to each person.

EGGS, OMELETTES, ETC.

How to Choose.

FRESH eggs when held to the light, the white will look clear, and the yolk distinct; if not good they will have a clouded appearance.

Another way to test good eggs is to put them in a pail of water, and if they are good they will lie on their sides always; if bad, they will stand on their small ends, the large end always uppermost, unless they have been shaken considerably, when they will stand either end up. Therefore, a bad egg can be told by the way it rests in the water—always up, never on its side. Any egg that lies flat is good to eat, and can be depended upon.

When eggs are stale, the white will be thin and watery, and the yolk will not be a uniform color, when broken; if there is no mustiness, or disagreeable smell, eggs in this state are not unfit for making cakes, puddings, etc.

Eggs for boiling should be as fresh as possible; a new laid egg will generally recommend itself by the delicate transparency of its shell.

Eggs a-la-Coque: or, Plain-Boiled.

This being beyond question the most popular way of serving eggs, we must commence by giving it in the most approved French method. Get ready a saucepan of boiling water, place in it some fresh eggs, immediately retire the saucepan from the fire, put on the lid, and let the eggs remain exactly four minutes. Take them up and serve them in a napkin, well warmed and folded in a dish. The eggs, if so preferred, may be put into cold water over a quick fire, and when the water comes to a boil, they are done.

Egg Sandwiches.

Hard boil some very fresh eggs and, when cold, cut them in thin slices, and lay them between some bread and butter; season them well with pepper, salt, and nutmeg.

Eggs and Sausage.

Cut some slices of Bologna or Spanish sausage; toss them in butter or olive oil. Fry some eggs, trim them nicely, and lay one upon each piece of sausage; arrange among them some parsley leaves, fried crisp, and serve as hot as possible.

Mixed Eggs and Bacon.

Take a nice rasher of mild bacon; cut it into squares no larger than dice; fry it quickly until nicely browned, but on no account burn it. Break half a dozen eggs into a basin, strain and season them with pepper, add them to the bacon, stir the whole about, and when sufficiently firm turn it out into a dish. Decorate with hot pickles.

Eggs and Beet-Root.

Take some slices of dressed beet-root; toss them in some good fresh olive oil made perfectly hot; arrange them in a dish; place some poached and trimmed eggs *en couronne* (in a circle) round the beet-root; add pepper; squeeze lemon-juice over, and serve directly.

Eggs with Onions.

Boil some eggs hard, preserve the yolks whole; cut the whites into slips, and add them to a few small onions which you have first fried in butter; give all a stir up, pour off the superfluous fat; dredge in a little flour; moisten it sufficiently with gravy; add seasoning to taste; let it come to a boil; put in the yolks, and when they are quite hot, serve.

Poached Eggs.

Get ready some boiling water in a sauce-pan; put in a little salt; break some new-laid eggs, one at a time, into teacups; lay them gently in the water, as near the surface as possible; place the sauce-pan over the fire, and let the eggs boil for from three to four minutes, according to fancy; drain them, and serve them hot, upon pieces of toast.

Eggs in Croquets.

Boil eighteen eggs, separate the yolks and whites, and cut them in dice; pour over them a sauce a-la-creme, add a little grated bread, mix all well together, and let it get cold; put in some salt and pepper, make them into cakes, cover them well on both sides with grated bread, let them stand an hour, and fry them a nice brown; dry them a little before the fire, and dish them while quite hot.

Baked Eggs.
TIME, FIVE MINUTES.

Well butter a dish, and break five eggs very carefully on it; put on the top of each a little pepper and salt and a bit of butter, and put them into a slow oven until well set. Serve them up hot.

Scrambled Eggs.

Break eight or more eggs into a basin, add to them a tablespoonful of sweet butter, cut into bits, and a teaspoonful of salt; make a little bit of butter hot in a frying-pan, pour in the eggs and let them cook. Stir them with a spoon until they are just set without becoming hard or brown; serve over toast.

Eggs a-la-Sicilienne.

Take the yolks of a half dozen hard boiled eggs, roughly chop them; cut the whites into rings; put the yolks into the middle of a dish, with the whites round them; lightly sift some bread crumbs over; sprinkle some essence of anchovy upon the top; add a dessertspoonful of salad oil and a little red pepper; place it in an oven for five minutes, and serve.

Egg Omelette aux Confitures.

Beat the yolks of nine eggs and the whites of six; add a little sugar and rasped lemon rind. Put them into a frying-pan well buttered, and, when set tolerably firm, spread over the top surface some apricot, orange, or other marmalade, strawberry jam or currant jelly, etc. Fold the omelette in two, and with a red-hot skewer just press it together. Serve upon a napkin arranged in a dish.

Omelette of Ham, Tongue or Sausage.

There are three methods of making a ham or tongue omelette; firstly, by simply cutting the meat into small dice, tossing it in butter, and pouring the well-beaten and seasoned eggs upon it in the pan, and letting them remain until set, when serve; or pound the meat to a paste in a mortar and beat it up with the eggs, and fry in the usual manner. The third method is to beat the eggs and fry them, then lay upon them the meat (which has been previously tossed in butter), fold in the ends of the omelette, and serve as hot as possible.

Egg Omelette and Rum.

Mix eggs, sugar, rasped lemon rind, etc., together as for a sweet omelette, and, when dressed, turned upon a dish, and glazed, pour a glass of rum over it, and set a light to the spirit just before placing the omelette upon table; serve it flaming.

Omelette—American Mode.

Beat the yolks of six and the whites of four eggs; season with salt and spice according to taste. Cut some nice little pieces of bread, no larger than dice; fry them in butter till they are well browned, then throw them quickly into boiling gravy or milk, or sauce of any particular flavor; mix them with the beaten eggs, and fry as an ordinary omelette.

Egg and Cheese Omelette.

Cut the cheese into small pieces, using about a dessertspoonful to two eggs, and for the rest proceed in the ordinary way. Parmesan cheese should be grated and beaten up with the seasoned eggs, oil being used for frying it. Gruyère cheese should be cut into dice and strewn upon the eggs directly after they are poured into the pan; a little fresh butter chopped up and added to the eggs while they are being beaten is a great improvement.

Pickled Eggs.

Hard boil a dozen eggs, and, when cold, remove their shells; put them into a wide-mouthed stone jar. Boil a quart of strong vinegar, seasoned with whole pepper, allspice, ginger, and a few cloves of garlic; pour this over the eggs while it is scalding hot, and, when cold, bung down tight. Use as an accompaniment to cold meat, or slice and toss them in salad oil as a relish to be eaten with deviled meats.

To Preserve Eggs.

By adopting the following method, eggs have been kept good two years: One bushel of quick lime, thirty-two ounces of salt, eight ounces of cream of tartar. Mix the whole together, with as much water as will reduce the composition to such a consistency that an egg, when put into it, will swim.

Another way is: Procure shallow baskets which are rather coarse or open (they should hold about eight or ten dozen eggs), hang them on nails or hooks driven into the beams of the cellar. The lighter and more airy the cellar is, the longer the eggs will keep good.

COFFEE, TEA, CHOCOLATE, ETC.

Hints to Coffee and Tea Drinkers.

COFFEE is used at breakfast, after dinner, and also as an evening beverage. To most persons it proves at all times refreshing. When its use is succeeded by heartburn, or other unpleasent symptoms, it should be discontinued. It is of great service to the laboring man, or those who do hard and laborious work, as it is a great stimulant, and is invaluable in removing a feeling of exhaustion. Those who " waste the midnight oil," may, by its use resist a tendency to fall asleep. Those who are desirous of obtaining early and sound sleep should not drink coffee immediately before bed-time. Persons troubled with indigestion should avoid it altogether. In attacks of spasmodic asthma it is useful.

Avoid highly flavored teas, especially green, as these generally derive their flavor from pernicious ingredients. *All* green tea is more or less injurious; it acts powerfully on the nervous system and injures the stomach. Good black tea is not only safe but wholesome; but it should always be taken with a suitable proportion of milk and sugar added to it as correctives.

To Roast Coffee.

Have either a Patent Roaster, or an ordinary sheet-iron pan. To every three pounds of coffee you put in the roaster add a piece of good fresh butter, a little larger than a marble, and two teaspoonsful of powdered sugar; then roast the berries. This little addition develops the aroma of the berry. Many people prefer having chicory added to their coffee—the proportion is about a quarter of a pound of chicory to a pound of coffee.

To Make Coffee.

To make good common coffee, allow a tablespoonful of it, when ground, to each pint of water. Turn on the water boiling hot, and boil the coffee in a tin pot, from twenty to twenty-five minutes—if boiled longer it will not taste fresh and lively. Let it stand, after being taken from the fire, four or five minutes to settle, then turn it off carefully from the grounds into a coffee-pot or urn. When the coffee is put on the fire to boil, a piece of fish-skin or isinglass, of the size of a nine-pence, should be put in, or else the white and shell of half an egg, to a couple of quarts of coffee.

To Make French Coffee.

French coffee is made in a German filter, the water is turned on boiling hot, and one-third more coffee is necessary than when boiled in the common way. Where cream cannot be procured for coffee, the coffee will be much richer to boil it with a less proportion of water than the above rule, and weaken it with boiling hot milk, when served out in cups.

Coffee Milk.

Boil a dessertspoonful of ground coffee, in nearly a pint of milk, a quarter of an hour; then put into it a shaving or two of isinglass, and clear it; let it boil a few minutes, and set it on the side of the fire to grow fine.

This is a very fine breakfast; it should be sweetened with sifted sugar of a good quality.

Coffee as Made in India.

Put a quarter of a pound of ground coffee into a jug, and pour over it four quarts of boiling water; stir until the froth disappears; then cover up carefully with a towel, folded several times, so as to retain the steam, and let it remain twelve hours; then pour it off, and test as required, without boiling. It will keep several days.

The Art of Tea Making.

Use soft water, and be sure it boils. If you are compelled to use hard water, throw into the kettle a pinch of carbonate of soda; but the latter should never be used unless the water requires correction, and then very moderately, for it is apt to destroy the delicate roughness of the flavor. Put your tea into the empty pot, and be sure you use enough. Some persons practice a foolish economy in this matter, and use so little that the product is not much better than plain hot water. Then place the pot before the fire, or on the hob, or, still better, on the hot plate of an oven, till the tea is well heated, but, of course, not burnt; then pour upon it the boiling water, and a fragrant infusion of good strength is instantly produced.

Tea—Ordinary Mode.

Scald the tea-pot, and if the tea is a strong kind, a teaspoonful for a pint of water is sufficient—if it is a weak kind, more will be required. Pour on just enough boiling water to cover the tea, and let it steep. Green tea should not steep more than five or six minutes before drinking—if steeped longer it will not be lively. Black tea requires steeping ten or twelve minutes to extract the strength.

To Make Chocolate.

Scrape or grate the chocolate, take a tablespoonful of it for half a pint, half-and-half milk and water; put it in a perfectly clean stew-pan, make the chocolate a smooth paste with a little cold milk, and stir it into the milk and water when it boils, cover in for ten minutes or longer; add sugar to taste, unless French chocolate is used, which is prepared sweet enough.

Serve soda biscuits or rolls, or toast, with it.

Chocolate—Philadelphia Mode.

Allow three spoonsful of scraped chocolate to a quart of water; boil about twenty minutes, and stir while boiling; pour in rich cream or milk and let it boil up, and it is ready for the table.

Cocoa.

This is a very delicate drink. Persons who cannot drink coffee and tea, make use of this with impunity.

Take two ounces of cocoa-shells and put them in a coffee boiler (but which has never been used for making coffee,) with two pints of water; allow it to simmer for eight hours by the side of the fire, and then pour it gently off for use, leaving the shells in the boiler, to which, if another ounce is added, it will make other two pints, but it should not be used oftener than twice.

Cocoa—Prepared.

This beverage is prepared the same as chocolate, omitting the sugar. Milk may be used altogether if preferred. Never boil prepared cocoa more than one minute. Too much boiling makes it oily. The quicker it is used after making, the better it will be.

WINES AND BEVERAGES..

How to Manage Wines and Beer.

ALL wines, particularly the light-bodied and sparkling, require to be kept on their side, and at a uniform temperature of about fifty-five degrees.

The sparkling wines are in their prime in from eighteen to thirty months after the vintage, depending on the cellaring and climate. Weak wines of inferior growths, should be drunk within twelve or fifteen months.

Wines should be decanted very carefully in removing them from the bin when about to be used, otherwise the deposit is liable to become mixed with the liquid, and the flavor destroyed. Old bottled wines will lose many of their properties unless carefully decanted.

Wines old in bottle should be drunk immediately on being decanted. If allowed to remain open for any length of time, the delicate aroma, so much esteemed, will be lost, and the wine becomes vapid.

Various methods are employed for improving home-made wines which seem to require it. The leaves of the sweet bay and the peach, kernels of fruit, almonds, cloves, ginger, etc., are used to impart to it both flavor and perfume; brandy is mixed with it to give strength; and bruised raisins soaked in spirits are employed to improve the liquor when it is flat.

The usual domestic and foreign fruits, from which wines are made are gooseberries, currants, sloes, damsons, elderberries, grapes, strawberries, raspberries, blackberries, cherries, raisins, oranges, and lemons; also, various other fruits.

To Make English Sherry.

Put to thirty pounds of good moist sugar ten gallons of water. Boil it half an hour, skim it well, and then let it stand till quite cold. Add eight quarts of ale from the ale vat while fermenting, stir it well together, let it remain in the tub till the next day; then put it into the barrel with six pounds of raisins, one quart of brandy, one pound of brown sugar candy, and two ounces of isinglass. Let it remain three weeks before the barrel is closed, and it must stand twelve months before it is put into bottles.

Raisin Wine.

TIME TO STAND, TWELVE DAYS.

Half a hundred of Valencia raisins; ten gallons of soft water.

Take half a hundred of Valencia raisins, pick them from the stalks, and chop them very small, then put them into a tub, and pour over them ten gallons of hot soft water. Let this be strained twice or thrice every day for twelve days successively, then pour the liquor into a cask, make a toast of bread, and while it is hot spread it on each side with yeast, and put it into the vessel. It will be fit to drink in four months.

Orange Wine.

To six gallons of spring water, put fifteen pounds of loaf-sugar, and the whites of four eggs well beaten; let it boil for a quarter of an hour, and as the scum rises take it off; when cold, add the juice of fifty Seville oranges and five lemons; pare twelve oranges and five lemons as thin as possible, put them on thread, and suspend them in the barrel for one month, then take them out, and put in two pounds of loaf-sugar and bung it up.

Grape Wine.

Bruise the grapes which should be perfectly ripe. To each gallon of grapes put a gallon of water, and let the whole remain a week without being stirred. At the end of that time, draw off the liquor carefully, and put to each gallon three pounds of lump-sugar. Let it ferment in a temperate situation—when fermented, stop it up tight. In the course of six months it will be fit to bottle.

Raspberry Wine.

To each quart of well-picked raspberries put a quart of water; bruise, and let them stand two days; strain off the liquor, and to every gallon put three pounds of loaf sugar; when dissolved, put the liquor into a barrel, and when fine (which will be in about two months), bottle it, and to each bottle put a tablespoonful of brandy.

Red Currant Wine.

Take thirty-six pints of fruit and one pint of raspberries. Mix with them twenty pints of water. When these have fermented, add twenty pounds of good sugar; and after the wine is casked, two pints of brandy or whisky without any special flavor.

Red Gooseberry Wine.

Take equal quantities of water and bruised fruit, and to every twenty pints of the mixture add fifteen pounds of loaf sugar and one pound of sliced beet-root. When fermented, put into the cask a quart or more of brandy or flavorless whisky.

Wine of Mixed Fruits.

Take equal measures of water and fruit, such as white, black, or red currants, raspberries, cherries, strawberries, and gooseberries; bruise, strain, and ferment the juice, adding fifteen pounds of sugar for every twenty gallons of the liquor. A handful of sweet marjoram and a quarter of a pound of ginger will give flavor and perfume. Add two quarts of brandy or whisky, but do not put any flavoring.

Damson Wine.

Gather the fruit dry, weigh and bruise it, and to every eight pounds of fruit add one gallon of water; boil the water, pour it on the fruit scalding hot; let it stand two days; then draw it off, put it into a clean cask, and to every gallon of liquor add two and a half pounds of good sugar; fill the cask. It may be bottled off after standing in the cask a year. On bottling the wine put a small lump of loaf sugar into every bottle.

Cherry Wine.

Gather the cherries when quite ripe. Pull them from their stalks, and press them through a hair sieve. To every gallon of the liquor add two pounds of lump sugar finely beaten, stir all together, and put it into a vessel that will just hold it. When it has done fermenting, stop it very close for three months, and then bottle it off for use.

Rhubarb Wine.

In the month of May, when rhubarb is green, the stalks of the leaves should be used in the following proportions: Five pounds of stalks are bruised in a suitable vessel, to which is added one gallon of spring water; and after lying in mash three or four days, the liquor juice is poured off, when to every gallon of this juice three pounds of sugar are added, and allowed to ferment for four or five days in a suitable vat; as soon as the fermentation has ceased, the liquor must be drawn off into a cask and allowed to remain until the month of March, when all fermentation will have finished; it must then be racked off, and more loaf sugar added.

Good Elderberry Wine.

Strip the berries clean from the stalks, and put them into a tub; pour boiling water on them, in the proportion of two gallons to three of the berries, press them down into the liquor, and cover them closely. Let them remain in this state until the following day, when the juice must be strained from the fruit; then squeeze from the berries the juice remaining in them, and mix it with what was poured off at first. To every gallon of this mixture of juices add three pounds of sugar, one ounce of cloves, and one ounce of ginger; boil twenty minutes, keeping it thoroughly skimmed. While still hot, put it into a cask, or large stone bottles; fill entirely, and set the wine immediately, with a large spoonful of new yeast put into the bung-hole, and stirred round in the liquor.

Blackberry Wine—My own Receipt.

Place your fruit in a large vat, mash and strain them through a hair sieve, or wine press, so as to extract the juice. To every quart of pure juice add two quarts of water and three pounds of sugar. Fill your barrel or keg entirely full. Reserve some of the mixture, in order to refill the vessel as it is fermenting. Continue refilling until fermentation has ceased. Close the bung hole. If the barrel or vessel is undisturbed, it does not require to be racked off. To rack it off will not injure the wine, it will rather improve it.

Parsnip Wine.

Sliced parsnips, twenty pounds; boiling water, five gallons; when cold, press out the liquor, and to each gallon add cream of tartar half an ounce, and sugar two pounds and three-quarters; ferment, rack, and add brandy at discretion.

Ginger Wine.

To three gallons of water put three pounds of sugar, and four ounces of race ginger, washed in many waters to cleanse it; boil them together for one hour, and strain it through a sieve; when lukewarm, put it in a cask with three lemons cut in slices, and two gills of beer yeast; shake it well, and stop the cask very tight; let it stand a week to ferment, and if not clear enough to bottle, it must remain until it becomes so; it will be fit to drink in ten days after bottling.

To Improve Poor Wines.

This is the cant term of the wine trade, under which all the adulteration and "doctoring" of wine is carried on. A poor sherry is improved by a little almond flavor, honey, and spirit; a port deficient in body and astringency, by the addition of some red tartar (dissolved in boiling water), some kino, rhatany, or catechu, and a little honey and brandy.

To Restore Musty Wine.

Bruised mustard seed, half pound; camphor, quarter ounce; bruised cloves, half ounce. Add them to ninety or one-hundred gallons of the wine, then bung close.

To Rack Wine.

This should be performed in cool weather, and preferably early in the spring. To avoid disturbing the dregs, a clean syphon, well managed, will be found better than a cock or faucet. The bottoms, or foul portion, may be strained through a wine-bag, and added to some other inferior wine.

To Restore Flat Wine.

Add four or five pounds of sugar, honey, or bruised raisins, to every hundred gallons, and bung close. A little spirits may also be added.

How to Imitate Sherry Wine.

Take twelve gallons prepared cider, nine quarts imported pure sherry wine, six quarts native wine, three-eighths drachm oil of bitter almonds dissolved in alcohol, nine pints rectified whisky, one and a half pounds sugar, one and a half ounce tincture of saffron. Mix and manage as before.

How to Make Apple Wine.

To every gallon of cider, immediately as it comes from the press, add two pounds of sugar. Boil it as long as any scum arises, then strain it through a sieve and let it cool; add some good yeast, mix it well; let it work in the tub two or three weeks, then skim off the head; draw it off close and tun it; let stand one year, then rack it off, and add two ounces isinglass to the barrel; then add half pint spirits of wine to every eight gallons.

Raspberry Brandy.

Pick fine dry fruit, put into a stone jar, and the jar into a kettle of water, or on a hot hearth, till the juice will run;

strain, and to every pint add half a pound of sugar, give one boil, and skim it; when cold put equal quantities of juice and brandy, shake well and bottle. Some people prefer it stronger of the brandy.

Cherry Brandy.

Get equal quantities of morello and common black cherries; fill your cask, and pour on (to a ten gallon cask) one gallon of boiling water; in two or three hours, fill it up with brandy—let it stand a week, then draw off all, and put another gallon of boiling water, and fill it again with brandy—at the end of the week, draw the whole off, empty the cask of the cherries, and pour in your brandy with water, to reduce the strength; first dissolving one pound of brown sugar in each gallon of your mixture. If the brandy be very strong, it will bear water enough to make the cask full.

Blackberry Brandy.

TIME, FIFTEEN DAYS TO FERMENT.

One pound of sugar to two pounds of blackberry juice; a quarter of a pint of gin or brandy.

Cover a quantity of blackberries with water, and put them into an oven to draw the juice out. Strain them through a sieve and leave them to ferment for fifteen days. Afterwards add a pound of sugar to two quarts of juice, with a quarter of a pint of gin or brandy. When bottled, do not cork it too close.

Method of Cider Making.

As soon as the apples are ripe, collect them in heaps on the grass; by no means house them, or the cider will inevitably be musty. After they are ground and pressed strain off any bits of skin or core that may have passed through the sieve of the press, put it at once into casks; do not touch it until it has done fermenting, then put in the bungs. Any addition is injurious; and the sulphuring of casks cannot be recommended.

To Keep Cider Sweet.

When barreling the cider, put into each barrel or keg a gill (eight large tablespoonsful) of white mustard seed. This will retard its becoming hard or sour. There is also a chemical ingredient, the sulphate of lime, which is a complete stopper to the fermentation of new cider, arresting it just when one wishes.

Champagne Cider.

Good pale vinous cider, one hogshead; proof spirit (pale) three gallons; sugar, fourteen pounds; mix, and let them remain together in a temperate situation for one month; then add orange flower water, one quart, and fine it down with skimmed milk, half a gallon.

To Keep Cider Good for Years.

Take the cider when you think it will suit your taste, put it into a kettle, and boil it very little. Make a bag and put into it quarter of a pound of hops, then put the bag with hops into the kettle with the cider, and tie it fast to the handle so that the bag with hops will not touch the bottom of the kettle; scum off the cider while you have it on the fire, and after it has boiled a short time take it off the fire, and let it cool down lukewarm; put it into a sweet barrel, and add one pint of good brandy, bung it up, and it will keep the same as you put it into your barrel for years.

Ginger Beer, or Pop.

Pour two gallons of boiling water on two pounds brown sugar, one and a half ounce of cream of tartar, and the same of pounded ginger; stir them well, and put it in a small cask; when milk warm, put in half a pint of good yeast, shake the cask well, and stop it close—in twenty-four hours it will be fit to bottle—cork it very well, and in ten days it will sparkle like champagne—one or two lemons cut in slices and put in, will improve it much. For economy, you may use molasses instead of sugar—one quart in place of two pounds. This is a wholesome and delicious beverage in warm weather.

Spruce Beer.

Boil a handful of hops, and twice as much of the chippings of sassafras root, in ten gallons of water; strain it, and pour in, while hot, one gallon of molasses, two spoonsful of the essence of spruce, two spoonsful of powdered ginger, and one of pounded allspice; put it in a cask—when sufficiently cold, add half a pint of good yeast; stir it well, stop it close, and when fermented and clear, bottle and cork it tight.

Sarsaparilla and Lemon Pop.

"Sarsaparilla Syrup."—Twelve pounds crushed sugar, one gallon of water, quarter of an ounce of oil of sassafras, quarter of an ounce of oil of wintergreen, a little lemon; heat thirty minutes, but not boil; color the syrup with burnt sugar.

"Lemon syrup."—Twelve pounds crushed sugar, one gallon of water, half an ounce oil of lemon; heat as above.

For eight gallons of water, one pound of carbonate of soda, the whites of six eggs, beat to a foam, mix together, and strain through a coarse cloth; use half a teaspoonful of tartaric acid to each bottle, also a tablespoonful of the syrup to each bottle; then fill up with the mixture of water and eggs.

Molasses Beer.

Six quarts of water, two quarts of molasses, half a pint of yeast, two spoonsful of cream tartar, stir all together. Add the peel of a lemon grated, and the juice may be substituted for cream of tartar. Bottle after standing ten hours, with a raisin in each.

Beer of Essential Oils.

Mix a couple of quarts of boiling water with a pint and a half of molasses. Stir in five quarts of cold water, then add ten drops of the oil of sassafras, ten of spruce, fifteen of wintergreen, and a teaspoonful of essence of ginger. When just lukewarm, put in half a pint of fresh lively yeast. When fermented, bottle and cork it, and keep it in a cool place. It will be fit to drink in the course of two or three days.

Silver Top Beer.

To three pounds of crushed sugar, take one pint of hot water and place over a slow fire until dissolved, then add the whites of five eggs, with one spoonful of flour, beat to a foam, and a teaspoonful of lemon oil; then divide the syrup into two equal parts, and add to one part five ounces carbonate of soda, and to the other four ounces tartaric acid; bottle tight, and use a tablespoonful of each syrup with a gill of water. It is a delicious drink.

Excellent Mead.

Three pounds brown sugar, one pint molasses, one-fourth pound tartaric acid; mix, pour over them two quarts boiling water, stir till dissolved. When cold, add half ounce essence sassafras, and bottle. When you wish to drink it, put three tablespoonsful of it in a tumbler, fill half full with ice water, add a little more than one-fourth teaspoon soda. An excellent summer beverage.

Lemon Ice Cream.

One pint of sweet cream, three pints of new milk, one pound of loaf sugar, and two lemons; boil and stir the sugar in gradually. If you have no lemons use four eggs. Put into a freezer, and surround the freezer with ice and coarse salt, on all sides; while freezing stir it well, scraping it down from the sides.

Vanilla Ice Cream.

Boil a vanilla bean in a quart of rich milk, until it has imparted the flavor sufficiently—then take it out, and mix it with the milk, eight eggs, yolks and whites beaten well; let it boil a little longer; make it very sweet, for much of the sugar is lost in the operation of freezing.

Strawbery Ice Cream

Is made in the same manner—the strawberries must be very ripe, and the stems picked out. If rich cream can be procured, it will be infinitely better—the custard is intended as a substitute, when cream cannot be had.

Cocoanut Ice Cream.

Take the nut from its shell, pare it, and grate it very fine; mix it with a quart of cream, sweeten, and freeze it. If the nut be a small one, it will require one and a half to flavor a quart of cream.

Chocolate Ice Cream.

Scrape a quarter of a pound of chocolate very fine, put it in a quart of milk, boil it till the chocolate is dissolved, stirring it continually—thicken with six eggs. A vanilla bean boiled with the milk will improve it.

Pineapple Ice Cream.

INGREDIENTS.—Half a pound of preserved pineapple, one pint of cream, the juice of a small lemon, one gill of new milk, a quarter of a pound of sugar.

Cut the pineapple into small pieces, bruise it in a mortar, add the sugar, lemon-juice, cream, and milk; mix well together, press through a hair sieve, and freeze twenty-five minutes.

To Make Ices.

Ices are composed of the juice of fruits, creams, and liquors, prepared and congealed by means of pounded ice mixed with salt, or with nitre or soda. The freezing-pot should be always of pewter, because it prevents the contents of the vessel from congealing too quickly, and gives time to mix them thoroughly. In ices that are badly mixed the sugar sinks to the bottom, and they have necessarily a sharp, unpleasant taste.

Raspberry Vinegar.

Put a quart of ripe red raspberries in a bowl; pour on them a quart of strong well flavored vinegar—let them stand twenty-four hours, strain them through a bag, put this liquid on another quart of fresh raspberries, which strain in the same manner—and then on a third quart: when this last is prepared, make it very sweet with pounded loaf sugar; refine and bottle it. It is a delicious beverage mixed with iced water.

To Make Whisky Vinegar.

Take six gallons of soft, pure water, three quarts of whisky, two and a half quarts Orleans molasses, and half a pint of good yeast; put the mixture in a keg, and let it stand in the sun one month, and it is fit for use. If made in winter, let it stand by fire.

Sugar Vinegar.

Mix together a little yeast, two pounds of brown sugar, and a gallon of water. Let it stand in the sun a few months, say three, and it is fit for use.

Cider Vinegar.

This is best when apples are plenty; everybody can make their own, merely by converting these apples into cider, and letting it stand six months.

Weights and Measures.

TESTED AND ARRANGED BY MYSELF. CALCULATED SIXTEEN OUNCES TO THE POUND.

Wheat Flour,...................one pound of sixteen ounces is one quart
Indian Meal,...................one pound two ounces.........is one quart
Butter, when soft,.............one pound one ounce...........is one quart
Loaf Sugar, broken up,.....one pound..........................is one quart
White sugar, powdered,....one pound one ounce...........is one quart
Best Brown Sugar............one pound two ounces.........is one quart
Eggs,..................................ten eggs.....................weigh one pound

LIQUID MEASURE.

Four large tablespoonsful.............are..........................half a gill
Eight large tablespoonsful............are.............................one gill
Two gills ....are...........................half a pint
A common-sized tumbler.............holds.......................half a pint
A common-sized wine-glass..........holds about..............half a gill
Two pints....................................are............................one quart
Four quarts................................are...........................one gallon

About twenty-five drops of any thin liquid will fill a common-sized teaspoon.
Four tablespoonsful generally fill a common-sized wineglass.
Four wineglasses will fill a half-pint tumbler, or a large coffee-cup
A quart black bottle holds in reality about a pint and a half; sometimes not so much.
A tablespoonful of salt is about one ounce.

DRY MEASURE.

Half a gallon..........................is.................a quarter of a peck
One gallon.............................is.................half a peck
Two gallons...........................are................one peck
Four gallons..........................are................half a bushel
Eight gallons.........................are................one bushel

THE ART OF WASHING, IRONING, &c.

Duties of the Laundry Maid.

THE laundry-maid is charged with the duty of washing and getting-up the family linen,—a situation of great importance where the washing is all done at home; but in large towns, where there is little convenience for bleaching and drying, it is chiefly done by professional laundresses, who apply mechanical and chemical processes to the purpose. These processes, however, are supposed to injure the fabric of the linen, and in many families the fine linen, cottons and muslins, are washed and got up at home, even where the bulk of the washing is given out. In country and suburban houses, where greater conveniences exist, washing at home is more common, and in country places universal.

Hints on Washing.

The linen for Monday's wash should be collected on Saturday, sorted and put to soak in cold water according to the various kinds. The body linen should be put into one tub, the bed and table linen in another, and the fine things separately. Plain collars, cuffs, wristbands, should be strung through the button-holes on a piece of bobbin long enough to enable the articles to be easily divided for rubbing, starching, &c. Colored muslins, prints and flannels, must be laid aside to be washed in a different manner from white calico or linen. Properly boiled suds are far better than soap for washing, particularly if a washing machine be employed. The suds should be prepared in the following manner: Shred into an earthenware jar the best yellow soap cut into very fine shavings, and pour boiling water to the quantity required. One pound of soap is plenty for one gallon of water. Add to this quantity half a pound of the best Scotch soda, and set the jar (covered) on a stove or at the back of the kitchen range till the soap is quite dissolved. If this be done on Saturday evening, the soap will be a smooth jelly fit to use on Monday morning.

To Wash Muslins and Piques.

In getting up muslins and piqués, the failure is not generally in the washing, but in the starching. A good-sized panful of starch should be used, in which three or four inches of composite or other candle has been melted whilst hot. The articles should be thoroughly squeezed from the starch, and folded whilst wet between folds of old sheeting or table linen. They should then be passed beneath the rollers of a mangle, or through a wringing machine. All lumps of starch are thus removed.

Piqués should be ironed as lightly as possible, and the iron ought never to come into contact with the outside surface of the piqué. An old cambric handkerchief is the best thing to use under the iron where absolutely necessary to iron on the right side.

To Wash Flannels and Woolen Articles.

Have the suds ready prepared by boiling up some good soap in soft water with washing crystal, but do not use the suds when boiling; let them be as hot as the hand will bear when the articles are put in. The flannels should not be rubbed with soap, nor should the material itself be rubbed, as in washing linen, etc.; the fibres of the wool contain numberless little hooks, which the rubbing knots together; hence the thickening of the fabric and consequent shrinking in its dimensions. Sluice the articles up and down in plenty of suds, which afterwards squeeze (not wring) out. The clothes-wringers are a great improvement upon hand labor, as, without injury to the fabric, they squeeze out the water so thoroughly, that the article dries in considerably less time than it otherwise would do. After rinsing, squeeze out the water, and dry in the open air, if the weather is such as to admit of the articles drying quickly; if not, dry in a warm room, but avoid too close proximity to a fire. Let any dust or mud be beaten out or brushed off prior to washing. All flannels for shirts should be shrunk previously to making up, or they will speedily become too small.

To Wash Woolen Shawls.
SCOTCH METHOD.

Scrape one pound of soap, boil it down in sufficient water. When cooling, beat it with the hand; it will be a sort of jelly. Add three tablespoonsful of spirit of turpentine, and one of spirit of hartshorn. Wash the articles thoroughly in it, then rinse in cold water until all the soap is taken off, then in salt and water. Fold between two sheets, taking care not to allow two folds of the article washed to lie together. Mangle, and iron with a very cool iron. Shawls done in this way look like new. Only use the salt when there are delicate colors that may strike.

To Wash White Merino Shawls.

Wash the shawl in fair suds made beforehand, rub no soap on the shawl, rinse in clear warm water, with two changes if you please; then take a solution of gum arabic, and add to it warm water till you think it will produce a little stiffness like starch when dry. Press with a moderately hot iron, before quite dry, laying a clean cotton or linen cloth between the iron and the shawl.

To Wash Point Lace.

FRENCH RECEIPT.

Mix a teaspoonful powdered borax in a basin of strong white Castile soap-suds. Baste the lace to be washed, very carefully, with *fine* cotton, upon two thicknesses of flannel. Soak the lace, thus arranged, in the soap-suds mixture for twenty-four hours, or longer if very dirty, changing the suds two or three times. Then let it remain for two or three hours in clean water to rinse, changing the water once. *Squeeze* it out (do not ring it), and, when partially dry, place the flannel with the lace on it, lace downwards, on two thicknesses of dry flannel laid on a table, and smooth it with a hot iron. During the whole process, the lace must remain basted on the flannel; and when it is pressed, must lie between the dry and damp flannel, and pressed upon the latter. When the lace is perfectly dry, rip it off, when it will be done.

To Wash and Starch Lawns.

Lawns may be done in the same manner as the former, only observe to iron them on the wrong side, and use gum arabic water instead of starch, and, according to what has been directed for sarsanets, any colored silks may be starched, abating or augmenting the gum water, as may be thought fit according to the stiffness intended.

To Wash Calicoes, Quilts, &c.

AUTHOR'S OWN METHOD.

For as many clothes as will well boil in a six-bucket boiler, take sufficient water to wet the clothes well. Beat into this as much soap ("or the first trial a little more") as would be used for the entire washing of the same clothes the old way. Dissolve a piece of borax the size of a large hickory-nut in boiling water, taking care to see it is all dissolved. Borax will not dissolve in cold water. Pour this dissolved borax in with the prepared soap and water. Put the clothes in, and let them soak twelve or twenty-four hours. Then put them on to boil, and after they get well to boiling let them boil one hour. The boil-water must be the soak-water, with enough other water to make a good boil-water. Take out into sufficient cold water to make a good warm suds and wash out, looking a little to the collars and wristbands. After this put them through two other waters, and hang out. The calicoes should be soaked in a part of this same soak, but separate from the white clothes, and boiled after the white clothes. Most calicoes will be dulled the first and second washings; after that they will brighten out. Quilts and comforts should be folded ready for wringing, and tacked in a few places with twine previous to wetting, and not untacked until ready to hang out. A quilt or comfort will require working about five minutes in each water to make it beautifully clean. To make calicoes look bright like new, a large tablespoonful of turpentine should be put in the soak instead of the borax. The white clothes will not look quite as well as with the borax. The clothes must be soaked in wood. The two first waters must be either rain or brook-water. There must be soap enough in so that, when the clothes boil, they boil foamy. Washing done in this manner is not quite half the work as when done in the old way: and I think clothes will last nearly or quite twice as long. I do not perceive that either borax or turpentine rot the clothes in the least.

Washing Occupying One Hour.

Have a preparation made from two tablespoonsful alcohol, two tablespoonsful turpentine, half pound brown soap, cut fine and mixed in one quart hot water. Pour the same into a large tub of boiling water, and allow the clothes to soak for twenty minutes. Then take them out and put them in a tub of clean cold water for twenty minutes. Afterward boil them in a like quantity of the above preparation for twenty minutes, and rinse in cold water.

To Make Starch.

Allow half a pint of cold water, and one quart of boiling water to every two tablespoonsful of starch.

Put the starch into a tolerably large basin; pour over it the cold water, and stir the mixture well with a wooden spoon until it is perfectly free from lumps and quite smooth. Then take the basin to the fire, and whilst the water is *actually boiling* in the kettle or boiler, pour it over the starch, stirring it the whole time. If made properly in this manner, the starch will require no further boiling; but should the water not be boiling when added to the starch, it will not thicken, and must be put into a clean saucepan, and stirred over the fire until it boils. Take it off the fire, strain it into a clean basin, cover it up to prevent a skin forming on the top, and when sufficiently cool that the hand may be borne in it, starch the things. Many persons, to give a shiny and smooth appearance to the linen when ironed, stir round two or three times in the starch a piece of wax-candle, which also prevents the iron from sticking.

Gum Arabic Starch for Making Shirt-Bosoms Glossy.

Procure two ounces of fine white gum arabic, and pound it to powder, put it into a pitcher, and pour on it a pint or more of boiling water, according to the degree of strength you desire, and then, having covered it, let it set all night. In the morning, pour it carefully from the dregs into a clean bottle, cork it, and keep it for use. A tablespoonful of gum water stirred into a pint of starch that has been made in the usual manner will give a beautiful gloss to shirt-bosoms, and to lawns (either white or printed) a look of newness to which nothing else can restore them after washing. It is also good for thin white muslin and all kinds of laces.

To Wash Silks.

Silks, when washed, should be dried in the shade, on a linen-horse, taking care that they are kept smooth and unwrinkled. If black or blue, they will be improved if laid again on the table, when dry, and sponged with gin, or whisky, or other white spirit.

A black silk dress, if very dirty, must be washed; but, if only soiled, soaking for twenty-four hours will do; if old and rusty, a pint of common spirits should be mixed with each gallon of water, which is an improvement under any circumstances. Whether soaked or washed, it should be hung up to drain, and dried without wringing.

Satin and silk ribbons, both white and colored, may be cleaned in the same manner.

To Iron Clothes.

In ironing a shirt, first do the back, then the sleeves, then the collar and bosom, and then the front. Iron calicoes generally on the right side, as they thus keep clean for a longer time. In ironing a calico dress, first do the waist, then the sleeves, then the skirt. Keep the skirt rolled while ironing the other parts, and set a chair to hold the sleeves while ironing the skirt, unless a skirt-board be used. Silk should be ironed on the wrong side, when quite damp, with an iron which is not very hot, as light colors are apt to change and fade. In ironing velvet, turn up the face of the iron, and after dampening the wrong side of the velvet, draw it over the face of the iron, holding it straight; always iron lace and needlework on the wrong side, and put them away as soon as they are dry, because if the least damp yet, they are apt to collect dust, which causes them to turn yellow very quick.

TO CLEAN WEARING APPAREL.

To Clean Black Cloth.

Dissolve one ounce of bicarbonate of ammonia in one quart of warm water. With this liquid rub the cloth, using a piece of flannel or black cloth for the purpose. After the application of this solution, clean the cloth well with clear water, dry and iron it, brushing the cloth from time to time in the direction of the fibre.

To Take Out Spots of Ink.

As soon as the accident happens, wet the place with juice of sorrel or lemon, or with vinegar, and the best hard white soap.

To Take Iron-moulds Out of Linen.

Hold the iron-mould on the cover of a tankard of boiling water, and rub on the spot a little juice of sorrel and a little salt; and, when the cloth has thoroughly imbibed the juice, wash it in lye.

To Take Out Spots on Silk.

Rub the spots with spirits of turpentine; this spirit exhaling, carries off with it the oil that causes the spot.

To Remove Mildew from Linen.

Moisten a piece of soap, and rub it thickly into the part affected. Then scrape fine chalk, or rather whitening, and rub that also in. Lay the linen on the grass, and from time o time, as it becomes dry, wet it a little. If the spots are not quite removed repeat the process.

FAMILY MEDICINES.

THAT this work may be complete in all its parts, and no portion of it without a species of useful domestic instruction, I propose to add to its value of practical utility the advantage of a *Family Physician* and *Household Surgeon* and give some general and specific remedies for ailments of every-day occurrence; it being understood that, in all serious cases, the guidance of a physician is indispensable. Advice and directions are given for the treatment of some severe cases requiring prompt action, that may be followed with benefit until the arrival of the doctor. No particular school of medicine is adhered to, the efficacy of each receipt being the primary consideration in inserting it. The list includes many popular and domestic remedies, together with prescriptions of celebrated and leading physicians. Not crude and popular nostrums, but sound and scientific advice, conveyed in such a form that a parent may, with the utmost safety and confidence, administer what is prescribed either to an infant or an adult, with that certainty of benefit as if ordered by the family practitioner.

This is not done with the idea of superseding the medical man, where families have the means of employing one, but for the use of those who may not be so fortunately situated. The information we purpose giving will be of incalculable advantage, and of great utility and assistance in all cases of emergency, or where professional aid is not attainable.

To make this department of my work more immediately acceptable to parents, I propose treating the diseases of infancy and childhood first in my series, to be followed by those affections that generally attack maturer years and age. With this brief prospectus of my intentions I will at once proceed to the consideration of the different diseases and their remedies.

Rules for Treatment of the Child after Birth.—Give the breast within twelve or eighteen hours after birth at latest.

Foment the breasts with warm water if the milk does not flow; avoid rubbing the breasts with spirits.

If there be too much milk, drink little, and take opening medicine.

As a nurse, wear easy dresses about the bosom and chest.

Keep down the tendency of the abdomen to enlarge, by exercise.

If the nipple is small, or turned in, have it drawn by an older or stronger infant, not by artificial means, but let the new-born child have the first milk.

Choose a hired wet nurse (when required) nearly of the same age with the mother, like her in constitutional peculiarities, and who has been confined about the same time.

When nursing, live on nutritious but not on heavy diet. A full habit requires less nutriment than a delicate constitution. Stimulating liquors are to be avoided. Simple diluents, such as tea, are quite enough as drinks for many mothers.

The mother's milk is the best food for the new-born child for three months.

An infant from two to four months old requires to be suckled once about every three hours.

The best substitute for the breast, but as temporary as possible, is asses' or diluted cow's milk; but on no account should farinaceous food be given at this early period.

Apply a flannel bandage to the lower part of the body in bowel complaints. A warm bath soothes irritation.

After six months an approach may be made to more solid diet.

Raise up the child after feeding.

Give no stimulants, carraway seeds, carminatives, &c.; they are most pernicious.

Give as little medicine to a child as possible, and always by advice.

Never over-feed, and never stop crying by feeding.

Avoid rough jolting and patting of the back.

Train an infant to regularity in all its wants.

Rules for Weaning.—Wean gradually, discontinuing suckling in the night; the gradual change is beneficial to both mother and child. Avoid weaning in severe weather. Take for yourself a cooling purgative, and refrain from fluids and stimulating diet.

In weaning, apply to the breasts three ounces compound soap liniment, three drachms laudanum, one drachm camphor liniment. If this be too irritating, foment with warm water, or poppy-heads and chamomile flowers boiled together in water. Avoid tightness or pressure from the dress, and all roughness, for fear of abscess. Avoid drawing the breasts: avoid exposure to cold.

Rules for Treatment after Weaning—Food.—Study the child's constitution, digestive powers, teeth, strength, and proportion the kind and quantity of food.

Animal food, in small quantity, once a day, if the teeth can masticate, is necessary when there is rapid growth.

Avoid too nourishing a diet with a violent tempered child.

Give a nourishing diet to a white looking, lymphatic child.

Both over-feeding and under-feeding produces scrofula and consumption.

The spoiled and petted child is injured both in health and temper.

Avoid seasoned dishes, fried and salted meats, pastry, uncooked vegetables, unripe fruits, wine and rich cake.

Insist on thorough chewing or mastication.

Never tempt the appetite when disinclined.

Vary the food from day to day, but avoid variety at one meal.

Animal food should be tender, and eaten with a little salt, vegetables, and bread.

Take care that the child's food is well cooked. Give no new bread.

Sweetmeats and confections are only to be given to children in a very sparing manner, if given at all. Never pamper or reward with eatables.

Rules for Sleep.—Allow the child plenty of sleep, without disturbance.

Avoid accustoming the child to sleep on the lap; it will not sleep in bed if so accustomed.

Establish times for regular sleeping.

Keep the hands, feet, and face comfortably warm—blankets are better than sheets.

Support every part of the body, raising by a slope the head and shoulders.

Avoid laying the child in the same bed with an adult, unless for a short time, to restore warmth if it fail.

Never rouse the child by play when taken up during the night.

Rules for Clothing.—In the first stage of infancy, warmth depends on clothing alone, for there is no muscular movement.

Avoid a degree of warmth which produces sensible perspiration.

Flannel and calico are the best materials in all seasons.

Dress the child loosely and fasten with strings, not with pins.

The umbilical cord, navel, and belly-band, require much attention.

Avoid keeping the child's head too warm, or its feet cold.

Avoid chilling the child, or taking it abroad in cold weather.

Attend to the form and size of the child's shoes, so that the feet shall not be cramped.

The practice of plunging infants into cold water, to render them hardy, is exceedingly dangerous.

Let a child's washing be very completely and carefully performed. Keep the child always perfectly clean and neat.

Be very attentive to ventilate the apartment where a child lives but never expose it to draughts of air.

Begin early to form habits of personal cleanliness and delicacy.

Vaccination.—Let the child be vaccinated from six weeks to two months after birth, and that by a proper medical attendant. Vaccination should take place before teething.

Deformities and Distortions.—Consult the surgeon upon the first appearance of any deformity; and do not allow fears for giving pain to the child prevent the use of the necessary remedies.

Be very vigilant with rickets or soft bones. Never allow the rickety child to support its own weight. It ought to be kept on its back for many months, and carried about on a little mattress, on a board or tray, and have nourishing diet, and the proper medicines to give solidity to the bones.

Never jerk or swing children by the arms; much mischief has been done by this practice.

When a child falls, or meets with any accident, it is highly culpable in a nurse to conceal it. If she do not immediately mention it, she may be the cause of the child's deformity and lameness for life.

With proper attention, a tendency to be left-handed may be easily cured in a child.

Prevent all tricks and ill-habits which injure the features and organs; such as stuffing the nostrils, ears, etc., distending the mouth with too large a spoon.

Curvature of the spine is of very frequent occurrence from mismanaging children, by tight lacing, long sitting without support to the back—(all school seats and forms should have backs). Take all deformities of the spine in time, before they get fixed.

Visiting the Sick.—Do not visit the sick when you are fatigued, or when in a state of perspiration, or with the stomach empty, for in such conditions you are liable to take the infection. When the disease is very contagious, take the side of the patient which is next to the window. When you come away, take some food, change your clothing, and expose it to the air.

To Purify the Air of a Sick Chamber.—Dr. J. C. Black obtained £5,000 from Parliament for the following receipt: "Take six drachms of powdered nitre, and the same quantity of oil of vitriol; mix them together by adding to the nitre one drachm of the vitriol at a time; placing the vessel in which you are mixing it on a hot hearth, or plate of heated iron, stirring it with a glass rod, a tobacco-pipe, etc. Then place the vessel in the contaminated room, moving it about to different parts of the room."

Ointment for Sore Nipples.—Take of tincture of Tolu two drachms; spermaceti-ointment half ounce; powdered gum, two drachms. Mix. Make an ointment.

The white of an egg mixed with brandy is the best application for sore nipples. The person should at the same time use a nipple-shield.

Teething.—The first sign of teething is heat in the mouth of the child—felt by the mother during sucking—flow of saliva—biting and grinding the gums. A piece of india rubber is better than coral, ivory, or any hard substance, for rubbing the gums.

When the child is much distressed, have recourse to medical aid.

When the bowels are confined, give without delay a gentle purgative, such as castor oil, manna, magnesia, or senna. The warm bath at ninety-six degrees soothes the child.

A child's mouth should be often examined, even after three years of age. Wayward temper, cough, and even croup, have been traced to cutting a double tooth.

Do not hesitate to allow the child's gums to be lanced.

Exercise.—Very little motion, and that of the gentlest and most careful kind, is all the infant should have for a considerable time after birth.

Avoid the upright posture as much as possible.

Avoid all sudden and violent jerking, and long-continued positions.

Allow the child to move its limbs freely, on the floor or in bed.

Watch the first efforts of the child to walk alone, and interfere rather with eye and hand than by exclamations of caution and alarm; these last do much harm.

Avoid sympathising too strongly with a child when hurt; assist quietly, and show how the accident happened. Children who are angry when hurt, should see that you do not sympathize with their rage, although you do with their sufferings.

Abjure all leading-strings and go-carts, or other artificial means of teaching the child to walk. Never drag the child by one hand, or lift it either by one or both arms.

When the child walks alone, it should not be permitted to over-fatigue itself.

The mother should have her eye both on the child and its attendant out of doors, and be as much as she can in her child's company.

Cholera Infantum.—In this disease the stomach and bowels must be evacuated, and afterwards give charcoal and magnesia, or the latter alone. When there is much irritability clysters of flaxseed tea, mutton broth, and starch, with a little laudanum in them, will give ease. Fomentations to the bowels and abdomen are useful. After the violence of the symptoms is over, give the Peruvian bark in powder or decoction, adding a little nutmeg. Or, use a tea of avens, or bayberry-root, or the leaves of red raspberry. The removal of children to the country—abstaining from fruit—the use of flannel and the cloth bath—are the means prescribed for prevention.

Summer Complaint.—Take two tablespoonsful of grated comfrey root and the white of one egg, beaten well together; then have ready a pint of boiling milk, into which stir the comfrey and egg. It will thicken like "pap," and it is not unpleasant to take.

Navel Soreness in Children.—This sometimes arises from inattention, or from some local irritation, which may be easily removed. REMEDY. Keep the bowels gently open, and keep the part very clean. Dress the sore with a piece cf fine soft old linen, dipped in port wine. If the sore looks black and emits an offensive smell, dress it with a bleaching liquid, made by stirring a quarter of a pint of chloride of lime into three pints of water. A teaspoonful of this mixture to be put into a wineglassful of water.

Nipples, inflamed, in Children.—An inflamed nipple in children's breasts is a common complaint immediately after birth. It affects male and female infants alike, and extends to the breast underneath. FIRST REMEDY. Mix spirits of camphor with lard, and occasionally rub on the part. SECOND REMEDY. Cut a piece of soft brown paper the size of a crown piece, make a hole in the centre for the nipple to go through, cover the paper with pure treacle, and place it over the inflamed part.

Convulsions.— Children are liable to convulsions from teething, wearing tight clothes, small-pox, measles, etc. Bathing in warm water, with a mild clyster, will soon relieve them; and to make the fit still shorter, cold water may be poured over the face and neck while the rest of the body is in the warm bath.

Ointment for Scurf on the Head.—Lard, two ounces; sulphuric acid, diluted, two drachms; rub them together, and anoint the head once a day.

Griping in Children may be remedied by a little magnesia administered once or twice a day. If the gripings are severe, put the child into a warm bath, and give one grain of calomel every three hours until relief is afforded, then give a teaspoonful of castor oil.

Mouth Sore.—Take of honey two tablespoonsful; borax, powdered, half drachm; mix well together, and take a teaspoonful twice a day. The mixture should be placed in the mouth, little by little, touching the various ulcers that are visible, or can be got at.

Vermin in the Hair of Children.—The most effectual mode of destroying vermin in the hair, is to dissolve five grains of bichloride of mercury (corrosive sublimate) in half a pint of distilled water, and wet the hair well with the solution.

This lotion must be used with caution, as it is a deadly poison if taken into the stomach.

Soothing Syrup for a Cough.—Half a pound of muscatel raisins, opened, but not stoned; half a pint of the best olive oil, and half a pint of good Jamaica rum. These ingredients to be simmered over the fire for about half an hour, but not to boil. A teaspoonful may be taken at a time, and often.

Worms in Children.—Make a strong sage tea, and dissolve in it a little saleratus; sweeten it, and, if preferred, add a little milk. Salt and water is also good, especially if there are symptoms of fits. Allow them no sugar or sweetmeats, but plenty of salt in their food, which should be plain, but abundant.

ANOTHER REMEDY.—Give three to five grains of calomel in sugar, over night, and a dose of castor oil the next morning. Repeat once a week until the worms are wholly removed.

Croup.—Spirits of turpentine is a sovereign remedy for croup. Saturate a piece of flannel with it, and place it on the throat and chest, and send for your family physician. If the case be very urgent, and the child in great distress, and the distance to the doctor's residence very great, drop three drops of the turpentine on a lump of sugar, and give it internally. Or a good emetic of blood-root, or lobelia, or both combined, should be given. Every family should keep a bottle of spirits of turpentine in the house.

ANOTHER REMEDY.—This remedy is simply alum: Take a knife or grater and shave or grate off in small particles about a tablespoonful of alum, mix it with about twice the quantity of sugar or honey to make it palatable, and administer as quickly as possible. The doses should be separated at intervals of fifteen minutes, until the phlegm is cut and cast off. This will give almost immediate relief. The patient should also bathe his feet in hot water and apply cloths wet in cold water to the throat and chest, changing as often as they get warm.

Whooping Cough.—A teaspoonful of castor oil to a teaspoonful of molasses; a teaspoonful of the mixture to be given whenever the cough is troublesome. It affords relief at once, and in a few days effects a cure. The same medicine relieves croup, however violent the attack.

ANOTHER REMEDY.—Sulphurate of copper, one-half grain; syrup of poppies, one-half ounce; anise-seed water, one and a half ounce; mix. Dose—one to two teaspoonsful.

Scarlatina and Measles.—Sesquicarbonate of ammonia is antidote to scarlatina and measles. The dose in these complaints varies from three to ten grains, according to the age of the patient, given at longer or shorter intervals, according to the mildness or severity of the attack. The suitable dose dissolved in as small a quantity of cold water as will admit of its being swallowed with as many grains of loaf sugar, merely to make it palatable, is all that is required.

Scarlet Fever Remedy.—One-half ounce each chlorate of potassa and hydrochloric acid, and one-half ounce spring water. Dose—ten drops in a wineglassful of cold water every two hours.

Cure for Smallpox.—Take one grain each of powdered foxglove (digitalis) and sulphate of zinc. Rub together thoroughly in a mortar with five or six drops of water; this done, add four or five ounces of water, and sweeten with loaf sugar. Dose—a tablespoonful for an adult, and one or two teaspoonsful for a child, every two or three hours, until symptoms of disease vanish.

Lotion to prevent pitting in Smallpox.—Take of nitrate of silver, two grains; rose water one ounce—dissolve. Let every vesicle on the face, neck, and bosom be touched with a brush wetted in this lotion.

Each spot as it dries will become black, but that of course will peel off with the eruption at the proper time.

Chicken Pox.—The symptoms are slight feverishness, succeeded by a number of red spots, which break out on the face and back, followed in a few days by watery bladders.—*Remedy.* Magnesia, one drachm; rhubarb, half-drachm; powdered ginger, ten grains; divide into twelve doses, and mix each dose in a little water; administer occasionally while the disease is prevalent. Give cooling drinks, and let the diet be mild.

To Relieve Lockjaw.—Let any one who has an attack of lockjaw take a small quantity of spirits of turpentine, warm it, and pour it on the wound, no matter where the wound is, or what its nature is, and relief will follow in less than one minute. Nothing better can be applied to a severe cut or bruise than cold turpentine; it will give certain relief almost instantly.

A White Swelling on the Joints.—Pump on the part half an hour every morning, This cures also pains in the joints. It seldom fails.

ANOTHER REMEDY.—A stream of cold water one day, and warm the next, and so on by turns. Use these remedies at first, if possible. It is likewise proper to intermix gentle purges to prevent a relapse.

ANOTHER REMEDY.—Boiled nettles applied to the part.

To Dissolve White or Hard Swellings.—Take white roses, elder flowers, leaves of fox-glove, and of St. John's-wort a handful of each; mix them with hog's lard, and make an ointment.

ANOTHER REMEDY.—Hold them morning and evening, in the steam of vinegar, poured on red-hot flints.

Asthma Remedy.—Gather brakes (by some called ferns) in the woods; dry them, place some under the sheet and sleep on them. Add a few fresh ones every few weeks, and not abandon it as soon as a little better; continue a year or more. This is an old Indian remedy.

Mixtures for Asthma.—Syrup of squills, four ounces; milk of gum ammoniacum, six ounces; wine of ipecacuanha, two ounces; mix. The dose is a small teaspoonful four or five times daily. *Expectorant.* Infusion of gentian, four ounces; infusion of cascarilla, six ounces; simple syrup, two ounces; mix. Dose—two tablespoonsful three times a day. *Tonic.*

Erysipelas.—Take an ounce of cream of tartar to a quart of cold water. Dose—half a wineglass full every two-hours, day after day; keep the bowels open with epsom salts. Apply copperas water to keep from spreading.

Remedy for Bronchitis.—Croton oil it is said will entirely remove this complaint. One drop daily rubbed over the surface of the throat produces a singular but powerful eruption of the skin, but in course of time restores the voice and thoroughly removes all mucus from the part affected.

ANOTHER REMEDY.—For soreness in the lower part of the throat, and in the breast. Take a dose of senna and salts, apply a plaster of burgundy pitch to the breast, and use light diet; rub the throat with a coarse cloth, and avoid exposure and heavy exercise of the lungs. If the burgundy pitch is not at hand, the ordinary pitch, melted and spread on a piece of muslin or sheepskin, may answer.

To Cure Salt Rheum.—Mix in an earthen vessel, one ounce aqua-fortis, with one ounce quicksilver; when effervescence has ceased, incorporate with it one pound lard and one ounce dissolved hard soap; then work into the mixture one ounce prepared chalk and one-half tablespoonful spirits of turpentine.

To Cure Hoarseness.—When the voice is lost, as is sometimes the case, from the effects of cold, a simple, pleasant remedy is furnished by beating up the white of one egg, adding to it the juice of one lemon, and sweetening with white sugar to the taste. Take a teaspoonful from time to time. It has been known effectually to cure the ailment.

Sore Throat.—Those subject to sore throats, etc., should bathe the neck with cold water in the morning, and use the flesh-brush at night, which will be found to relieve them very soon.

An Infallible Remedy for Sore Throat.—Make a poultice of wormwood, boiled in sweet milk, and apply it to the throat. I have known this to give relief in the worst cases in eight hours.

For a Consumptive Cough.—Take half a pound of double refined sugar, finely beat and sifted, wet this with orange-flower water, and boil it up to a candy height; then stir in an ounce of cassia-earth finely powdered, and use it as with any other candy.

For a Cough and Shortness of Breath.—Take elecampane roots, one ounce; saffron, quarter ounce; ground ivy and hyssop, of each one handful. Boil this in two quarts of water until it is above half consumed; strain it out, and sweeten it with sugar-candy, and take three spoonsful often.

Excellent Remedy for a Cough.—Take one ounce Syrup of White Poppies; half an ounce each of Paregoric Elixir and Tinc. Squills, and one-quarter of an ounce of Tinc. Tolu. Mix. Dose, a teaspoonful in barley-water.

Catarrh, or Cold.—This is attended with a cough, copious discharges of mucus from the nose, hoarseness and pain in the head—take a purge of senna, manna, and salts, drink freely of flaxseed tea, slightly acidulated with lemon, and take about twenty drops of antimonial wine three times a day; if there is pain in the breast, the pitch plaster is very beneficial; a tea made of a teaspoonful of Cayenne pepper is also very good. If it is attended with much cough, make a mixture of an ounce of syrup of squills, two drachms of antimonial wine, half an ounce of paregoric, with a half pint of water, and take two teaspoonsful every quarter of an hour till relieved.

Dropsy of the Abdomen.—This may be known by a swelling or enlargement of the belly, a watery rattling when touched; hardy and scanty urine. It is a most obstinate disease to cure, except in the early stage and the early part of life; steaming and warm baths, such as promote free perspiration, are beneficial; it has been frequently cured by taking five grains of calomel with two of gamboge, every two days; an ounce and a half of cream of tartar, taken in a little water, daily, has been found a valuable remedy; wear thick flannel, drink no more fluids than are absolutely necessary, and use light and digestible animal food, avoiding salted meats, etc., all such as create a thirst.

Excellent Remedy for the Dropsy.—Take sixteen large nutmegs, eleven spoonsful of broom ashes dried and burnt in an oven, an ounce and a half of bruised mustard-seed, and a handful of scraped horse-radish; put the whole into a gallon of strong mountain wine, and let it stand three or four days. A gill, or half a pint, according to the urgency of the disease and strength of the patient, is to be drank every morning fasting, taking nothing else for an hour or two after.

Biles.—Take frequent purges of salts—a poultice of soap and sugar is frequently used, and is active in drawing the bile to a head; but this preparation is generally too severe; a mush poultice, or one of bread and milk, is generally the best; to this, if the pain is severe, a little sweet oil and a teaspoonful of laudanum, may be added; if the bile does not break, it should be opened with a lancet; it should then be healed by a plaster of simple cerate, and a compound of beeswax and lard.

Blotches on the Skin, Pimples, etc.—Take repeated doses of salts, or sulphur and cream of tartar; keep the person pure by frequent warm baths, avoid all stimulating drinks, and poisonous drugs and powders for the face, and use a light diet; if all this should fail, use the syrup of sarsaparilla.

Deshler's Original Healing Salve.—As this salve is so well known in all parts of the country for its healing properties, we append the original receipt for making the same.

RECEIPT. Take of mutton tallow, rosin and beeswax, each one pound, flaxseed oil two gills, thick turpentine (such as exudes from pine trees or boards) four ounces. Melt the rosin and beeswax together first, and stir them well till thoroughly dissolved and incorporated: Then put in the other ingredients and keep *constantly* stirring the whole together over a slow fire, till they are all melted and well incorporated; then remove it from the fire and continue *stirring* the whole mass till it is *cold*, otherwise the ingredients will separate and spoil the article. It may now be put by for use, as it will keep for any length of time.

If it is intended to draw it should be spread thick, but if only for healing it should be spread thinly.

A Cure for Ringworm.—Take yellow-dock root; cut in small pieces, and simmer them in vinegar, and, when the strength is extracted, strain off the vinegar, which apply to the part affected at least three times a day. At the same time, it is well to drink a tea made of the same root; or take some of the extract of yellow dock-root, which can be found at any drug store. This is infallible.

A Cure for Tetter.—Take as much mustard as will make into a salve mixed with honey; spread it on a rag, and lay it on the sore for twenty-four hours. If the sore is not dead, make new salve, and lay it on three or four hours longer.

Then take the inside of elder-bark and stew it in lard; put in beeswax enough to make a salve; set it by until it gets cold. This is to heal the sore. Don't let the sore get wet.

Then take mullein and boil it in water, and wash with after the wound is healed. This is to harden the tender skin again.

To Remove Proud Flesh.—The following recipe has been practised in England for years with great success. It is simply this—pulverize loaf sugar very fine, and apply it to the part affected.

Cancer.—Take a quantity of red-oak bark, burn it to ashes; to this add water; boil to the consistence of molasses; apply it freely to the part affected; leave on for an hour; afterward cover the plaster with tar; remove in a few days, and if protuberances appear in the wound, apply the plaster and tar, alternately, until they all disappear; after which apply any healing salve.

Remedy for Scrofula.—Put one ounce aqua-fortis in a bowl or saucer; drop in it two copper cents; when the effervescence ceases, add two ounces strong vinegar. The fluid will be of a dark green color. It should and will smart. If too severe, dilute it with a little rain water. Apply it to the sore, morning and evening, by a soft brush or a rag. Before applying it, wash the sore with water. This receipt comes well recommended for curing old sores and other scrofulous eruptions.

To Cure Itch.—*First Remedy.* Rub into the part affected, at night, sulphur ointment; wash this off thoroughly in the morning, and re-anoint the parts; continue to adopt this plan until the affection disappears.—*Second Remedy.* Liquor of ammonia, one ounce; camphorated alcohol, one drachm and a half; bay salt, half an ounce; water, one pint; mix, and rub it well into the parts; afterwards use olive oil.

Pile Ointment.—Take of balsam of copaiva, forty drops; lard, one ounce; pulverized nut galls, half an ounce; extract of lead, twelve drops; opium, six grains. Make into an ointment.

Use this, and at the same time keep the bowels open with small doses of castor oil or balsam copaiva.

ANOTHER REMEDY FOR PILES.—Make daily use of a syringe, with warm water and castile-soap—a mild and sure cure if persevered in. A decoction made of "balm of gilead" buds, with alcohol, has cured inveterate cases.

Liniment for Piles.—Take two ounces emollient ointment; half an ounce laudanum. Mix these ingredients with the yolk of an egg, and work them well together, and then anoint the diseased part or sore.

Bruises.—Bruises are too often neglected, from the fact that the extent of the injury is seldom visible. Soak a piece of bread in vinegar, then mash it into a poultice, add a few drops of laudanum, and apply it to the part; bruised wormwood and vinegar is also an effective application. Keep applying fresh poultices, and bathe the part with laudanum, sweet oil and vinegar.

To Prevent Swelling from Bruises.—Apply at once a cloth five or six folds in thickness, dipped in cold water, and when it grows warm renew the wetting.

Remedy for a Sprain.—Wormwood boiled in vinegar, and applied hot, with enough cloths wrapped around to keep the sprain moist. This is an invaluable remedy.

Liniment for Sprains.—Compound liniment of camphor an ounce and a half, tincture of opium half an ounce. Mix. This is an admirable application for sprains and bruises after the inflammation has disappeared, and for rheumatism and colic when unattended by inflammation.

Soundness of the Lungs.—The following is one of the most unmistakable tests of the soundness or unsoundness of the lungs. The patient is directed to draw in a full breath, and then begin to count, as far as he can, slowly and audibly, without again drawing his breath. The number of seconds he can continue counting is then to be carefully noted. In confirmed consumption the time does not exceed eight seconds, and often less than six. In pleurisy and pneumonia it ranges from nine to fourteen seconds. But when the lungs are sound, the time will reach as high as from twenty to thirty-five seconds.

German Cure for Consumption.—Take a pound of pure honey, and let it boil gently in a stew-pan; then, having washed, scraped clean, and finely grated with a sharp grater, two large sticks of fresh horse-radish, stir into the honey as much as you possibly can. It must remain in a boiling state about five minutes, but stirred so as not to burn; after which put it into small earthen pots, or a jar, and keep it covered up for use. Two or three tablespoonsful a day, or more, according to the strength of the patient, and some time persisted in, is said to perform wonders, even where there is a confirmed phthisis pulmonalis, or consumption of the lungs. It is also serviceable in all coughs where the lungs are greatly affected.

Another Cure for Consumption.—The following is said to be an effectual remedy, and will in time completely eradicate the disorder. Live temperately—avoid spirituous liquors—wear flannel next the skin—and take, every morning, half a pint of new milk, mixed with a wineglassful of the expressed juice of green hoarhound. One who has tried it says—"Four weeks' use of the hoarhound and milk relieved the pains of my breast, gave me to breathe deep, long, and free, strengthened and harmonized my voice, and restored me to a better state of health than I had enjoyed for years."

Perfect Cure for a Burn.—Take essence of peppermint and whisky, in proportions of one part peppermint and three of spirits, and apply with cloths, and it gives perfect relief instantly. Peppermint and sweet oil is equally good, put on with cotton. This should be always at hand, whenever there is danger from such accidents, as it acts like a perfect charm, and will not fail to relieve.

Best Cure for Burns or Scalds.—The best application in cases of burns or scalds is a mixture of one part of carbolic acid to eight of olive oil. Lint or linen rags are to be saturated in the lotion, and spread smoothly over the burned part, which should then be covered with oiled silk or gutta-percha tissue to exclude the air. The dressing may be left on from two to three days, and should then be re-applied, exposing the burn as short a time as possible to the air.

Another Cure.—Of all applications for a burn, we believe that there are none equal to a simple covering of common wheat flour. This is always at hand; and while it requires no skill in using, it produces most astonishing effects. The moisture produced upon the surface of a slight or deep burn, is at once absorbed by the flour, and forms a protection.

Body in Flames.—Lay the person down on the floor of the room, and throw the table cloth, rug, or other large cloth over him, and roll him on the floor.

Liniment for Rheumatism.—Olive oil and oil of turpentine of each an ounce and a half, spirit of vitriol three drachms. Mix. This will be found excellent for rheumatism, sprains, chilblains, and other cases in which active application is needful.

Mixture for Chronic Rheumatism.—Oxymuriate of mercury, four grains; spirits of wine, eight ounces. Rub well together, and when perfectly dissolved, add antimonial wine, fifty drops. *Dose*—One teaspoonful twice a day.

Remedy for Inflammatory Rheumatism.—Take one ounce pulverized saltpetre and put it into a pint of sweet oil. Bathe the parts affected, and a sound cure will speedily be effected.

Cure for Rheumatic Gout.—Take half an ounce nitre, half ounce sulphur, half ounce flour of mustard, half ounce Turkey rhubarb, and two drachms powdered gum guaiacum. Mix. A teaspoonful to be taken every other night for three nights, and omit three nights, in a wineglassful of cold water—water which has been well boiled.

Bilious Fever.—The approach of this disease is indicated by a full, hard, and quick pulse, hot skin, white tongue, sickness of the stomach, and pain in the head. The patient should be bled till the pulse is reduced, and take from ten to fifteen grains of calomel, followed by a Seidlitz Powder; the bowels should still be kept open by salts and senna, and the patient take no other nourishment than rice or barley and cold lemonade.

Typhus Fever.—If the apartment is large, airy, and clean, there is little danger from infection. The simple process spoken of in another part of this work will prevent any bad effect from the disease. The sheets and body linen should be changed.

Cure for Fever and Ague.—The following, brought from the Spanish Main, and said to be an unfailing cure for fever and ague is highly recommended. Just before the chill comes on, have a pot of very strong coffee made and keep it hot, and when the first chill is felt, pour out about a pint and squeeze the juice of a couple of lemons into it, and a little sugar to make it palatable, and drink it off, go to bed and cover up warm. One trial of this often cures, whilst two or three trials never fail.

Cooling Drink for Feverish Thirst.—One tablespoonful of cream of tartar; juice of two large lemons; a pint of boiling water; sugar to taste; one wineglass of gin. Mix all together.

Intermittent Fever.—Treat first with an emetic of ipecacuanha, twenty grains. Work off with chamomile tea, or warm water. After which give a gentle purgative of calomel, three grains; compound rhubarb pill, ten grains. Divide into three pills, to be taken immediately. Then give the following:

Sulphate of quinine, two scruples; aromatic confection, one drachm. Mix and divide into twenty pills; three to be taken morning, noon, and night, and continued for four or five days, and repeated afterwards at intervals, to ensure success. The bowels must be carefully attended to.

Apoplexy.—When medical aid is not procurable, rather copious bleeding from the arm should be resorted to; cold water should be poured upon the head, and the bowels opened by means of active purgatives; ten grains of calomel may be immediately given, and its action promoted by the use of saline purgatives and stimulating clysters. The legs may be placed in pretty warm water, and blisters applied between the shoulders.

Turn of Life.—Keep the bowels free from costiveness by taking two teaspoonsful of white English mustard seed, whole, three times a day. If giddiness and occasional pains in the head, leeches to the temple will be found very beneficial; and if ulcers should break out on any part of the body, they ought by no means to be healed up, unless a drain, by means of a seaton or issue, be established in some other part.

Felon.—Soak the finger in strong, warm lye, for half an hour at a time, frequently. Also make use of strong poultices.

A Safe Remedy for a Felon.—Take a pint of common soft soap, and stir it in air-slacked lime till it is of the consistency of glazier's putty. Make a leather thimble, fill it with this composition, and insert the finger therein, and change the composition once in twenty minutes, and a cure is certain.

Cure for a Wen.—The following has proved to be effectual. Make a very strong brine, dip in a piece of flannel two or three times doubled, and apply it to the wen; keep it constantly wet, night and day, until suppuration takes place.

Pills for Nervous Headache.—Socotrine aloes, powdered rhubarb, of each one drachm; compound powder of cinnamon, one scruple; hard soap, half a drachm; syrup, enough to form the mass. To be divided into fifty pills, of which two will be sufficient for a dose; to be taken occasionally.

Neuralgia.—The fumes of sugar snuffed up the nose will cure ordinary cases of neuralgia. Put a small quantity of sugar on a hot shovel and try it.

Neuralgia and General Pain Killer.—Take two quarts of 95 per cent. alcohol, and add to it the following articles: Oils of sassafras, hemlock, spirits of turpentine, balsam of fir, chloroform, and tincture of catechu and guaiacum, of each one ounce; oil of origanum, two ounces; oil of wintergreen, half ounce, and gum camphor, half ounce. The above is a noble liniment, and may be successfully employed in rheumatism, bruises, neuralgia, sprains, headache, burns, and spinal affections.

To Promote the Growth of the Hair.—Eau de cologne, two ounces; tincture of cantharides, two drachms; oil of rosemary and oil of lavender, of each ten drops.

For Baldness.—Fill a bottle with powdered lobelia, then pour in as much as it will contain of equal parts of brandy and sweet oil. In a few days it will be fit for use. Bathe the head once a day with this, and it will prevent the loss of hair. It is said to restore it when lost.

A Cure for Earache.—Take a bit of cotton-batting, put upon it a pinch of black pepper, gather it up and tie it, dip it in sweet oil and insert it in the ear. Put a flannel badge over the head to keep it warm. It will give immediate relief.

BEST CURE FOR THE EARACHE.—Drop some warm glycerine into the ear by means of a quill, and afterwards introduce a piece of wool. Wool plucked from a blanket is the most suitable; the fibres are elastic, and do not coalesce into a hard pellet as cotton is apt to do.

Deafness.—A mixture of ten drops of spirits of turpentine with one ounce of almond oil, introduced upon cotton into the ears, is serviceable in cases of deafness from a diseased action of the *ceruminous glands.*

ANOTHER REMEDY.—Oil of almonds, one pound, bruised garlic, two ounces, alkanet, half ounce; infuse and strain. Applied with a little cotton to the ear.

Sore Eyes.—Make a decoction of fresh wild turnip, or of lobelia; strain through a fine cloth, and use it for a wash. Or, dissolve twelve grains of white vitriol, and sixteen grains of sugar of lead in half a pint of water; or, instead of the water, in three gills of milk and use the whey.

To Strengthen Weak Eyes.—Put a teaspoonful of vinegar to half a pint of water and use it warm two or three times a day.

Salve for a Speck in the Eye, arising from Healed Ulcers.—Red precipitate and carbonate of zinc, one and a half drachms each; tutty, half a drachm; red sulphurate of mercury, one scruple; balsam of Peru, fifteen drops; lard, two ounces. Mix well.

Jaw Ache.—Take a dose of salts, and apply a warm poultice of hops and vinegar to the part. Steaming the part with the vapor of vinegar, keeping the body covered at the same time with blankets, till a perspiration comes on, is also very effectual.

For Filling Decayed Teeth.—Take of quicksilver, ten grains; pure silver filings, five grains. The mercury and silver will unite and form an amalgam, which after being stuffed into the tooth will, in two hours, turn as hard as the tooth itself.

Cure for Tooth-Ache.—It is said that drops prepared as follows will cure the worst tooth-ache ever known:—One ounce of alcohol, two drachms Cayenne pepper, one ounce kerosene oil; let it stand twenty-four hours after mixing.

Tooth-Ache Drops.—Laudanum, three parts; alcohol, five parts; camphor, one part; pellitory of Spain (powdered), two parts; cassia, one part; opium, one part. Digest for a few days, and decant the clear liquid. Apply by means of a little lint.

Doctor Stoy's Cure for the Bite of a Mad Dog.—Take one ounce of red chicken-weed, (gathered and dried in the shade during the month of June,) put it into one quart of strong (or brewer's) beer, boil it down to one pint. Strain the tea through a clean linen cloth, then stir into the tea one ounce theriac so that it will be well mixed. The theriac is not to be boiled.

Dose.—For a man with a strong constitution, one half pint taken in the morning, sober, and the next morning the other half pint, also sober.

The patient ought to fast three hours after he has taken the medicine; then he can eat bread and butter, or bread and molasses, for at least a week or ten days; he must not eat any pork, nor any fish or water-fowls, and must not drink any water. He can drink any kind of tea, and he must not get angry or overheat himself for two weeks.

For a person of a weak constitution, make three doses out of the above-prepared quantity, and also for children in proportion. Three doses will be sufficient for a cure.

For animals, the medicine must be doubled; and its food water and wheat bran, to be given warm.

(This is the original receipt of the celebrated Dr. Stoy, which has rendered such valuable service through Pennsylvania, and we cannot think of letting it pass without notice in this work.)

Hydrophobia.—Wash and cleanse the wound immediately, and apply to every part of it "nitrate of silver." This destroys the poison which will come away. If faithfully applied, a celebrated physician declares the sufferer perfectly safe.

Cure for Liver Complaint.—Take half an ounce each extract of taraxacum (dandelion) and tartrate of potossa; forty-five grains carbonate of soda; half ounce sweet tincture of rhubarb, and six ounces spring water. Dose, a teaspoonful three times a day.

Inflammation of the Intestines.—Severe pain in the abdomen, increased upon pressure, and shooting in a twisting manner round the navel; hardness of the abdomen; obstinate costiveness. There is sometimes vomiting or straining at stool, according as the inflammation happens in the superior or inferior portions of the intestine. The pulse is quick, hard, and contracted, and the urine high-colored, and there are other symptoms of fever with great prostration of strength. All those inducing inflammation of the stomach; also, strangulated hernia, colic, long-continued costiveness. It is distinguishable from colic by being accompanied with fever, and by increase of pain from pressure. The indications of cure are: 1. To reduce the inflammation by bleeding once or twice from the arm, by a large blister laid over the belly, by the warm bath, and by total abstinence from stimulating articles of diet or medicine. 2. To move the bowels by gentle purges, as castor oil, salts, or cream of tartar; and by clysters of salt water.

Bleeding at the Lungs.—Eat of raw table salt freely. Or take equal parts of powdered loaf sugar and rosin four times a day; or drink freely of a decoction of yellow dock root.

Spitting of Blood.—Syrup of poppies a quarter of an ounce; diluted sulphuric acid, ten drops; infusion of red roses, two ounces and a half. One or two tablespoonsful four times a day.

Genuine Syrup for Coughs, Spitting of Blood, &c.—This excellent remedy for such frequently very alarming symptoms, cannot be made too public. It is thus made:—Take six ounces of comfrey roots, and twelve handsful of plantain leaves, cut and beat them well; strain out the juice; and, with an equal weight of sugar, boil it up to a syrup.

To Arrest Bleeding at the Nose.—Introduce, by means of a probe, a small piece of lint or soft cotton, previously dipped into some mild styptic, as a solution of alum, white vitriol, creosote, or even cold water. This will generally succeed; but should it not, cold water may be snuffed up the nostrils. Should the bleeding be very profuse, medical advice should be procured.

ANOTHER REMEDY.—Two small arteries branching up from the main arteries on each side of the neck, and passing over the outside of the jawbone, supply the face with blood. If the nose bleed from the right nostril, for example, pass the finger along the edge of the right jaw till the beating of the artery is felt. Press hard upon it for five minutes and the bleeding will cease.

Bleeding at the Chin.—A person often cuts himself in shaving; and perhaps just at the moment when he is in a hurry to make his toilet the blood continues to flow obstinately. *Remedy.*—A cobweb placed on the cut will speedily staunch the blood; or if the arms are raised aloft, and kept in that position for a moment or two, the blood will cease to flow.

A Cure for Diarrhœa.—Put into a bottle three ounces pimento, (allspice,) upon which pour one pint best French brandy; sweeten with sugar.

Dose.—A wineglassful every hour for three hours, for adults. For children, dilute, and give a tablespoonful each hour. This remedy has been known to cure violent cases of diarrhœa.

Cure for Summer Complaint.—Take two tablespoonsful of grated comfrey root and the white of one egg beaten well together; then have ready a boiling pint of milk, into which stir the comfrey and egg. It will thicken like "pap," and it is not unpleasant to take.

Dysentery.—One or two doses of rhubarb may be taken with good effect; the bowels must be regulated by a suitable diet.

Excellent Remedy for Cholera Morbus.—At the commencement of the disease give plentifully of thin broths, teas, or other diluting drinks, to promote the vomiting until the offending cause is expelled; clysters of the same may be given every hour. After these evacuations have been continued for some time, a decoction of toasted bread may be given, to stop the vomiting; or, take lemon-juice, loaf-sugar, and a little brandy, pour hot water to it, and drink it after puking. As the stomach and intestines are much weakened after this disease, an infusion of some tonic bitters in wine may be taken for some time.

Cholera Mixture.—Mix together one ounce essence of Jamaica ginger; two ounces each camphorated tincture of opium and aromatic spirits of ammonia; and one ounce spirits of camphor. Dose, a teaspoonful every hour.

Cramp.—An affection usually caused by exposure to cold and damp. *First Remedy*—Foment the part affected with warm water, with a little mustard mixed in it; drink nothing cold, and take a little brandy and water; put the feet in warm water, and endeavor to produce a perspiration, take two or three times a day a dose of Peruvian bark in a little wine, or a little ginger and water. *Second Remedy*—Take of water of ammonia or spirits of hartshorn, one ounce; olive oil, two ounces; shake them together till they unite, and rub it on the affected part with the hand.

Cramp in the Stomach.—A sharp, violent darting and drawing pain in the stomach; apply hot bricks to the stomach and soles of the feet, and give a teaspoonful of ether with from forty to seventy drops of laudanum or paregoric.

Pills for Costive Habits.—Extract of aloes, twenty grains; powdered ginger, half a drachm; powdered ipecacuanha, eight grains; syrup, sufficient quantity. Mix, and divide into sixteen pills. Dose, one about noon.

Treatment of Epilepsy or Falling Fits.—Take of ammoniate of copper, twenty grains; bread crumbs and mucilage of gum arabic, a sufficient quantity to form it into a mass; which is to be divided into forty pills. In the beginning, one of these is to be taken three times a day, and gradually increased to two, or even three pills, thrice a day.

Hysterics.—Assafœtida, one drachm; peppermint water, one ounce and a half; ammoniated tincture of valerian, two drachms; sulphuric ether, two drachms. Mix. A dose of this mixture is a tablespoonful every second hour.

Remedy for Disease of the Kidneys.—Boil one ounce pareira brava in three pints of water until it is only one pint. Dose, a wineglassful three times a day.

For Pains and Strictures in the Bladder.—Pulver. quassia, one drachm; carbonate of soda, one drachm; tinct. opium, half ounce; water, five ounces. Morning and evening one tablespoonful to be taken.

Incontinence of Urine.—Take from the hazel-nut the inner skin from the meat; make a decoction by steeping in hot water, and drink at intervals through the day. This strengthens the urinary organs, so that a cure is speedily effected.

ANOTHER REMEDY is a tea made from water melon seeds; drink a teacupful two or three times a day until relieved.

ANOTHER REMEDY.—Put four drops tincture of aconite root in a tumbler of water. Dose, a teaspoonful every hour until relieved.

Gravel.—A disease depending on the formation of stony matter in the kidney. *First Remedy.* The general treatment should consist in a hot bath and warm fomentations; a dose of castor oil should be administered, when the bowels have acted, if there be much pain, the following may be given: Solution of acetate of morphine, one drachm: spirit of hydrochloric ether, two drachms; syrup of roses, half ounce; camphor mixture, four ounces; dose, one-fourth part, to be taken at bedtime. Linseed tea or barley water should be drank freely. *Second Remedy.* Infusion of buchu, seven ounces; tincture of musk seeds, one ounce; sal-volatile, two drachms; mix; dose, two tablespoonsful once or twice a day.

Cure for Quinsy.—Simmer hops in vinegar a few minutes, until their strength is extracted, strain the liquid, sweeten it with sugar, and give it frequently to the patient, in small quantities, until relieved. This is said to be an excellent medicine.

Gargle for Quinsy.—Infusion of roses, five and a half ounces; syrup of roses, half an ounce; diluted sulphuric acid, twenty-five minims. Mix.

To prevent the acid from injuring the enamel of the teeth, it should be sucked through an acid-tube, or quill, and the mouth carefully washed after each dose.

Mumps.—These are swellings of the glands under the jaw, the ear, and down the neck. They render the act of swallowing difficult, and are attended with a slight degree of feverishness, foul tongue, and headache. *Remedy.* Apply warm fomentations to the swelling, and immediately afterwards wrap round with flannel to prevent cold chilling; sprinkle on the flannel compound liniment of turpentine. Let the diet be light, chiefly farinaceous, and keeping the bowels regular by applying mild aperients. After the fourth day, take one grain of quinine, in fifteen drops of diluted vitriolic acid, in a wineglassful of water, three times a day for a fort-night.

Remedy for Diptheria.—Permanganate of potassa has been administered with great success in cases of diptheria. The proportions used for external use are one drachm of the permanganate to a pint of water, the dose for internal use, one teaspoonful of a solution of one drachm in one and a half pints of water.

Hiccoughs.—Take a swallow or two of vinegar, or a long draught of cold water.

Powder for Hiccough.—Put as much dill-seed, finely powdered, as will lie on a shilling into two spoonsful of syrup of black cherries, and take it presently.

Heartburn.—What is commonly called heartburn is not a disease of the heart, but an uneasy sensation of heat or acrimony about the pit of the stomach, accompanied, sometimes, by a rising in the throat like water. *First Remedy.* One teaspoonful of the spirit of nitrous ether, in a glass of water or a cup of tea. *Second Remedy.* A large teaspoonful of magnesia taken in a cup of tea, or a glass of mint-water.

Heartburn Lozenges.—Prepared chalk, four ounces; crab's eyes prepared, two ounces; bole ammoniac, one ounce; nutmeg, one scruple, or cinnamon half an ounce. Make into a paste with dissolved gum arabic. When held in the mouth until they dissolve, they will afford effectual relief.

Cure for Dyspepsia.—Take one ounce pulverized rhubarb, one ounce caraway-seed, one tablespoonful grated orange peel. Put these into a bottle with one pint of pure whisky, shake it well together, and keep in a warm place. *Dose.* One tablespoonful in the morning, and at night when going to bed. Shake the mixture well before taking it.

CENTENNIAL CURE FOR DYSPEPSIA.—Close all the outer doors of a four-story house, open the inner doors, then take a long switch and chase a cat up and down stairs till she sweats.

Debility is a falling off from the usual power of the individual to perform those exertions in which he has been habitually engaged. *Remedy.* Nourishing food, change of air, careful regulation of diet, cold shower baths, and the following forms of medicine: Sulphate of magnesia, four ounces; sulphate of iron, eight grains; sulphate of quinine, ten grains; diluted sulphuric acid, one drachm; infusion of gentian-root, eight ounces; two tablespoonsful twice or thrice a day. Or, compound tincture of bark, one ounce; carbonate of ammonia, two scruples; water, eight ounces; two tablespoonsful three times a day.

Depression of Spirits.—Sal volatile, combined with camphor, is more efficacious than most remedies in affording relief in depression of spirits, heartburns, spasms, palpitations, etc.

For Nervous Languors.—Cinnamon bark and nutmegs, of each one ounce; cloves, half an ounce; cardamon seeds, a quarter of an ounce; dried saffron, one ounce; prepared shells, eight ounces; refined sugar (powdered), one pound; water, half a pint. Rub the dry substances mixed together, into a very fine powder; then add the water gradually, and mix until the whole is thoroughly incorporated. Dose, from ten grains to a drachm.

Pain in Back.—Pains in the back are of many kinds, and may result from a variety of causes. *Remedy.* If weakness be the cause, cold bathing, the shower bath, and squeezing a sponge repeatedly down the back, together with vigorous rubbing with a rough towel, will be found efficacious. Rest, in a recumbent or semi-recumbent position, will also alleviate the pain and contribute to its removal.

Another remedy for persons suffering from pain in the back, is to place on the part affected either a porous or aconite plaster, procured at any drug store.

Sun-Stroke.—The obstruction of heat is the point of attack; wait for no doctor, as delay is dangerous; but strip the patient to the waist and pour cold water over the neck and chest until consciousness begins to return, or until the intense heat is abated. Let him also take the following mixture: Infusion of senna leaves, a teaspoonful; nitre, half a drachm. Mix. Half to be taken immediately, the other half in three hours. He should also drink plentifully of lemonade or of vinegar and water. Linen cloths dipped in cold water and vinegar of roses may be applied to the forehead, temples, or all over the head. As consciousness returns, slight stimulants may be carefully administered.

ANOTHER CURE.—Immediately bruise horseradish and apply it to the stomach, and give him gin to drink. Never-failing.

A Remedy for Snake Bites.—This remedy, it has been stated, is a positive cure for snake bites.

Take an egg and beat it up well, then stir in a tablespoonful of gun-powder, and the same quantity of salt. Spread on linen and apply on the wound. Soon after it is applied the back of the linen will show evidence of the poison by turning green; then apply a second plaster, and continue to change until the discoloration of the cloth ceases to be apparent. This remedy is said to have cured persons bitten by the most poisonous snakes. During this operation, if a decoction of lobelia be taken in small doses, it would be very beneficial.

Poison of the Rattlesnake.—Iodide of potassium, four grains; corrosive sublimate, two grains; bromine, five drachms. Ten drops of this mixture, diluted with one or two tablespoonsful of brandy, wine, or whisky, constitute a dose, to be repeated if necessary. It must be kept in glass-stoppered phials, well secured, as the air will affect it. The salts may, in case of emergency, be first dissolved in a little water, before adding the bromine, as this dissolves them very slowly.

List of the Principal Poisons, with their Antidotes or Remedies:—

OIL OF VITRIOL, AQUA FORTIS, SPIRIT OF SALT.—Magnesia, Chalk, Soap and Water.

EMETIC TARTAR.—Oily Drinks, Solution of Oak Bark.

SALT OF LEMONS OR ACID OF SUGAR.—Chalk, Whiting, Lime, or Magnesia and Water. Sometimes an Emetic Draught.

PRUSSIC ACID.—Pump on back, Smelling-salts to nose, Artificial Breathing, Chloride of Lime to nose.

PEARLASH, SOAP-LEES SMELLING-SALTS, NITRE, HARTSHORN, SAL VOLATILE.—Lemon-juice and Vinegar and water.

Arsenic, Fly Powder, or White Arsenic, King's Yellow, or Yellow Arsenic.—Emetics, Lime Water, Soap and Water, Sugar and Water, Oily Drinks.

Mercury, Corrosive Sublimate, Calomel.—Whites of Eggs, Soap and Water.

Opium, Laudanum.—Emetic Draught, Vinegar and Water, Dashing Cold Water on chest and face, walking up and down for two or three hours.

Lead, White Lead, Sugar of Lead, Goulard's Extract.—Epsom Salts, Castor Oil, Emetics.

Copper, Blue Stone, Verdigris.—Whites of Eggs, Sugar and Water, Castor Oil, Gruel.

Zinc.—Lime Water, Chalk and Water, Soap and Water.

Iron.—Magnesia, Warm Water.

Henbane, Hemlock, Nightshade, Foxglove.—Emetics and Castor Oil, Brandy and Water, if necessary.

Poisonous Food.—Emetics and Castor Oil.

To Cure the Stings of Hornets, Wasps, Bees and Spiders.—Swelling may instantly be arrested by an application of equal parts common salt and bicarbonate of soda, dissolved in warm water, and well rubbed in on the place bitten or stung.

The Painters' Cholic.—Pains and spasms in the belly and intestines; eructations or belching, frequent inclinations to go to stool, etc. It very frequently terminates in a palsy in the wrists and extremities, or other parts of the body. Castor oil in repeated doses is often effectual in producing stools. Mercury united with opium is very beneficial, by exciting salivation. Rub the belly with brandy and camphor mixed, and relieve the pain by doses of laudanum, of from forty to eighty drops. Bleeding is recommended in violent stages, if the patient is of a full habit. (Blister or mustard plasters have also proved efficacious.)

The following prescriptions are recommended :—1st. Take of calomel, half of a grain; prepared sulphuret of antimony, half of a grain; conserve of roses, five grains; make a pill to be taken three times a day. 2d. Take sulphate of alum and potash, one half scruple; infusion of roses, twelve drachms; syrup of roses, one drachm. Make a draught to be taken three times a day.

Cure for Flux.—Take four ounces of castor oil, two tablespoonsful of pulverized gum arabic; two teaspoonsful of pulverized gum kino; one teaspoonful of laudanum; mix with one pint of warm water, shake well, and take a tablespoonful three times a day. I have never known this to fail in the most severe cases.

Jaundice.—A disease arising from obstruction to the passage of the bile into the intestines, from disorders of the liver. *Remedy.* The diet should be cool, light, and diluting—consisting chiefly of ripe fruit and mild vegetables. The drink, barley water or linseed tea, sweetened with liquorice; the bowels must be kept gently open. When the disease has abated, constant doses of Peruvian bark should be given, with good port wine; plenty of exercise taken, and a mustard poultice placed occasionally over the liver.

To Relieve Night-Sweats.—Dissolve fifteen grains sulphate of quinine in half ounce essence of tansy, quarter ounce alcohol, quarter ounce water, and thirty drops muriatic acid. A teaspoonful taken two or three times during the day and at bed-time. In connection with this remedy, cold sage tea is recommended to be used freely as a drink.

Drowning.—Wipe the body dry and place it on a warm mattrass, covered with a blanket, and rub incessantly with flannels under the blanket; keep the head raised, apply hot bricks, or bottles full of hot water, under the arm-pits, to the feet and thighs, and place hot tiles under the spine. Irritate the nostrils with a feather and the smell of strong ammonia. An injection of warm gruel and turpentine should be thrown up the rectum; turn the body on its side, and use rapid friction along the spine with brandy and turpentine. Should these means not restore animation, remove the body to a hot bath for ten or fifteen minutes, keeping up artificial respiration the whole time, by closing the lips with the hand, and inserting the pipe of a small pair of bellows into one of the nostrils, and while an assistant presses back the larynx, or organ of voice, to let the air enter the wind-pipe, inflate the lungs steadily with the bellows, forcing out the air by pressing the hand on the stomach after every inflation. As soon as the patient can swallow, give a little weak wine and water, and when reaction commences, an emetic of half a drachm of white vitriol dissolved in a cup of warm water, or, if more convenient, an emetic of mustard. To relieve the headache that supervenes, bleed or apply leeches to the temples, or apply a blister to the nape of the neck.

To Restore Persons Struck by Lightning.—*First Remedy*.

When a person is struck by lightning strip the body and throw buckets of cold water over it from ten to fifteen minutes; inflate the lungs, as described in the directions respecting DROWNING, and apply continued frictions all over the body, apply also blisters to the breast, and administer stimulants, as brandy and sal-volatile. *Caution*—As trees, haystacks, and other elevated objects serve to conduct lightning rather than ward it off, a person overtaken by a thunderstorm should never seek shelter near these; it is much better to get wet to the skin, than expose one's self to this danger. It is also dangerous to stand near leaden spouts, iron gates, or pallisades, at such times, metals at all times having so strong a conducting power for lightning, as frequently to lead it out of the course which it would otherwise have taken. When in the house, avoid sitting or standing near a window or door; the nearer you are placed towards the centre of the room the better.

Chapped Hands.—This troublesome complaint arises generally from not wiping the hands perfectly dry after washing them. *Remedy*—Borax, two scruples; glycerine, half ounce; water, seven and a half ounces; mix, and apply as a lotion twice a day.

ANOTHER CURE.—Instead of washing the hands with soap employ oatmeal, and, after each washing, take a little dry oatmeal, and rub over the hands, so as to absorb any moisture. If oatmeal cannot be obtained, bran will answer the same purpose. Dry oatmeal or bran is also an excellent remedy for prickly heat.

Excellent Wash for Numbed or Trembling Hands.— These disagreeable complaints are said to be soon remedied by the very simple expedient of frequently washing the hands, so effected in a strong decoction of wormwood and mustard seed; to be strained, and used when cold.

Lip Salve.—White wax, three drachms; spermaceti, one and a half drachms; olive oil, six drachms; alkanet root, one drachm. Melt the wax and spermaceti in a cup, then the oil and root in another, near the fire; then strain through muslin or fine linen, and mix with the wax; then add balsam of Peru, one drachm; essence of bergamot, ten drops; otto of roses, five drops. Mix well together.

Cold Cream.—Oil of almonds, one pound; white wax, four ounces; melt, pour into a warm mortar, add by degrees, rose water, one pint. It should be light and white. Used as a mild unguent to soften the skin, prevent chaps, etc.

Frost Bites.—Friction with snow or cold water merely should be used, until the circulation is somewhat restored, and then equal parts of brandy or some other spirit mixed with cold water may be applied, until the restoration is completed. Frost bites are apt to leave troublesome sores, which are difficult to heal. The red precipitate ointment is the best application; and if much inflamed, they should be poulticed.

Chilblains.—These sores are caused by frost, and are often very painful. Where the skin is not broken, bathe the part in strong alum water; this will cure if continued a week or two. Copal varnish is good. Also pig's foot oil will effect an immediate cure.

ANOTHER REMEDY.—Bathe the feet with a strong solution of alum, or a mixture of equal parts of oil of turpentine and balsam copaiva. Or, dip a piece of white chalk in vinegar, and frequently rub the chilblains with it. Or, bind on thin white skin which comes from suet.

To Cure Itching Feet from Frost Bites.—Take hydrochloric acid, one ounce; rainwater, seven ounces; wash the feet with it two or three times daily, or wet the socks with the preparation until relieved.

Cure for Ingrowing Nails on Toes.—Take a little tallow and put it into a spoon, and heat it over a lamp until it becomes very hot; then pour it on the sore or granulation; the effect will be almost magical. The pain and tenderness will at once be relieved. The operation causes very little pain if the tallow is properly heated; perhaps a repetition may in some cases be necessary.

Corns.—Take half an ounce of verdigris, two ounces of beeswax, two ounces of ammonia; melt the two last ingredients together, and just before they are cold, add the verdigris. Spread it on small pieces of linen, and apply it after paring the corn. This has cured inveterate corns.

Cure for Soft Corns.—Dip a bit of soft linen rag into turpentine, and wrap it around the soft corn; wet the cloth in it night and morning, and in a few days the corn will have disappeared; but the relief of the throbbing, burning pain, comes almost immediately after the first or second application. Wear cotton between the toes, and the corns will not reappear.

Corn Plaster.—Beeswax, one pound; resin, four ounces; Venice turpentine, eight ounces; sulphate of copper, eight ounces; arsenic, one ounce. Mix with heat.

Bunions.—Bunions can be treated the same as corns.

Offensive Feet.—The unpleasant smell which the feet of some persons give out is generally attributable to some defect in the pores of the skin. *Remedy*—Wash the feet in warm water, to which a little hydrochloric acid, or chloride of lime has been added.

Swollen Feet.—Usually a sign of debility. *Remedy*—Put on a bandage moderately tight, from the toe upwards, giving a uniform degree of pressure; take also the following medicine: Squill pill and extract of colocynth, of each half a drachm; calomel, one scruple; digitalis, ten grains; mix, and make into twenty pills. Take two every day.

What Shall We Eat?—Here are some of the common articles of food, showing the amount of nutriment contained, and the time required for digestion:

	Time of Digestion.	Amount of Nutriment.
Apples, raw	1 h. 50 m.	10 per cent.
Beans, boiled	2 h. 30 m.	37 per cent.
Beef, roasted	3 h. 30 m.	26 per cent.
Bread, baked	3 h. 30 m.	60 per cent.
Butter	3 h. 30 m.	96 per cent.
Cabbage, boiled	4 h. 30 m.	7 per cent.
Cheese	5 h. 15 m.	70 per cent.
Cucumber, raw	— —	2 per cent.
Eggs, hard boiled	5 h. 30 m.	25 per cent.
Fish, boiled	2 h. 00 m.	20 per cent.
Milk, fresh	2 h. 15 m.	7 per cent.
Mutton, roasted	3 h. 15 m.	30 per cent.
Pork, roasted	5 h. 15 m.	24 per cent.
Poultry, roasted	2 h. 45 m.	27 per cent.
Potatoes, boiled	2 h. 30 m.	13 per cent.
Rice, boiled	1 h. 00 m.	38 per cent.
Sugar	3 h. 30 m.	96 per cent.
Turnips, boiled	2 h. 30 m.	4 per cent.
Veal, roasted	4 h. 00 m.	25 per cent.
Venison, boiled	1 h. 30 m.	22 per cent.

According to the above table, cucumbers are of very little value. Some vegetables and fruits should, however, enter into family consumption, even if purchased for sanitary reasons. Among those which contain the most saccharine matter, sweet potatoes, parsnips, beets, and carrots are the most nourishing.

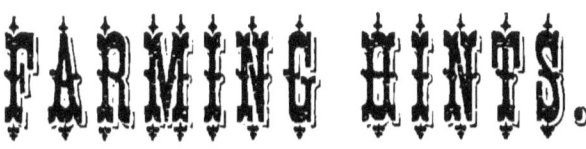

"Upon Agriculture, the foundation of individual happiness and national prosperity must rely for support."—JACKSON.

AS publisher of this work, I have been allotted, by the author, this portion of her book, for the purpose of giving some of my views under this head, and for the purpose of conveying to the public some hints in relation to Agriculture and the Farm. Being an "ex-farmer," and having had twenty years practical "experience" and "hard work," in that school, I will give a few suggestions on the art of cultivation; but I shall dwell more particularly on the raising of stock of all classes; the modes of curing different diseases, and invaluable receipts in general in relation thereto. Also a few hints in regard to orchards, fruits, the dairy, etc.

DIG DEEP FOR GOLD.—The following anecdote contains some profitable advice:—" An old farmer, on his death-bed, told his sons, who were not very industrious lads, that he had deeply buried his money in a particular field, which was the most barren land on his farm. In consequence of this information, soon after the old man's death, the sons began to dig (and they dug deeply too) all over the field—and this they did again and again; for it was long before they quite despaired of finding the money. At length, however, they gave up the search, and the land was planted with corn; when, from the deep digging, pulverization, and clearing which it had received in the search for the money, it produced a crop which was indeed a treasure." It might result to the profit of some of our farmers' sons, should they imagine their fathers had deeply buried a bag of dollars in some barren field, and be led to dig in search of the treasure—and though they might not find the expected wealth, their exertions would be amply rewarded, as is illustrated in the anecdote.

Shallow plowing or "skinning," operates to impoverish the soil, while it decreases production.

Deep plowing improves the productive powers of every variety of soil, and finds nourishment so much below the surface as will avoid the effects of drought. It supplies a good and firm foundation for all kinds of grains. It does not expose the roots to be cut off those crops that need cultivation. Good soil is made by exposure of earth to the atmosphere, and whoever wishes to make permanent improvements in the way of farming will not fail to plow deep.

PROPER QUANTITY OF SEEDS REQUIRED PER ACRE.

Wheat,	1½ to 2	bushels.	Peas,	2 to 3	bushels.
Oats,	3	"	Blue Grass,	2	"
Buckwheat,	½	"	Garden Grass,	2	"
Rye,	1½	"	Red Top,	1 to 2	pecks.
Barley,	2	"	White Clover,	4	quarts.
Corn, in drills,	2 to 3	"	Red Clover,	8	"
Corn, in hills,	4	"	Timothy,	6	"
Broom Corn,	½	"	Red Beets,	3	pounds.
Potatoes,	10 to 15	"	Rutabagas,	¾	"
Beans,	1½	"	White Turnips,	2	"

SOUND LOGIC.

No food; no cattle—no cattle, no dung—no dung, no grain, is a maxim that ought to be firmly fixed in every farmer's mind.

TO PRESERVE GRAIN.

A discovery of considerable importance has been announced, with regard to preserving grain. To preserve and secure it from insects and rats, nothing more is necessary than not to fan it after it is thrashed, and to stow it in the granaries mixed with the chaff. In this state it has been kept more than three years, without experiencing the smallest alteration, and even without the necessity of being turned to preserve it from humidity and fermentation.

TO CORRECT MUSTY GRAIN.

Take a bushel of grain, and pour on it two bushels of boiling water. Let them stand until cold, then skim off the floating grains and husks, and discard them; drain off the water, and dry the remainder in a kiln. The musty quality rarely penetrates through the husk.

MIX STRAW WITH CLOVER.

Farmers who have straw or coarse old hay, will find a great advantage in mixing them in layers, with hay that is not thoroughly made; the dry stuff will prevent the clover from injuring by moisture, and it imbibes sweetness so that the cattle will eat it with a good relish.

EARLY POTATOES IN THE SPRING.

A method how to get extra early potatoes in the kitchen garden. Plant the potatoes in the fall, about eight inches deep, put a handful of leaves in with each potato; then cover the ground with fresh horse-manure about six inches thick, and you will have potatoes before any spring planting.

REMEDY FOR FROZEN POTATOES.

In the time of frosts, potatoes that have been affected thereby, should be laid in a perfectly dark place for some days after the thaw has commenced. If thawed in open day, they rot; but if in darkness, they do not rot; and they lose very little of their natural properties.

TO PRESERVE CARROTS, PARSNIPS AND BEETS ALL WINTER.

A little before the frost sets in, draw your beets or parsnips out of the ground, and lay them in the house, burying their roots in sand to the neck of the plant, and ranging them one by another in a shelving position; then another bed of sand, and another of beets, and continue this order till the last. By pursuing this method, they will keep very fresh. When they are wanted for use. draw them as they stand, not out of the middle or sides.

SIX REASONS FOR PLANTING AN ORCHARD.

1. Would you leave an inheritance to your children? Plant an orchard. No other investment of money and labor will, in the long run, pay so well.

2. Would you make home pleasant—the abode of the social virtues? Plant an orchard. Nothing better promotes, among neighbors, a feeling of kindness and good will, than a treat of good fruit, often repeated.

3. Would you remove from your children the strongest temptations to steal? Plant an orchard. If children cannot obtain fruit at home, they are very apt to steal it; and when they have learned to steal fruit, they are in a fair way to learn to steal horses.

4. Would you cultivate a constant feeling of thankfulness towards the Great Giver of all good? Plant an orchard By having constantly before you one of the greatest blessings given to man, you must be hardened indeed if you are not influenced by a spirit of humility and thankfulness.

5. Would you have your children love their home, respect their parents while living, and venerate their memory when dead—in all their wanderings look back upon the home of their youth as a sacred spot—an oasis in the great wilderness of the world? Then plant an orchard.

6. In short, if you wish to avail yourself of the blessings of a bountiful Providence, which are within your reach, you must plant an orchard. And when you do it, see that you plant good fruit. The best are the cheapest.

GENERAL HINTS ON PLANTING AN ORCHARD.

Plow the ground deep before planting. Let the land be high. Lowlands are liable to spring frost, and the fruit blossoms are often blighted by them. High situations are also more easily drained, which is absolutely essential to the well-being of the trees.

Be careful in planting to give the trees a fair chance for life and health by digging the holes in which they are set wide and large, so that they may be surrounded by loose earth, that can be easily penetrated by the tender fibres of the roots which are to convey nourishment for their sustenance and growth. A tree properly planted will grow as much in five years as one carelessly and badly set in will in ten; and often the chance of survivorship is dependent on slight circumstances. Fill up with the surface soil around the roots, placing each rootlet in the most natural position. Do not use any barnyard manure.

Top dress the land with compost, ashes, plaster, or other fertilizers. The orchard, after the trees are planted, must have a shallow and careful plowing, so as not to destroy the roots of the trees. An excellent plan for preventing young fruit trees from becoming hide-bound and mossy, and for promoting their health and growth, is to take a bucket of soft soap, and to apply it with a brush to the stem or trunk, from top to bottom, this cleanses the bark and destroys the worms or the eggs of insects; and the soap, becoming dissolved by rains, descends to the roots, and causes the tree to grow vigorously.

PREMATURE FRUIT.

All immature apples, plums, or other fruit, that fall from the trees, ought to be eaten by hogs, or be carefully gathered up and burnt to destroy the eggs or worms therein contained, which will otherwise produce insects to commit depredations next year on your fruit trees.

TO DESTROY THE PEACH WORM.

It is said that a mixture of one ounce of saltpetre and seven ounces of salt, applied on the surface of the ground, in contact and around the trunk of a peach tree seven years old and upwards, will destroy the worm, prevent the *yellows*, and add much to the product and quality of the fruit.—Also, sow the orchard with the same mixture, at the rate of two bushels to the acre.

FRUIT TREES NEAR BARN-YARDS.

We have known peach trees to grow four feet in a year when planted on the margin of a barn-yard, and others every way else alike, away from the barn-yard but eight inches. Fine crops of peaches and apples may be had by setting the trees around such yards.

TO DESTROY CATERPILLARS ON GOOSEBERRY TREES, &c.

Get a quantity of elder leaves, and boil them in as much water as will cover them, until the liquor becomes quite black, then clear and cool it, and to every gallon of this liquor add one gallon of tobacco water. When the trees are quite dry lay it on with a fine rose water pot, and in ten minutes the caterpillars will fall off. Another way is to syringe the infested trees with a decoction of *black hellebore*.

TO PRESERVE FRUIT TREES FROM MICE AND INSECTS.

Apply, early in the fall, around the root a thick layer of lime and ashes. It would be well to sink the earth around the tree about six or eight inches; throw in a few shovelsful of the lime and ashes, and then cover up with earth, tramping it well down.

ANOTHER PREVENTIVE FOR INSECTS.—Dissolve aloes in warm water and paint the trees with it; then the insects and vermin will find them so bitter that they will go away. Tar water, or whitewashing the stems with lime is also a good preventive.

TO PROTECT YOUNG TREES FROM HARES.

Young trees in orchards or plantations, where hares can get into, should have prickly bushes tied round their stems, that the hares may be prevented from gnawing the bark off.

TO STOP VINES FROM BLEEDING.

The most effectual way to do this is to cut the part clean with a sharp knife, and afterwards sear it over with a red-hot iron. Pruning vines late in autumn, or early in winter, will prevent this in a great measure.

TO DESTROY INSECTS IN VINES.

Soft soap, two pounds; flowers of sulphur, two pounds; powdered tobacco, two pounds; boil for half an hour in water, six gallons. Apply lukewarm.

NEW METHOD OF GRAFTING.

Mr. Kent, of Manchester, has published the following method of grafting:—" In the first place, I prepare the stock and the graft in the same way as for grafting with clay in the common way. I then take a long slip of India rubber, three-quarters of an inch broad, and about the thickness of a shilling. I tie one end of this elastic ribbon with a thread, well prepared by rubbing with shoemakers' wax, to the stock, a little below where it is cut for being joined to the graft. I then make the joint as neatly as possible, and wrap it round with the ribbon, taking due care to keep the India rubber fully stretched, and to make it overlap at each turn fully one-half of the breadth of the previous round, till the whole is covered. I then tie the top with a thread in the same manner that I tied the bottom, and the operation is finished."

After the graft is completely set, remove the rubber bands and preserve them for next year's grafting.

TO MAKE AN EVERGREEN GROW COMPACT.

If you have an evergreen, or Norway spruce, balsam fir, American spruce, or any of the pines, and desire to make it grow more compact, just pinch out the bud from every leading branch, all around and over it. Repeat this process again next year, at this time, and your evergreens will thereafter grow thickly.

HOW TO PRUNE FLOWERING SHRUBS.

Flowering shrubs may be pruned when their leaves fall off. Cut off all irregular and superfluous branches, and head down those that require it, forming them into handsome bushes, not permitting them to interfere with, nor overgrow other shrubs, nor injure lower growing plants near them. Put stakes to any of them that want support, and let the stakes be so covered with the shrub, that the stake may appear as little as possible.

TO CLEAR ROSE TREES OF BLIGHT.

Take sulphur and tobacco dust in equal quantities, and strew it over the trees of a morning when the dew is on them. The insects will disappear in a few days. The trees should then be syringed with a decoction of elder leaves.

TO EXPAND TULIPS AND OTHER FLOWERS.

Tulips, and many other flowers, when cut early on a dull, cold morning, are seldom very well expanded. If they are afterwards placed in a warm room, and their stems put to stand in warm water, it will cause them to expand their flowers as well as they would have done on the bed on the brightest day in spring. This is not only applicable to tulips, but to many other flowers as well.

HOW TO DESTROY THE POTATO BUG.

Paris green. has proved itself to be the best exterminator, but as it has been found objectionable to use it dry on the stalks, from the fact of the dust being injurious to health, the following mode of using it will be more advisable: To one barrel of water take three-quarter pounds of paris green; take a common watering can, stirring the mixture well before filling it, and apply it to the stalk or vine. It has been found, upon applying it twice, that all the bugs would be killed by the process.

TO FREE PLANTS FROM LEAF-LICE.

Mix one ounce of flowers of sulphur with one bushel of sawdust; scatter this over the plants infected with the insects, and they will soon be freed, though a second application may possibly be necessary.

THE QUICKEST WAY TO PROCURE GRAPES.

The quickest method of procuring grapes is to graft into the body, near the ground, or which is preferable, into the roots of large vines. In the following year, if the graft has taken, fruit will be produced. Thus every farmer, who has wild vines growing on his ground, may, by procuring cuttings of hardy foreign or native kind, and paying a little attention to the grafting and training, be soon and amply supplied with grapes for market or wine making.

GROWING TOBACCO.

As soon as the frost is out of the ground, burn a brush heap, and while it is hot, rake in the seed. When the plants have leaves about an inch long, transplant to rich, warm soil, and set them out about four feet each way. Keep the weeds down, and by all means keep off the "tobacco-worm." Nip off the seeds as fast as they come, and let the plants stand until they become spotted with yellow spots the size of a five-cent piece; then cut them close to the ground, and hang them over a pole in the shed to dry. When sufficiently dry, so as not to break the leaves, pack them in a pile so that they can sweat; then hang them up again.

TO PROTECT DRIED FRUIT FROM WORMS.

It is said that dried fruit put away with a little bark of sassafras (say a large handful to the bushel), will save for years, unmolested by those troublesome little insects, which so often destroy hundreds of bushels in a single season. The remedy is cheap and simple, but we venture to say a good one.

TO PRESERVE GRAPES.

First, pick off all unsound or unripe grapes, and lay the clusters in an empty room on papers until dry, for in all packages some will be crushed and dampen others. Then any empty crate will do to pack them in. First a layer of grapes, then a thickness of paper, so as to exclude the air and keep them separate, then grapes and then paper, and so on until you have three or four layers—no more than four. If the box is to hold more, put in a partition to support the others that are to be packed. I have known grapes to keep until April or May, if preserved in this way.

TO PREVENT THE GROWTH OF BUTTERCUPS, TO THE INJURY OF GRASS.

Geese are very fond of the plant, and the goslings eat the flowers and seed-vessels, thus preventing the plants seeding; while the old geese scoop up the roots, biting off the leaves and rootlets. They eat the bulb with much relish, and if kept in sufficient numbers, in proportion to the ground, they will very soon root up every buttercup. Thus the geese may be fed, and the pastures at the same time improved.

TO PREVENT THE DEPREDATIONS OF RATS, &c., IN CORN STACKS.—FIELD MICE, &c.

Take one pound of nitre, and one pound of alum; dissolve them together in two quarts of spring water; get about a bushel of bran, and make a mash thereof, putting in two pints of the above liquid, and mixing all together. When you build your stacks, every second course, take a handful or two of the mash and throw upon them till they come to the casing.

For *Field Mice* bore holes in the ground to the depth of twenty inches, letting the holes be wider at the bottom than the top; drop into these holes some favorite food, and they may be captured in enormous numbers.

KILLING WEEDS.

Spading the garden in the fall, though beneficial in other respects, will not kill weeds. The seeds of the weeds are not to be frozen out. The only way to get rid of weed seeds in the soil is to allow them to germinate, and then kill the young plants. If taken at the right time this may be done in the garden with the rake. Do not hope to destroy the vitality of weed seeds either by freezing or by burying; as soon as the influences are favorable they will grow as sure as fate.

STANDARD WEIGHTS.

Wheat,..........Lbs. per Bushel, 60	Hemp Seed,...Lbs. per Bushel, 42
Rye,............. " " " 56	Blue Grass.... " " " 14
Barley,......... " " " 48	Dried Peaches, " " " 33
Oats,............ " " " 32	Dried Apples, " " " 25
Corn,............ " " " 56	Canary Seed... " " " 60
Corn, (on Ear) " " " 70	Millet,.......... " " " 50
Potatoes........ " " " 60	Bran............. " " " 25
Onions,......... " " " 50	Hominy......... " " " 60
Onion Sets..... " " " 35	Beans............ " " " 62
Clover Seed,.. " " " 64	Barley Malt... " " " 34
Timothy Seed, " " " 45	Rye Malt...... " " " 40
Flax Seed...... " " " 56	Apple Butter.......per Gallon, 10
Grass Seed, Hungarian, " 50	

DAIRY SCENE.

THE DAIRY—BUTTER MAKING, Etc.

There is no one article of family consumption, now in use, that is of greater consequence than butter.

Improvement in the art of making good butter is rapidly becoming a more important consideration to the American dairyman and farmer, as the very marked advance in the developments of dairy husbandry attests.

It will be generally conceded that the production of choice butter has never been equal to the demand, evidencing that the art of making it uniformly good is as yet comparatively limited.

The first requisite, of course, in making good butter is to have good stock, not necessarily full-blooded stock. For rich, highly-colored butter, graded cows of the Alderney breed are to be chosen; whereas, if the quantity of milk only is to be regarded, irrespective of its quality, the Ayrshire is the best. But whatever may be the breed, the cows must be well treated in every particular in order to insure a good article of butter.

If the cows upon which the farmer depends for his butter cannot be treated humanely, be well protected from the extremes of heat and cold, be fed regularly, and with the food experience has shown to be the best adapted for the purpose of producing rich milk, he will never earn for himself the reputation of being a first-class dairyman. Cows *must* be well protected and fed with great regularity, as well as to the quantity and quality of the food, as to the times of feeding, in order to insure good butter. Indeed, too much emphasis cannot be laid' upon the fact, that as the cows are fed and treated so will the quantity and quality of the milk be. Poor feed and poor treatment will produce poor butter, however elaborate and convenient are the arrangements for making it.

SUMMER PASTURE FOR COWS.

A mixture of timothy and clover, in proportion of one-fourth of the latter to three-fourths of the former, produces the most and the best butter,—for color, texture, and taste. Clover alone, from an excess of water in the plant, has a tendency to make butter too soft, and consequently, to injure its keeping qualities; but mixed with timothy, in the proportions above given, it adds to the butter sufficient moisture, which is lacking where timothy alone is given.

Be sure, also, they can have plenty of pure, running, spring or well-water, and as often as they want it. Do not allow them to drink impure, stagnant water, unless you desire impure, stagnant butter. Let them, also, have free access to salt, both summer and winter; their instincts will be a better guide for the amount they actually need for the purposes of health, than any theories upon the subject.

Have shade-trees for protection during the heat of the day; or, what would be still better, keep them housed during the hottest part of the day, for two or three hours, where they can be kept cool and free from flies.

WINTER FOOD FOR COWS.

The food best adapted in winter is sweet, well cured hay, not musty, and free from dust. In the scarcity of hay, clean oat straw is adaptable. Bean straw, (which, however, is scarce among farmers,) produces very rich milk and cream. Corn meal, it is a well known fact, produces a good quality of milk and cream, and a rich and yellow-colored butter. Roots, turnips, carrots, and cake meal are also well adapted for making rich milk and cream, and produce increased quantities of it. In giving water to cows in winter, it should be reduced to the same temperature as in a summer's day. It will add greatly to the quality of milk and cream.

MILKING OF COWS.

In the first place the bag should be washed clean before milking,—not with the milk of the cow,—but with lukewarm water, in order more effectively to remove the dirt. The cow should be stripped clean, as the last milk is the richest, and experiments seem to prove that the highest results are attained, both as to quality and quantity of milk, by milking three times daily. As soon as the milk pail, which should be made of tin, as most easily kept clean, is full, it should be removed at once to the milk-room, in order to avoid the milk being tainted by the atmosphere of the stable, and in order that it may become cool as soon as possible by being strained into the milk-pan.

MILK-ROOM, TEMPERATURE, ETC.

Free ventilation, yet with an equable temperature, are essential points in determining the value of the milk-room. As soon as the milk is brought into the milk-room it should be strained through a fine wire strainer into the milk-pans, to the depth of five inches in each pan. The size of the pans will be determined by the amount of milk to be set. The pans should then be set on a shelf made of slats, which will allow the milk to cool sooner than if placed on a solid board shelf. It is very important that the animal heat in the milk should be evaporated as soon as possible, and the greater the surface of the bottom of the pan that can be exposed to the direct influence of the air, the sooner will this result be attained. After the milk is placed upon the shelf, the pans should be kept perfectly still until they are ready to be skimmed. When an even temperature of sixty-two degrees is maintained in the milk-room, the time necessary for the cream to rise will be from forty to forty-eight hours in winter, and from twenty to twenty-four hours in summer. But it should be closely watched, and if, before that time, white specks appear on the surface of the cream, it should be skimmed at once, no matter whether the milk is sour or not; for though the temperature of the milk-room may be equable, a variation in the quantity of the elements of the air, as the presence of more or less oxygen, ozone or electricity, will cause the cream to rise at times more quickly than at others. The food of the cow, also, produces like results. The milk, therefore, must be watched closely, and skimmed at the expiration of the above-mentioned times, if the white specks upon the surface of the cream have not previously appeared.

CHURNING THE BUTTER.

The length of time the cream should remain before being churned will depend upon the amount of milk skimmed each day. If there is enough cream each day for a churning, it should, of course, be churned. If not, the cream must be set aside in a cool place, where it can have a temperature of sixty degrees, be kept covered, and when more cream is added, it should be stirred thoroughly, adding a little salt, not more than half an ounce to a churning. But it is not well to keep cream that has taken from forty to forty-eight hours to rise, longer than two days before churning it. As, however, the milk is to be watched closely, in order to determine the time for skimming it, so the cream must be watched as closely, in order to decide the time for churning it. The best practice is to allow it to become only slightly acid before churning. Having thoroughly cleansed and scalded the churn and dash, the cream should be put in at a temperature of fifty-eight deg.; for the motion of churning will bring it up to sixty deg. before the butter comes. The old-fashioned way of throwing scalding water into the churn, to make butter come more quickly, has gone by. It should never be resorted to, as it is a sure means of making the butter white and cheesy, and extracting the nutriment and substance from it.

WORKING, WASHING AND SALTING BUTTER.

After the butter has come, a quart or two of cold, soft water, should be put into the churn, for the purpose of hardening the butter, but if extremely hot weather, a lump of ice will greatly facilitate the hardening process, and cause it to be more easily gathered and taken from the churn. After it has been gathered as much as possible with the dash, it should be removed with the butter-worker to the table or bowl where it is to be worked. It then should be immediately worked thoroughly with the butter-worker (never with the hand, for the insensible perspiration from it will more or less taint butter), using an abundance of cold, soft water to wash out the butter-milk, and at the same time to harden the butter. By washing thoroughly, the butter need not be worked so much to free it from the buttermilk, and hence there will not be so much danger of injuring the grain of the butter by excessive working, wash freely, especially where the butter is to be packed, as it will keep longer by being washed. Where it is to be used immediately there is not the same necessity for washing.

The butter having been thoroughly washed with cold, soft water, it should be salted during the first working, using a little salt at a time and working it in, and then adding more, by this means securing a uniformity of salting. The salt should, previous to its use, be thoroughly pulverized by rolling it, and all foreign substances removed from it. If the butter is intended for immediate use, one half ounce of salt to a pound of butter is sufficient. If it is to be packed, from three-fourths of an ounce to an ounce will be necessary. The best salt to use is the Liverpool salt of the Ashton brand. It may cost more at first, but it is cheaper in the end.

After the butter has been salted and worked for the first time, it should be removed from the vessel in which it has been worked to another, covered entirely with cotton cloth, soaked in brine, in order to exclude all air, and placed in an even temperature of sixty deg., where it should remain ten or twelve hours, when it is ready to be worked again. This second working should be as light as possible, just enough to get out the buttermilk left by the first working. The buttermilk must, however, be all worked out, or else all the previous labor spent upon the butter will be in vain. It may look and taste well for a time, especially where an abundance of salt has been used, which will absorb a good deal of it, but it will not keep well when there is any buttermilk in—the acid of the buttermilk after a time causing the butter to become rancid. At the end of the second working of the butter it should be immediately placed in the package in which it is intended to be sent to market.

BUTTER IN ROLLS AND PRINTS.

Butter prepared in these forms is more for immediate consumption. A few of the principal markets in the United States prefer rolls and prints still, but I think the time is not far distant, when both the dealer and consumer will prefer alone solid packed butter in tubs, pails and firkins, and discard entirely rolls and prints. The process of making is the same as for solid packed butter, but owing to its being more exposed to the atmosphere a greater quantity of salt is used in preparing it, for the purpose of keeping it sweet.

TO COLOR BUTTER.

Scrape a large yellow carrot into a tin vessel with two quarts of new milk; let it simmer an hour. When cool, strain it into the cream, just before churning. This will do for a small churning.

Increase the quantity of carrot according to the amount of cream. This is preferable to annetto, which can be used where carrots are not to be had.

IMPROVING STRONG AND RANCID BUTTER.

Butter can be greatly improved in quality and taste, by washing and working it over thoroughly with lime-water, and then cleaning out the lime-water by a good washing in cold spring water. The lime-water is made by allowing a small lump of pure lime to slake in a bucket of water, then stir it well and allow it to settle.

TO FRESHEN SALT BUTTER.

Churn it over in new milk and treat it as if making new butter.

BUTTER PACKING AND SHIPPING.

The package, before the butter is put into it, should have been soaked ten or twelve hours in strong brine, sufficiently strong to float an egg, and the butter should be pressed in it hard and evenly, having first put in a thin layer of salt in the bottom of it. If the package is not filled by the first packing, put it away in a cool place, excluding the air from the butter by putting over it a cotton cloth saturated in brine, and by covering carefully the package itself. As soon as the package is filled, having been careful to pack the butter hard and uniformly, it should be covered with a white cotton cloth, from which the sizing has been washed, and which has previously been soaked in strong brine. Nail up the package and put it away in a cool place till such time as it is convenient to market it, taking care not to expose it to the heat of the sun during its transportation to market.

CHEESE MAKING.

The materials employed in making cheese, are the curd formed from milk and rennet; but certain processes are requisite to the due preparation of it. It is necessary for this purpose that the curd, which is the basis of cheese, and exists not in the cream, but in the milk, be separated from it. This is done by artificial coagulation, and when the curd is entirely freed from the whey, by means of pressing and otherwise, it becomes cheese, and will keep for a great length of time free from all danger of decomposition.

TO PREPARE RENNET TO TURN MILK.

Take out the stomach of a calf as soon as killed, and scour it inside and out with salt. After it is cleared of the curds always found in it, let it drain a few hours; then sew it up with two handsful of salt in it, or stretch it on a stick, well salted; or keep it in the salt wet, and soak a piece for use, which will do over and over again by washing it in fresh water.

TEMPARATURE AMD PREPARATION OF MILK.

The milk intended for cheese as well as for butter ought to be carefully passed through a fine canvas sieve, to deprive it of any impurities, such as hairs, etc. That which is produced at a single milking is the best, and when brought warm from the cow it is the more readily effected by the rennet. The natural heat it possesses when taken from the udder is from eighty-five to ninety degrees. If it is below eighty-five degrees it must be raised to that temperature either by mixing hot water with the milk, or placing a vessel containing some of the milk in a copper of boiling water, and mixing the milk so heated with the rest. Much of the success of cheese-making depends upon the milk being of a proper degree of heat when the rennet is put into it.

PROCESS OF MAKING.

Put the milk into a large tub, warming a part till it is of a natural degree of temperature, same as described in above paragraph. Put in as much rennet as will turn it, and cover it over. Let it stand till completely turned; then strike the curd down several times with the skimming-dish and let it separate, still covering it. There are two modes of breaking the curd, and there will be a difference in the the taste of the cheese, according as either is observed; one is to gather it with the hands very gently towards the side of the tub, letting the whey pass through the fingers till it is cleared, and ladeling it off as it collects; the other is to get the whey from it by early breaking the curd. The last method deprives it of many of its oily particles and is therefore less proper.

Put the vat on a ladder over the tub, and fill it with curd by a skimmer, press the curd close with your hand, and add more as it sinks, and it must be finally left two inches above the edge. Before the vat is filled, the cheese-cloth must be laid at the bottom, and when full drawn smooth over on all sides.

There are two modes of salting cheese: one by mixing salt in the curd while in the tub after the whey is out: and the other by putting it into the vat and crumbling the curd all to pieces with it after the first squeezing with the hands has dried it. The first method appears best on some accounts, but not on all, and therefore the custom of the country must direct. Put a board under and over the vat, and place it in the press; in two hours turn it out, and put a fresh cheese-cloth, press it again for eight or nine hours, then salt it all over, and turn it again in the vat, and let it stand in the press fourteen or sixteen hours, observing to put the cheeses last made, undermost. Before putting them the last time into the vat pare the edges if they do not look smooth. The vat should have holes at the sides and at the bottom to let all the whey pass through. It now only remains to wash the outside of the cheese in warm whey or water, wipe it dry, color it with annatto, and place it in a cool place to mature or ripen.

TO MAKE CREAM CHEESE.

This is made from the last of the milk drawn from the cow at each milking, or of a mixture of milk and cream. It is usually made up into small pieces, and a gentle pressure applied to press out the whey. After twelve hours it is placed upon a board or wooden trencher, and turned every day, until dried. In about three weeks it will be ripe. Nothing but raw cream, turned with a little rennet, is employed, when a very rich cheese is wanted. A little salt is generally added, and frequently a little powdered sugar. The vats employed for cream cheeses are usually square, and of small size.

TO MAKE SAGE CHEESE.

Bruise the tops of young sage in a mortar, with some leaves of spinach, and squeeze the juice; mix it with the rennet in the milk, more or less, according as you like for color and taste. When the curd is come, break it gently, and put it in with the skimmer, till it is pressed two inches above one vat. Press it eight or ten hours. Salt it, and turn every day.

DUTCH CHEESE.

Muriatic acid is used to coagulate the milk instead of rennet, and this is said to impart the pungent taste peculiar to the Dutch cheese, and also to preserve it from mites. Much of the Dutch cheese is made of skimmed milk, and is intended for sea stores, as it keeps well, from being much less rich than the higher class cheese.

ROOM FOR CURING CHEESE.

A dark room is not best adapted for curing cheese. Cheese should be exposed to light to obtain the best flavor, and besides it can be examined more minutely from time to time, and freed from the depredations of the skipper. The best means to protect cheese from these pests is to make a mixture of oil and Cayenne pepper, and apply it to the outside of the cheese, as may be required.

TO PRESERVE CHEESE SOUND.

Wash in warm whey, when you have any, and wipe it once a month and keep it on a rack. If you want to ripen it quick, a damp cellar will bring it forward. When a whole cheese is fresh cut, the larger quantity should be spread with butter inside, and the outside wiped to preserve it. To keep those in daily use moist, let a clean cloth be wrung out from cold water, and wrapt round them when carried from table. Dry cheese may be used to advantage to grate for serving with macaroni or eating without. These observations are made with a view to make the above articles less expensive, as in most families where much is used there is waste.

CATTLE AND STOCK SCENE.

Remedies for Cattle, Sheep & Swine.

COW.

RULES FOR SELECTING A GOOD MILCH-COW.

Her head should be rather long and small; cheeks thin; muzzle fine; nostrils large and flexible; eyes mild, clear, and large; neck rather long, and *slim* near the head; horns long and small, and of an orange color; small ear, inside of a yellowish tinge; small breast; back level and broad, and straight to the rump; well ribbed; wide in the loin; flank low; thighs thin and deep; hind legs small, standing well apart; forelegs rather small below the knee, above the knee large; large teats, of a dark orange-color; bag, when empty, lean, soft, and long; large milking veins; hair short and thick; large hind-quarters; color brindle, bright red, dun, or a light brown.

RULES FOR ADMINISTERING MEDICINES TO CATTLE.

When administering medicines, the age and constitution of the animal are to be considered, for a strong and healthy beast can bear much more than a weak one. A beast under three years old is not to be treated like one of five or six years of age, for its bowels are tender. As for a bull of four years old, he is to be treated in the same manner as an ox of the same age. There are some very small specimens of cattle, whose strength and constitution are in proportion to their size, and they should be treated accordingly.

TO MAKE TAR-WATER FOR CATTLE.

Take one quart of tar, put to it four quarts of water, and stir it well for fifteen minutes; let it stand for half an hour, and pour it off for use. Do not put water to the same tar more than twice, and give as hereafter prescribed.

PHYSIC.

Purgatives are among the most useful of medicines and, when properly administered, are of incalculable benefit to the husbandman in arresting and curing most of the diseases to which his cattle are subject. Great care should however be taken that the ingredients used are good, and that too large quantities are not given at one time.

Purging drinks are good for inflammatory complaints, for jaundice or for costiveness. They can be given moderately to old cattle once in six or eight weeks with much benefit.

PURGING DRINK.

Take one pound glauber salts, two ounces powdered ginger, half pint molasses; put all the ingredients together, pour three pints boiling water upon them, and give the whole at once, at blood-warm temperature.

BLEEDING.

Bleeding is necessary, and of great service, in all inflammations, fevers, bruises about the eyes, and sprains when accompanied with inflammatory symptoms. It is hazardous to bleed when the spirits are too much exhausted or weakened. Experience has warranted the rule, that not more than two quarts should be taken away at *one time*.

POISONS.

There are several vegetables that are poisonous to animals, such as foxglove, wild saffron, deadly nightshade, poison hemlock, branches of the yew, wilted leaves of the wild cherry, laurel, crowsfoot, and some others.

Take two ounces salts tartar, and twelve ounces Epsom salts, dissolve in six quarts of water, and give four times a day in four equal parts. Give freely of salt in all cases.

CATTLE CHOKING.

Turnips and potatoes, and some other substances, often lodge in the throat of cattle, and are sometimes difficult to remove.

Remedies.—Give a pint of strong soap-suds, holding the head high. Another: sometimes by stopping the breath a moment by holding the windpipe, and starting the animal very suddenly, the obstruction will be carried down.

FLESH WOUNDS.

Take four ounces linseed oil, three ounces fine salt, half pint molasses, one ounce copperas; boil ten minutes, let it stand until nearly cold, add three ounces turpentine and half an ounce oil of vitriol; make the whole into a salve, and bind on a small quantity at a time, changing it daily. When a wound has been a length of time in healing, proud flesh will sometimes appear. This can be eaten off with a very small quantity of red precipitate or blue vitriol.

RED WATER.

Take away two quarts of blood, and give physic as prescribed; and likewise give injections, if necessary, to bring the bowels to a proper state. After bleeding, as above, give four ounces Epsom salts, two ounces ginger, half ounce saltpetre, three ounces linseed oil, in two quarts of warm water, and keep the animal housed for two days.

LICE ON CATTLE.

Remedy.—Sprinkling snuff moderately on the animal will generally effect a cure. Another: take two ounces tobacco leaves, boil in two quarts of water, and apply cold; this, however, is not considered as safe for the animal as fresh buttermilk applied lukewarm.

INFLAMMATION OF THE BOWELS.

As soon as the disease shows itself, bleed two quarts; and in six hours give a small dose of physic, and give light food for three days.

HOVEN, OR SWELLING.

Give half a teacupful spirits turpentine, add to it half pint lamp oil. Or, another remedy is eight ounces melted butter, give all at one dose.

COLIC.

Take two quarts water, add one ounce ginger, one gill rye whisky, half pint molasses or half pound coarse brown sugar, and give while moderately warm.

YELLOWS, OR JAUNDICE.

Take two ounces aniseed, two ounces tumeric root, one ounce salt tartar, one ounce castile soap,—one gill molasses; add one quart boiling water, and give blood-warm.

BLACK TONGUE.

When it first makes its appearance, put the beast in a warm stable; take the inside bark of white-pine, boil it half an hour, add two ounces cream of tartar, and wash the mouth freely; take a small quantity of blood from the neck, and give a quarter of a pound of epsom salts; in two hours give two quarts of weak tar-water, and repeat it every eight hours.

HOLLOW HORN.

Take spirits of turpentine and vinegar of equal parts, rub round the roots of the horns and back of the ears. Keep the animal in a warm stable, well blanketed.

Take one pint of flaxseed, boil in three pints water for twenty minutes, add one pint new milk, strain, and add half pint linseed or castor oil, and two tablespoonsful of fine salt, and give as an injection.

BLACK LEG.

House the beast in a cool stable and bleed two quarts; foment the parts affected with salt and vinegar; take half pint linseed or castor oil, one ounce ginger, one drachm aloes, and give with one quart warm water.

WEAK AND INFLAMED EYES.

Wash them with a tea made of raspberry-leaves and sassafras bark, adding a small quantity of castile soap. Apply it cold.

HIDE BOUND.

Take two ounces allspice, two ounces ginger, two ounces mustard, one pint molasses; mix with two quarts warm water, and give in two doses, night and morning, after the beast has fasted for four hours.

LOCK-JAW.

Dash a large quantity of cold water over the animal, repeating every four hours, keeping the beast moving about. Another: bleed very freely, and follow by a moderate dose of physic.

LOSS OF CUD.

Where there is but little fever, give a small dose of salts and ginger, or take half pint gin and two ounces ginger; make a cud of boiled clover, or take a cud from another beast and divide it. Afterward make a decoction of oak bark, hoarhound, and balm, and give for one day with dry food.

STINGS OF HORNETS AND BEES.

Dissolve salt in vinegar and bathe for fifteen minutes.

BITE OF POISONOUS SNAKES.

Cleanse the wound thoroughly with strong soapsuds, then apply a mixture composed of one and a-half ounce hartshorn and one ounce olive oil, every four hours for one day; at the same time administer a large dose of physic.

SORE TEATS.

Bathe the teats with weak soap-suds, then apply cream, new milk, or goose oil, night and morning.

SHEEP.

LICE AND TICKS ON SHEEP.

These are found to attack sheep that are poorly kept. The only effectual cure is to make a strong brine, or, take half a barrel of cold water, adding half pound tobacco leaves boiled in four quarts water, and dip the sheep (all except the head), pressing as much of the liquid out of the wool as possible after dipping.

ROT.

Make a strong decoction of the bitter-sweet branches, and give half a teacupful every morning, with a good supply of salt, and feed on dry food for three days.

FOOT ROT.

Whenever the disease appears, let the foot be washed, and the hoof pared off as much as possible, not to make it bleed. Let the sheep stand upon a dry stable-floor, sprinkled with lime, for four hours; after this he may be kept in a dry pasture without further danger.

PELT-ROT.

The only remedy for prevention is good feeding, warm keeping, and anointing the parts from which the skin is off with a thin ointment of tar and grease.

STAGGERS.

Take half pint fresh butter or lard, and give in a melted state. Another: dissolve two ounces assafœtida in three quarts of warm water and give two tablespoonsful three times a day.

FOUL NOSES.

Lobelia (Indian tobacco), either dry or green, given in a weak tea. Or, applying warm tar to the nose, and giving a small quantity of tar water, will soon effect a cure.

SCOURS IN SHEEP.

Give fifteen drops of laudanum in a teaspoonful of ginger.

COSTIVENESS.

Give half ounce epsom salts or two tablespoonsful of castor oil, or feed on green clover for one day.

INFLAMMATION OF THE LUNGS.

Put the sheep into a warm enclosure, bleed freely, and give a tablespoonful of castor oil, or the same quantity of lard; after which give warm nourishing drinks.

SORE AND SWOLLEN MOUTH.

Tar-water, or putting tar in the mouth, and a teaspoonful of sulphur in oats or bran. Or, an ointment of fresh butter and sulphur applied to the affected part will usually effect a cure.

EATING POISON.

This is occasioned by eating laurel, wilted leaves of the wild cherry, and some other shrubs and plants.

Take of the twigs of the white-ash, boil for two hours, and give half a teacupful of the liquor with a gill of molasses, in a lukewarm state, to each sheep. Unless relief be obtained within one hour, the dose may be repeated, reducing the quantity one half.

TO PROTECT SHEEP AND LAMBS FROM DOGS, FOXES, AND WOLVES.

Take equal parts of sulphur and tar, adding a small quantity of aloes, powdered, and smear their necks and legs once a month through the summer.

This is said to be a positive means for keeping these "pets" at a proper distance, but for myself, if I was a "little lamb" I think if I had a lot of "seven shooters" somewhere about me, I would be better protected. (My assistant T. L. K. agrees with me perfectly in that.) J. B. M., *Pub.*

SWINE.

All the different breeds of swine raised in this country are so numerous, that it will be impossible to give all the detailed or particular descriptions of them. It is, however, practically sufficient to say, that the Old English and the Berkshire are considered as decidedly the best, and are to be found in all sections of the United States. Under the following headings will be found the proper remedies practically required for curing such as the ailments are demanding.

HOW TO CHOOSE A PIG.

Whatever the breed may be, it is requisite, in order to make a judicious selection, to give attention to certain particulars such as the following :—the loin and breast ought to be broad, so as to allow abundant scope for the functions of breathing, etc.; the bones ought to be small, and the joints fine; this affords evidence of high breeding, and the better a pig is bred the more rapidly will it come to maturity, and the more readily it will fatten; the feet should be firm and sound, the toes lying well together and pressing evenly upon the ground; the snout not too elongated but somewhat short and convex, rather than flat.

MEASLES.

Remedy.—Give quarter an ounce Epsom salts after fasting twelve hours. Another: take two grains powdered antimony and give in new milk. Another: give half an ounce sulphur twice a week with their food.

SORE THROAT.

Remedy.—Take a teacupful of molasses, half a teacupful of vinegar, a tablespoonful of melted butter and a teaspoonful of black pepper, and give when nearly cold. Feed for two days with fresh clover or potatoes and turnips.

COLDS, COUGHS, OR INFLAMMATION OF THE BRAIN.

Remedy.—If the cold or cough is not severe, moderate purgatives and a warming diet will generally effect a cure, but if the disease appears to affect the lungs, bleed one pint, and give gentle physic, of Epsom salts or castor oil and sulphur.

QUINCY.

Remedy.—Bring them into a warm enclosure, and see that the issues are well open; take one quart corn-meal; one and a half ounce Epsom salts, one ounce castor oil, one tablespoonful of sulphur, one quart new milk, and give at once, keeping salt and tar in their troughs.

SWELLING OF THE THROAT IN HOGS.

Remedy.—Take half a pint of molasses and a tablespoonful of hog's lard; to these add a piece of brimstone an inch in length; melt it over the fire, and when cold, or in a liquid state, drench the hog with it, and nine times out of ten it will be found to have the desired effect.

BLACK TEETH.

Remedy.—As the black teeth not only injure the general health as well as the sound teeth, they ought to be extracted. Examine and see that the issues are open, give one ounce sulphur and one ounce pulverized charcoal, with tar-water, and fresh green food. Keep the diseased swine separate from the rest for a few days.

BLIND STAGGERS.

Remedy.—Examine and see that the issues on the legs are open, purge freely, and in six hours after give one gill of brandy or rum, and a teaspoonful of pepper.

ITCH, SCAB, OR MANGE.

Remedy—Immerse the pig in lukewarm water, and, after drying, apply to all the parts affected an ointment made of half a pound of lead, and a quarter of a pound of sulphur. If the pig is old enough to drink, put a small quantity of sulphur in his food.

SWINE-POX.

This shows itself by a fine eruption of the skin near the joints, and by a redness of the eyes.

Remedy.—Take half an ounce saltpetre, dissolve it in half pint vinegar and a teacupful of sweet or linseed oil, and a tablespoonful of honey, and give lukewarm, in three parts, every morning.

UNIVERSAL REMEDY.

Many farmers, when their swine show signs of illness, feed them with corn-meal, mixed with two ounces sulphur and the same quantity of tar, charcoal, and salt, removing them to a warm, dry shelter. This, of course, will not cure all diseases, but will prevent most of them assuming a violent form.

THE HORSE.

TO CHOOSE A HORSE.

To those unacquainted with this animal, and the arts and deceptions often practiced by the horse dealer, it may appear unaccountable that as definite instructions cannot be given for the purchase of a *horse* as of other animals. A few general directions are all the limits of this work will allow. A short trial is the best way of estimating his worth; but where this is not allowed, the following suggestions are submitted, and, if followed, will be as sure a safeguard as it is possible to have.

THE EYES are the first things to attend to, and should be well examined, as the best judges are often deceived in them. *Clearness of the Eyes* is a sure indication of their goodness;

but this is not all that should be attended to: the eyelids, eyebrows, and all the other parts, must also be considered; for many horses whose eyes appear clear and brilliant, go blind at seven or eight years old. Therefore be careful to observe whether the parts between the eyelids and the eyebrows are free from bunches, and whether the parts round the under eyelids be full, or swelled; for these are indications that the eyes will not last. When the eyes are remarkably flat, or sunk within their orbits, it is a bad sign; also when they look dead and lifeless. The *Iris* or circle that surrounds the sight of the eye, should be distinct, and of a pale, variegated cinnamon color, for this is always a sure sign of a good eye.

THE TEETH will give a pretty correct idea of the age of a horse. Every horse has six teeth above and below; before three years old he sheds his middle teeth; at three he sheds one more on each side of the central teeth; at four he sheds the two corner and last of the fore-teeth. Between four and five the horse cuts the under tusks; at five will cut his upper tusks, at which time his mouth will be complete. At six years the grooves and hollows begin to fill up a little; at seven the grooves will be well nigh filled up, except the corner teeth, leaving little brown spots where the dark brown hollows formerly were. At eight the whole of the hollows and grooves are filled up. At nine there is very often seen a small bill to the outside corner teeth; the point of the tusk is worn off, and the part that was concave begins to fill up and become rounding; the squares of the central teeth begin to disappear, and the gums leave them small and narrow at top.

THE FEET should be smooth and tough, of a middle size, without wrinkles and neither too hard and brittle, nor too soft; the heels should be firm, and not spongy and rotten; the frogs horny and dry; and the soles somewhat hollow, like the inside of a dish or bowl. Such feet will never disappoint your expectations, and such only should be chosen.

THE LIMBS should be free from splents and windgalls. The knees should be straight, and not bending, or what is called a calf's knee: the back sinews strong and well braced: the pastern joints clean, and free from swellings of all kinds; and the hocks lean and dry, and free from spavins, corbs, and flatulent tumors.

THE BODY, OR CARCASS, should neither be too small or too large. The back should be straight, or have only a moderate sinking below the withers: for when the back of a horse is low, or higher behind than before, it is both very ugly and a sign of weakness. The back should also be of a proper length. The ribs should be large, the flanks smooth and full, and the hind-parts, or uppermost haunches not higher than the shoulders. When the horse trots before you, observe if his haunches cover his fore-knees. A horse with a short hind-quarter does not look well.

THE WIND is next to be regarded. A broken-winded horse always pinches in his flanks, with a very slow motion, and drops them suddenly, which may easily be perceived.

SORE TONGUE IN HORSES.

Take one part sugar of lead, one part bole ammoniac, and two parts burnt alum, the whole to be added to three quarts of good vinegar. With this wash out the mouth twice a day.

SURFEIT IN A HORSE.

First bleed from the neck; then give a mash of bran, say one gallon, mixed well with hot sassafras tea, in which a teaspoonful of saltpetre and a tablespoonful of sulphur has been added. To be given three times a week. Never give the horse to drink for half a day after having been fed with this mash. As a drink give sassafras tea, with a little saltpetre, say one-fourth of an ounce to the quart. As an ointment, equal parts of sulphur and hog's lard.

MIXTURE FOR SCOURS.

Suet cut fine and boiled in new milk, in the proportion of one-quarter of a pound to a pint of the milk. To this must be added of boiled starch, one pint; alum, in powder, one drachm. Given as a drench. Good both for horses and cattle.

DISTEMPER, OR EPIZOOTY.

This distemper usually attacks horses in the spring and fall. It first shows itself by discharges from the nose, a cough, difficulty of swallowing, soreness and swelling in the glands of the throat, and general debility. If it is attended to immediately, there is little danger; otherwise it often proves fatal. If the attack is not violent, thorough purging with bran-mashes may relieve him; but if the disease is very severe, bleeding, and afterward blistering must be resorted to. The horse must be kept warm; and if the swelling does not subside, a mild poultice may be applied. Also the following to be applied in the nostrils:—one ounce of roach alum, one ounce of white vitriol. Powder these well, put them into a pint of warm vinegar, and syringe about an ounce up his nostrils every day. This may do good if the disorder be newly caught.

A COLD OR COUGH.

Give a quarter of a pound of Epsom salts, and on the following day take the small boughs of the cedar, cut fine and mixed with meal or wet oats. Or, take two ounces sulphur, mix with human urine, and give with his food. Or, take a handful of arsesmart, chopped fine, with hay or grain. Or, boil one quart flaxseed half an hour, and give with meal mixed with bran.

ASTHMA.

Parsley root, twelve ounces; well clean, boil in one quart of water to a pint; strain, and add oil of sweet almonds, four ounces; tincture of opium, three drachms. Give every other morning.

CANKER IN HORSES.

Tar, one pound; tallow, one pound; powdered verdigris, four ounces. Mix and apply.

WASH FOR SORE EYES.

White vitriol, two scruples; sugar of lead, one drachm; water, one pint. Mix and apply.

CURE FOR LAMPASS.

Burn with a hot iron: never cut them out. If they are once burnt they will not return.

POLL-EVIL.

Bring the swelling to a head, as any other tumor, by the suppurating poultice, which is made as follows:—

Take four handsful of bran and three middling-sized turnips; boil them till soft, and beat them well together; then boil them again in milk to a thick poultice, adding to it two ounces linseed and half pound hog's lard.

THE STAGGERS.

Bleed the animal copiously, (the disease is a true apoplexy,) two and a half quarts at once; then give him half a pint linseed oil, the same of castor oil, forty grains calomel, sixty grains jalap, and two ounces tincture of aloes. Give him twice a day warm bran mashes.

FOUNDER IN HORSES.

Take a quarter of a pound of alum, dissolve it in hot water, let it cool, then pour it down the horse. Don't be afraid, it will cure. If the horse is stiff, put his feet in hot water, one at a time.

BROKEN WIND.

Feed with carrots, or parsnips, or beats; or use tar-water as a drink; some say lime-water; and when the cough is bad, bleed freely.

COLIC.

Castor oil, one pint; laudanum, one ounce; oil of pimento, one ounce; in a pint of warm ginger tea.

GRIPES.

Laudanum, one ounce; balsam copaiba, one ounce; oil of aniseed, one drachm; powdered camphor, two drachms; in a pint of warm ale.

BOTTS.

First drench your horse with sweet milk and molasses. Second, in a reasonable time drench him again with a quart of beef brine. Alum water is good; so is saltpetre water. A purge should always be given soon after the drench. A strong solution of salt and water, with a little alum, would perhaps be as good as the brine.

TO CHECK OVER-PURGING.

Take of prepared chalk, ginger, and aniseed, in powder, each one ounce; essential oil of peppermint, fifteen drops; rectified spirits of wine, half an ounce. Mix the whole in a pint and a half of warm linseed gruel, and give it.

GENERAL PURGATIVE MIXTURE.

Take four ounces epsom salts, half ounce nitre, quarter pound coarse sugar, dissolve them in one quart of warm water, then add six ounces castor oil; mix well, and give one gill, *blood-warm*, morning and evening, until a proper passage be obtained.

SPRAIN OF THE KNEE OR ANKLE.

Take six ounces tar, six ounces spirits of wine or vinegar, four ounces lard; melt these together by a slow heat (being careful not to have them take fire), add flaxseed, to make it into a poultice, and apply it until the swelling is removed.

SWELLINGS.

When a swelling first appears, bathe it well with vinegar having one ounce of saltpetre dissolved in it, after which take two ounces extract of lead, two ounces spirits of wine or vinegar, two ounces spirits of sal. ammoniac, five ounces vinegar, and half pint of water; mix and rub the parts well.

THRUSH, OR FROG-AIL.

Take six ounces tar, eight ounces whale-oil, four ounces spirits of turpentine, two ounces lard; mix well, and apply to the hoofs three times a week.

WIND GALLS.

Make a strong decoction of red-oak bark; add some strong vinegar and a little alum in powder. Bathe the parts with this decoction as warm as possible twice a day, and bind up comfortably tight with woolen cloths dipped in a warm decoction of the above.

SPAVIN.

Shave off the hair, and apply a blister of Spanish flies to the part affected. Bathe with warm strong vinegar, and let the horse have rest.

SCRATCHES IN HORSES.

Wash with strong soap-suds, then with strong copperas-water. Repeat this twice a day until he is cured : for a daily drink give sassafras or spice-wood tea, or a little saltpetre dissolved in his drink.

HOOF OINTMENT.

Tallow, one pound; tar, one pound; black resin, one pound; lard, two pounds; spirits of turpentine, one pound. Mix and apply.

RELIEF FOR STRING-HALT.

Bathe with warm vinegar and sweet oil, and rub well the part affected.

LINIMENT FOR GALLED BACKS OF HORSES.

White-lead moistened with milk. When milk is not to be procured, oil may be substituted. One or two ounces sufficed for a whole party for more than a month.

RINGBONE.

Take one ounce of camphor gum; one ounce oil of spike; one ounce hartshorn; one ounce spirits of turpentine. Shake well together, and it is fit for use; put it on above the ring, and rub it in with the finger. Use twice a day.

SAND-CRACK.

Remove the shoe, and ascertain carefully the extent of the injury. If the crack is superficial fill it with the composition below, and keep the foot cool and moist.

Take four ounces beeswax, two ounces yellow rosin, one ounce turpentine, and half ounce tallow or suet: to be melted together.

EXCELLENT HORSE AND CATTLE POWDER.

Take half pound fœnugreek-seed in powder, half pound flour of sulphur, half pound antimony, powdered, half pound cream of tartar, half pound saltpetre powdered. Mix all the ingredients thoroughly.

Dose.—One tablespoonful three times a week, mixed with their feed; and if the animal is sick, give every day.

EXCELLENT HORSE AND CATTLE OINTMENT.

Tar, one pound; resin, one pound; spirits of turpentine, one pound; tallow, three pounds; oil of vitriol, five ounces; sulphate of copper, five ounces; alum, five ounces. Mix very cautiously. An invaluable ointment.

POULTRY.

The hen is the most highly prized of all of the domestic tribes. There are many species of this fowl, each having its peculiar excellences, and being more or less productive, making it difficult to recommend any of them above the others. Hens properly kept, will pay three or four times their first cost and feeding yearly.

TO MAKE HENS LAY IN WINTER.

Provide a comfortable roost; plenty of sand, gravel and ashes, dry, to play in; a box of lime; boiled meat, chopped fine, every two or three days; corn and oats, best if boiled tender; all the crumbs and potato parings. This treatment has proved quite successful—and hens which, without it, gave no eggs, with it immediately laid one each, on an average, every two days.

TO DISTINGUISH THE SEX OF EGGS.

There are two classes of poultry-keepers—those who want female eggs only, to rear hens for the sake of their eggs, and those who want male eggs only, to produce cocks and capons for the table. There is only one outward sign which can be regarded as indicating the sex of the egg: it is this, that eggs containing the germs of males have generally wrinkles on their smaller end; while female eggs are equally smooth at both extremities.

TO FATTEN FOWLS IN A SHORT TIME.

Mix together ground rice well scalded with milk, and add some coarse sugar. Feed them with this in the day-time, but not too much at once: let it be pretty thick.

FATTENING TURKEYS.

Experiments have been successfully tried of shutting up turkeys in a small apartment made perfectly dark. They were fattened, it is said, in one-quarter of the usual time. The reason assigned is, that they are thus kept still, and have nothing to attract their attention. Yellow corn fed to turkeys, has a tendency to make the fat of a yellow color or appearance. White oats, or buckwheat, will produce a light color in the fat and flesh.

CURE FOR GAPES.

Dissolve in water as much soda as it will take up; then stir in your meal or feed until it is thick enough, and give your chickens all they will eat. This is a sure cure, if taken before they are too far gone.

PIP OR GAPES.

Remove the scab, or white blister, from the tongue, and apply salt and vinegar, and give some oily substance with their food. Spirits of turpentine, and ginger, mixed with their food, is a preventive.

CHOLERA IN POULTRY.

Take one tablespoonful of soda, one tablespoonful of Cayenne pepper, one tablespoonful of sulphur, one tablespoonful of pulverized charcoal; mix into a quart of coarse corn meal, and a pint of sweet milk, and let them eat freely. This is known to be an excellent cure for this disease.

SCABBY LEGS IN POULTRY.

The cause of scabby legs in poultry, is a parasitic insect, similar to the scab acarus of the sheep. The remedy is—wash the legs with a solution of potash, until the scabs are softened and peeled off, then dress them with an ointment of lard and sulphur, or wash them with carbolic soap suds.

FLUX, OR LOOSENESS.

Take ten drops of laudanum and half a pint of water, in which soak oats or corn, and give the hen. Or, take the yolk of an egg boiled hard, cut up fine, and give with food.

LICE.

These are destroyed by placing ashes and sand for the hen to wallow in, and by putting a little sulphur in their food. Or, immerse them in a weak decoction of tobacco-water, or sprinkle snuff over their bodies.

AND GENERAL GUIDE. 293

DESTRUCTION OF INSECTS IN POULTRY-HOUSES.

Fumigating poultry-houses with sulphur, thrown on glowing coals in an earthen vessel, and keeping the house closed for several hours, is said to be a perfect remedy for insects of all kinds. The poultry must, of course, be removed before the experiment.

HOW TO DRESS POULTRY.

Farmers and poultry shippers will find it greatly to their advantage by carrying out the following instructions in regard to killing and dressing poultry for market.

Turkeys.—Stick in the mouth or close to the ear, back of the head with a small pen-knife, so as not to show a gash; bleed thoroughly; pick dry while warm, being careful not to disfigure or tear the surface of the skin; leave the head and feet on, and entrails in.

Chickens should be dressed in the same way. Poultry, if scalded, will turn black in a very short time, which greatly disfigures and depreciates it in value in market.

Ducks and Geese may be scalded, only be sure to have it clean, and free from pin feathers and down. The small downy feathers may easily be removed by rubbing plenty of fine rosin over them; must be applied before they are cold.

CANARY BIRDS.

The following remedies for the diseases of Canary Birds will be found very efficacious. I have taken those diseases which are of most common occurrence, with the most simple and effective cures therefor.

INFLAMMATION OF BOWELS.

This disease may be known by the disappearance of feathers from the belly, showing the bare skin and veins. Feed altogether on lettuce seed and canary. Put a rusty nail into the water. This will effect a cure.

CONSTIPATION OR COSTIVENESS.

A bit of bread dipped in milk, and a blade of cabbage or lettuce will cure it. No seeds to be allowed at all.

EPILEPSY.

Repeated bathing in cold water will be found an excellent remedy for this disease.

ASTHMA.

Take a piece of baker's bread; soak it in water, and boil it well in milk; this to be given with cabbage or lettuce. No dry feed or seed.

DIARRHŒA.

Put a piece of rusty iron in your water dish. Change the water but once a week. Feed on bread boiled in milk, same as for asthma. For young canaries and other seed birds, some scalded rape seed is a very good remedy.

LOSS OF VOICE.

This is produced, not so much from physical defect, as from the escape of notes from the memory, generally transpiring after moulting. The best means to remedy this is to put the bird in close proximity to a good singer, when the voice will return after a short time. Do not wash your cage-bottom, but scrape it clean with a knife, and then put on some fresh gravel.

BEES.

But few persons are aware how early in the season bees eat honey faster than they produce it. By not attending to this in due time, learning from experience, observation, or the experiments of others, much is lost. When the weather is dry, bees usually consume honey faster than they collect it after the middle or 20th of July, unless they have access to buckwheat or other suitable flowers cultivated for their use; in this case they may gain honey in September

This subject is important to bee-masters who follow the old system, and destroy the bees when they take the honey. Some let them remain till the latter part of September, eating honey two months after they have ceased to collect any of consequence. In our short seasons for collecting honey, and long ones for consuming it, the habits of the bees must be studied very attentively, and there must be the most careful and economical management in order to make them profitable.

METHOD OF TAKING HONEY FROM BEE HIVES WITHOUT KILLING THE BEES.

Pour two teaspoonsful of chloroform into a piece of rag, double it twice, and place it on the floor-board of the hive, which must be lifted for the purpose, the entrance-hole being carefully secured. In about two minutes and a half there will be a loud humming, which will soon cease. Let the hive remain in this state for six or seven minutes, making about ten minutes in all. Remove the hive, and the greater number of the bees will be found lying senseless on the board; there will still be a few clinging between the combs, some of which may be brushed out with a feather. They return to animation in from half an hour to one hour after the operation. This plan possesses a great superiority over the usual mode of brimstoning, the bees being preserved alive; and over the more modern plan of fumigation by puff-ball; it is far less trouble, and the honey does not become tainted with the fumes.

TO DESTROY THE BEE MILLER.

To a pint of water, sweetened with honey or sugar, add half a gill of vinegar, and set it in an open vessel on the top or by the side of the hive. When the miller comes in the night, he will fly into the mixture and be drowned.

TO PURIFY HONEY.

Expose the honey to frost for three weeks, in a place where neither sun nor snow can reach it, and in a vessel of wood, or other substance which is not a good conductor of heat. The honey is not congealed, but becomes clear.

MISCELLANEOUS RECIPES.

SUPERIOR HERB BITTERS.—Take wild cherry bark, two pounds; juniper berries, one pound; Virginia snake root, half a pound; ginsing, two pounds; orange peel, one pound; cloves, quarter pound; sassafras, half pound. Grind all the ingredients fine. To make the tonic, add ten gallons pure rye whisky.

TO TAKE FROST OUT OF FRUIT AND VEGETABLES.—When a thaw approaches put the frozen articles into cold water, allowing them to remain in it until by their plump, fair appearance the frost seems to be out.

TO PREVENT MILDEW IN WHEAT.—Sulphate of copper, one pound; water, four gallons. Dissolve and steep the grain in it for one hour.

WARTS.—Frequently wash them with a strong decoction of oak bark, or wet lunar caustic, and rub it on the wart a few times.

BEST SHAVING SOAP EVER INVENTED.—Take four and a half pounds white bar soap, one quart rain water, one gill beef's gall, and one gill spirits turpentine; cut the soap thin and boil five minutes; stir while boiling, and color with half ounce vermillion: scent with oil of rose or almonds. Fifty cents worth of materials will make six dollars worth of soap.

TO SOFTEN HARD WATER.—A half ounce quick lime dipped in nine quarts of water, and the clear solution put into a barrel of hard water; the whole will be soft water as it settles.

TO TAKE THE RUST OUT OF STEEL.—Cover with sweet oil well rubbed on it: in forty-eight hours use unslackened lime, powdered very fine. Rub it till the rust disappears.

TO MEND CHINA.—To mend broken china, make a very thick solution of gum arabic, and stir it into the plaster of paris until the mixture becomes a viscous paste. Apply it with a brush, and in three days the article cannot be broken in the same place.

TO PRESERVE FURS.—When laying up muffs and tippets for the summer, if a tallow candle be placed on or near them, all danger of moths will be obviated.

TO CLEAN PLATED-WARE.—Make a paste with whiting and alcohol, apply it to the plated articles, and after it is dry, rub it off with a brush (if rough), or a soft rag, if smooth.

PASSOVER CAKES.—These are the unleavened bread of the Jews, and are made as thin as possible, and of a very large size. First mix and prepare a dough of four pounds of flour with one pound of water, roll it out very thin, and about ten inches in diameter, dock it well on both sides, and bake them in a very hot oven.

FURNITURE VARNISH.—White wax, eight ounces; oil of turpentine, one pint; melt the wax, and gradually mix in the turpentine.

THE BENEFIT OF TOADS.—Never destroy them; keep them in your garden to destroy the insects. They will do more to preserve a garden from such destruction than the labor of man.

TO PROTECT CHILDREN FROM BURNING.—Add one ounce of alum to the last water used in rinsing children's dresses, and they will be rendered uninflammable.

TO EXPEL RATS FROM HOUSES.—Smear their holes and haunts with a mixture of two parts of tar to one of lamp-oil, gently boiled together. They will not approach it.

TO REMOVE FRECKLES.—An ounce of alum, and an ounce of lemon-juice, in a pint of rose-water.

TO MAKE THE HAIR GROW RICH, SOFT, GLOSSY, ETC.—Take a half pint of alcohol, and castor oil quarter of a gill; mix, and flavor with bergamot, or whatever else may be agreeable. Apply it with the hand.

TO CURL FEATHERS.—Heat them gently before the fire, then, with the back of a knife applied to the feathers, they will be found to curl quickly and well.

FOR A BOIL.—Butter and oat-meal mixed to a rather thick paste, and laid on.

TO MAKE COMMON SEALING-WAX.—To every one ounce of shellac take half an ounce of rosin and vermillion, all reduced to a fine powder. Place them over a moderate fire and melt them.

TO PREVENT THE FORMATION OF A CRUST IN TEA KETTLES.—Keep an oyster-shell in your tea kettle. By attracting the stony particles to itself, it will prevent the formation of a crust.

TO PREVENT GRASS GROWING IN A PAVED YARD.—Pour boiling water over the stones whenever the grass shows itself.

TO EXTRACT INK FROM FLOORS.—Scour them with sand wet with water and the oil of vitriol, mixed. Rinse them with strong saleratus water.

TO PRESERVE FISH IN A LIVING STATE.—Fish may be preserved in a living state for fourteen days or longer without water, by stopping their mouths with crumb of bread steeped in brandy, pouring a little brandy into them, and then placing them in straw in a moderately cool situation.

FINE BLACKING FOR SHOES.—Take four ounces of ivory-black, three ounces of the coarsest sugar, a tablespoonful of sweet oil, and a pint of small beer; mix them gradually cold.

WATERPROOF COMPOSITION FOR BOOTS AND SHOES.—Boiled oil, half a pint; oil of turpentine, black rosin, and bees' wax, of each one ounce and a half. Melt the wax and rosin, then stir in the oil, remove the pot from the fire, and when it has cooled a little, add the turpentine.

TO MAKE ROSE POMATUM.—Melt one ounce white wax, with one ounce mutton suet, and add two ounces sweet oil; color the mass with alkanet, and perfume with oil roses.

TO EXTRACT GREASE SPOTS FROM PAPER.—Apply a little powdered pipe-clay, on which place a sheet of paper, then use a hot iron. Remove the adhering powder with a piece of India rubber.

TO MAKE FIVE GALLONS OF GOOD INK.—Take one-half pound of extract of logwood; dissolve it in five gallons of hot water; add one-half ounce of bichromate of potash; strain and bottle.

TO TAKE IRON STAINS OUT OF MARBLE.—An equal quantity of fresh spirit of vitriol and lemon-juice being mixed in a bottle, shake it well; wet the spots, and in a few minutes rub with soft linen till they disappear.

BLACK JAPAN FOR LEATHER.—Boiled oil, one gallon; burnt umber, five ounces; asphaltum, five ounces; lampblack, one pound, thin with spirits of turpentine.

TO PREVENT MOULD IN INK.—Take half a gill of spirits of wine, and add to the ink; or, infuse a piece of salt, as big as a hazlenut, on each quart.

TO EXPEL ANTS.—A small quantity of green sage, placed in the closet, will cause red ants to disappear.

MODE OF INCREASING THE POTATO CROP.—An English writer says, by carefully removing the buds as they appear on the potato vines, the crop of large ones is very much augmented. The theory is plausible, and worthy a fair trial.

LOW OR FEVER DIET.—Panada; gruel; milk, thickened with arrow-root; plain bread-pudding; arrow-root, salep, and tapioca jellies; rice-milk, chicken or veal-tea.

TOMATO KETCHUP.—Cut tomatoes in pieces, and between every layer sprinkle a thin layer of salt; let them stand a few hours, then add a little horseradish, garlic, pepper, and mace. Boil well and strain, then bottle, cork, and seal for use.

TO EXTRACT PAINT FROM COTTON, SILK, AND WOOLEN GOODS.—Saturate the spot with spirits of turpentine, and let it remain several hours, then rub it between the hands. It will crumble away, without injuring either the color or texture of the article.

COMPOSITION FOR MATCHES.—Take four parts glue, dissolve, and when it is hot, add one part phosphorus, and sift in a few spoonsful of whiting to bring it to a proper thickness. This is genuine.

TO RENEW RIBBONS.—Wash them in cool suds, made of soap, and iron when damp. Cover with a clean cloth and iron over it.

FOR KEEPING MEAT FRESH IN HOT WEATHER.—Place in a clean porcelain bowl, and pour very hot water over it so as to cover it. Then pour oil upon the water. The air is thus quite excluded and the meat preserved.

TO BLEACH STRAW.—Straw is bleached by the vapors of sulphur, or a solution of oxalic acid or chloride of lime. It may be dyed with any liquid color.

COLOGNE.—Take one gallon cologne spirits, proof, add of the oil of lemon, orange, and bergamot, each a spoonful; add also extract of vanilla, forty drops; shake until the oils are cut, then add a pint and a half of soft water.

PREVENTIVE FROM ANTS ON BARRELS.—A chalk mark around a sugar barrel protects it from ants.

TO PREVENT NIGHTMARE.—Avoid heavy suppers, and going to bed take the following mixture: Sal-volatile, twenty drops; tincture of ginger, two drachms.

SUPERIOR PAINT—FOR BRICK HOUSES.—To lime whitewash, add for a fastener, sulphate of zinc, and shade with any color you choose, as yellow ochre, Venitian red, etc. It outlasts oil paint.

TO CLEAN WHITE FEATHERS.—Wash them well in soft water, with white soap and blue; rub them through very clean white paper, beat them on the paper, shake them before the fire, dry them in the air, and afterward curl them.

TOOTH POWDER.—Mix equal portions of powdered chalk and charcoal, adding a quantity of powdered curd soap. This simple recipe not only cleanses the teeth, but is a preservative against decay.

GROWTH OF HAIR INCREASED AND BALDNESS PREVENTED.—Take four ounces of castor oil, eight ounces good Jamaica rum, thirty drops oil of lavender, or ten drops oil of rose, anoint occasionally the head, shaking well the bottle previously.

BLOATING IN CATTLE.—A tablespoonful of spirits of ammonia for an ox or cow; a teaspoonful for a sheep or calf.

TO PREVENT THE SMOKING OF LAMPS.—Soak the wick in strong vinegar and dry it well. They will of course smoke, even after this preparation, if the wicks are put up too high.

TO WAGONERS.—Take hog's lard, melt it over a gentle fire, and stir it in flour until it becomes a paste. Grease your wagons or carriages with it—and you will never use tar again.

JOCKEY CLUB, American.—Oil of jasmine, three ounces; oil of verbena, half drachm; oil of rose geranium, half ounce; oil of cassia, one drachm; alcohol, one pint.

SOAP FROM SCRAPS.—Dissolve eighteen pounds of potash in three pailsful of water; then add to it twenty-five pounds of grease, and boil it over a slow fire for a couple of hours. Turn it into a barrel, and fill it up with water.

BEST RED INK.—Take best carmine, two grains; rain water, half an ounce; water of ammonia, twenty drops. This is a beautiful ruling ink for ledgers and bank purposes. Add a little gum arabic.

POULTICE FOR A FESTER.—Boil bread in lees of strong beer; apply the poultice in the general manner. This has saved many a limb from amputation.

TO MAKE YELLOW BUTTER IN WINTER.—Just before the termination of churning, put in the yolk of eggs. It has been kept a secret; but its value requires publicity.

TO DESTROY FLEAS IN DOGS.—Rub olive oil into the dog's coat, let it remain on for half an hour, and wash it well out with the best yellow soap and warm water. A small portion of any sweet oil brushed into the coat of a woolly dog will effectually prevent its being infected with vermin.

TO ESCAPE FROM A ROOM OR HOUSE ON FIRE.—Crawl out on your hands and knees. The smoke always fills the upper part of the room first.

TO EXTINGUISH FIRE.—Dissolve pearlash, soda, wood-ashes, or common salt in the water, before it is put into the engine, and direct the jet on the burning wood work. The proportion may be twenty pounds to every fifty gallons; the more, however, the better.

PASTE FOR CLEANING METALS.—Take oxalic acid, one part; rotten stone, six parts. Mix with equal parts of train oil and spirits of turpentine to a paste.

TO TAKE OUT FRUIT SPOTS.—Let the spotted part of the cloth imbibe a little water without dipping, and hold the part over a lighted common brimstone match at a proper distance. The sulphurous gas which is discharged soon causes the spot to disappear.

TO CLEAN KNIVES.—One of the best substances for cleaning knives and forks is charcoal reduced to a fine powder, and applied in the same manner as brick dust is used. This is a recent and valuable discovery.

FOR THE SCARLET FEVER.—Bathe the patient with lye water, with a sponge all over, and it will have the most salutary effect

TO WASH COLORS.—For washing fine and elegant colors, the "Scientific American," advises ladies to boil some bran in rain water, and use the liquor cold. Nothing can equal it for ease upon color and for cleaning cloth.

COLORING EGGS.—Bind them round with narrow colored ribbons in a tasteful manner, and boil them about ten minutes. The ribbons will impart their color to them. Or logwood chips for purple, and onion peel for yellow, or loaf-sugar paper for purple.

TO KEEP GRAPES, PLUMS, ETC.—Put them in layers of cotton until your jar is full, cover close, and keep from frost.

GILDING WITH GOLD UPON SILVER.—Beat a ducat thin, and dissolve in it two ounces of *aqua regia;* dip clean rags in it and let them dry; burn the rags, and, with the tinder thereof, rub the silver with a little spittle; be sure first that the silver be cleansed from grease.

CEMENT FOR GLASS AND WOOD.—Steep isinglass twenty-four hours in common white brandy, then gently boil and keep stirring, until the composition is well mixed, and a drop, if cooled, will become hard as stone.

TO TAKE STAINS OUT OF MAHOGANY.—Spirits of salts, six parts; salts of lemon, one part; mix, then drop a little on the stains, and rub them until they disappear.

THE BEST WAY TO TAKE CASTOR OIL.—It is not generally known that castor oil may be most easily taken mingled with orange juice, a little sugar being added if the juice of the orange is not sweet. The difference between this and any other mode of taking this valuable medicine is surprising.

TO COLOR FRUIT YELLOW.—Boil the fruit with fresh skin lemons in water to cover them, until it is tender; then take it up, spread it on dishes to cool, and finish as may be directed.

TO POLISH STOVES.—Mix black lead with a little alcohol, and lay it on the stove with a piece of linen rag, then take a soft, dry brush, and rub it to a beautiful brightness.

MOSQUITOE BITES.—Dissolve sal soda (bleaching powder) in water, and with the tip of your finger apply it to the bite, letting it dry—the cure is complete. A teaspoonful of the solution is sufficient for a hundred of bites.

TO PREVENT WOUNDS FROM MORTIFYING.—Sprinkle sugar on them. The Turks wash fresh wounds with wine, and sprinkle sugar on them. Obstinate ulcers may be cured with sugar dissolved in strong decoction of walnut leaves.

TO KEEP MOTHS FROM CLOTHS.—Put a piece of camphor in a linen bag (or some aromatic herbs) in the drawers, among linen or woolen clothes, and neither moth nor worm will come near them.

POTATO SALAD.—Do not regard cold potatoes as waste, but cut them into slices, and dress with pepper, salt, oil, and vinegar. A little parsley, chopped, may be added. This forms an excellent salad for the supper table.

TO CLEAN CANARY BIRDS.—These pretty things may be effectually relieved of lice by placing a clean white cloth over their cage at night. In the morning it will be covered with small red spots, so small as hardly to be seen, except by the aid of a glass; these are the lice, a source of great annoyance to birds.

A SUBSTITUTE FOR CREAM.—Take two or three eggs, break them into a basin and beat them well, then add half a pint of good milk (hot), and beat them again until quite smooth. If milk cannot be procured, water may be used instead.

BED BUG POISON.—Take one pint alcohol, 2 ounces sal ammoniæ, one pint spirits turpentine, two ounces corrosive sublimate and two ounces gum camphor; dissolve the camphor in the alcohol, then pulverize the corrosive sublimate and sal ammoniæ, and add to it, after which put in the spirits of turpentine and shake well together.

TO RESTORE FADED FLOWERS.—Put the flowers into scalding hot water, sufficiently high to cover one-third of their stems; let them stand until the water is cold, then cut off the soft part of the stems and place them in cold water.

GENUINE WINDSOR SOAP.—Slice the best white soap as thin as possible, melt it in a stew-pan over a slow fire, scent it well with oil of carraway, and then pour it into a frame or mold made for that purpose, or a small drawer, adapted in size and form to the quantity. When it has stood three or four days in a dry situation, cut it into square pieces and it is ready for use.

SOAK YOUR SEED CORN IN A SOLUTION OF SALTPETRE.—It destroys the worm, is not relished by crows or squirrels, and yields much more abundantly than when planted without.

TO BRONZE IRON CASTINGS.—Thoroughly clean them, and then immerse them in a solution of sulphate of copper, when they acquire a coat of the latter metal. They must then be washed in water.

TO CLEAN CARPETS.—Having well beaten and brushed, scour with ox-gall, which will both extract grease and refresh the colors. A pint of gall in three gallons of soft water, warm, will do a large carpet.

SEIDLITZ POWDERS.—Tartrate of soda, one and a half drachm; carbonate of soda, one and a half scruple. Mix, and put it in a blue paper; tartaric acid, thirty-five grains, to be put into white paper. For half a pint of water.

TO PURIFY THE BREATH.—Gum catechu, two ounces; white sugar, four ounces; orris powder, one ounce. Make into a paste with mucilage, and add a drop or two of neroli.

METHOD OF CLEANING CHINA.—Mix a little pearlash or potters' clay, or soda, with your water, and it will give them a bright appearance.

ATMOSPHERIC LIQUID HAIR DYE.—Nitrate of silver, eleven dr., nitric acid, one dr., distilled water, one pt., sap green, three dr., gum arabic, one dr.

TO MAKE APPLE BUTTER.—The best apple butter is made by peeling, coring and slicing selected sweet apples and stewing them in sweet cider. Very little of this sort of apple butter, however, comes to market. The bulk of that sold is made from second-rate apples, peeled, sliced and stewed, and sweetened with brown sugar. A large quantity of such butter is made and sold for ships' stores, for use by the sailors.

SHINGLED ROOFS.—Whitewashed with lime, last nearly twice as long as roofs which receive no treatment to render them durable.

NEW ACID FOR DYEING.—Take of the root of the *aloe*, and by the action of *nitric* acid, a beautiful red color is produced, which will be found very useful to dyers.

TO FASTEN THE TEETH.—Put powdered alum, the quantity of a nutmeg, in a quart of spring water for twenty-four hours. Then strain the water and gargle with it.

REMEDY FOR MILK TURNING SOUR.—Add to each quart of milk fifteen grains of bi-carbonate of soda.

TO REMOVE THE SMELL OF ONIONS FROM THE BREATH.—Parsley eaten with vinegar will remove the unpleasant effects of eating onions.

THE BEST OATS ARE ALWAYS THE CHEAPEST.—Oats weighing thirty lbs. per bushel, contains sixteen lbs. of meal, and fourteen lbs. of husk. Those at thirty-six lbs. per bushel contain upwards of twenty lbs. of meal, and less than sixteen lbs. of husk; and, as the weight increases, the proportion of the meal to the husk is often greater.

TO GLAZE LINEN COLLARS.—To give linen collars, shirt bosoms and cuffs a nice glaze, add a teaspoonful of scraped white soap and one of salt to every pound of starch.

TO RESTORE RUSTY CRAPE.—Gin is an excellent thing. Dip it in and let it get saturated with it; clap it till dry; smooth it out with a hot iron, and it is as nice as when new.

MUSTARD POULTICE.—Mustard seed, and linseed, of each, in powder, half a pound; hot vinegar, a sufficient quantity. Mix them.

RASPBERRY SYRUP.—To every quart of fruit add a pound of sugar, and let it stand over night. In the morning boil and skim it for half an hour; then strain it through a flannel bag and pour into bottles, which must be carefully corked and sealed. To each bottle, add, if you please, a trifle of brandy, if the weather is so warm as to endanger its keeping.

TO EXTRACT RANCIDITY FROM BUTTER.—Take a small quantity, that is wanted for immediate use. For a pound of the butter dissolve a couple of teaspoonsful of saleratus in a quart of boiling water, put in the butter, mix it well with the saleratus water, and let it remain till cold, then take it off carefully, and work a teaspoonful of salt into it. Butter treated in this manner answers very well to use in cooking.

FLAXSEED TEA—DIET FOR THE SICK.—Take of flaxseed one ounce; white sugar, one and a half ounces; lemon juice, two tablespoonsful; boiling water, two pints. Infuse them in a pitcher some hours, and then strain off the liquor. An ounce of liquorice, shaved, may sometimes be used instead of sugar.

TO MAKE WHITE-WASH THAT WILL NOT RUB OFF.—Mix up half a pail full of lime and water, ready to put on the wall; then take a quarter of a pint of flour, mix it up with water, then pour on it boiling water a sufficient quantity to thicken it; then pour it, while hot, into the white-wash; stir all well together and it is ready.

AND GENERAL GUIDE.

EVENTS.

PHILADELPHIA IN "1609" AND "1876."

HILADELPHIA is located upon the Delaware River, about 50 miles from its mouth. A city of nearly two centuries growth; the second in the union in point of population, and the largest in area; it may also be classed as the sixth metropolis of the civilized world. It is also proudly clustered with memories enshrined, dear to every American heart. With joy and gratitude may we honor Philadelphia, the *birth-place* of liberty. Here occurred the most conspicuous "event" of all "events"—the immortal "Declaration of Independence." To give a minute history of Philadelphia since its infancy, (nearly two centuries ago) will be impossible, I will however, review a few of the well-known historical facts connected with Philadelphia, as far back as "1609." The Indian name of the place was " Co-a-que-na-que," or "Coaquanock." The banks of the Delaware were sparsely settled some time previous to the arrival of Penn's Colony, but not above Chester. Penn, however, went farther north, and pitched upon the peninsula as the site for the "great town," the river was discovered by Hudson, in 1609. "Delaware" river was named after Lord Delaware, (then governor of Virginia,) after visiting the "town" in the same year; the founding of the province of Pennsylvania was confirmed to Penn, January 5th, 1681, under the great seal of England; the "concession" made was no doubt at that time extraordinary, for the "Society of Free Traders" were induced to purchase, for four hundred pounds, the entire street, (now Spruce) from river to river, with all the lots situated thereon. The first colony of adventurous pioneers, principally of Friends, to this land, left England in the summer of 1681, in three

ships. The first arrival was by the ship *John and Sarah*, Captain Smith; the *Amity* was carried, in a terrific gale, to the West Indies, and did not land her crew until the following spring; and the *Factor* arrived late in the season, and remained below the future city during the entire winter, embedded in the ice. The little colony brought up by the *John and Sarah* suffered extreme distress and privation for a time. The founder did not set sail until August, 1682. He came in the ship *Welcome*, having previously dispatched William Markham as governor of the colony, with instructions to make the needful preparations for him upon his arrival. To this end the finer parts of the frame-work required in the construction of his cottage in Laetitia Court, (engraving of the original cottage in another part of book,) were sent out with Markham, and the building was erected on a spot which the founder was led to consider the most picturesque in the vicinity. This venerable structure, raised nearly two hundred years ago, still remains with but the merest semblance of its former self. It stands in a court penetrating the heart of a square bounded by Front, Second, Chestnut and Market Streets. It was the first brick building raised in Philadelphia, but to-day it is surrounded by a progeny of giants. The antique building has been modernized, and its sign "William Penn Hotel," is the only feature which, by contrast, suggests any idea of its departed grandeur. When Penn, upon his second visit in 1699, lodged in the slate roof house in Second Street, he made a present of his former residence to his daughter, Laetitia, "who, being a single woman and having no particular use for it," gave it up for colonial purposes. The founder, arriving at Newcastle, in 1682, proceeded at once to Upland, in Delaware County, where the Great Law of Pennsylvania was framed. Thence he came up the Delaware in an open boat, landing at the "Blue Anchor Tavern," which stood at the mouth of a little creek, long since filled up, and on a site which corresponds to the present intersection of Dock and Front Streets.

In selecting a title for the city, Penn found in "Philadelphia" a word which embodied in its inherent meaning the principles he had at heart. It was no arbitrary term, but implied, as the original in Greek has been translated, "brotherly love." He called the city after the ancient metropolis in Asia Minor, over the portal of whose time-honored temple was inscribed: "I have set before thee an open door, and no man may shut it."

The first settlers were mostly Friends; the population increased rapidly by emigration from Germany, the north of Ireland, and Sweden. The Germans made their settlement at Germantown, which was then called one of the *inland* towns of Pennsylvania—it is now the Twenty-second Ward of this city, and contains a larger population than did the city of Philadelphia in 1776. The Swedes made their settlement in the vicinity of Front and Carpenter; and the Friends began business about Dock Street.

The city as originally planned by Penn, and surveyed by his assistant Thomas Holmes, was a parallelogram two miles long, running from the Delaware to the Schuylkill River, by one mile wide, running from Cedar or what is now South Street, to Vine Street. This rectangle was quadrated by two magnificent thoroughfares, easily recognizable to-day in Market and Broad Streets, having at their intersection a large open area called Centre Square, upon which the new City Hall is now being erected. Each section formed by the interlacing of these two broad avenues was allotted its square. These four squares, Washington, Rittenhouse, Logan and Franklin,—taking the names of historic personages,—form to-day the pleasantest of our resorts.

Philadelphia County,—one of the three originally established by Penn,—extended in 1682-3 indefinitely to the northwest, having contiguous to it Chester and Bucks. Up to the year 1784 it included Montgomery County within its limits; but it extends now along the Delaware from Darby Creek to Poquesink Creek, and is bounded on the northeast by Bucks County, on the northwest by Montgomery County, and on the southwest by Delaware County, embracing a territory twenty-three miles long and averaging five and a half broad, having an area of one hundred and twenty-nine and one-eighth square miles. With a population of less than one thousand, two hundred years ago, it increased to twenty-one thousand in 1776, in this Centennial Year Philadelphia can boast of about one million inhabitants, occupying 150,000 dwelling houses. This exceeds the number of dwelling houses in New York by over 60,000; Baltimore by over 83,000. and Boston by over 94,000.

There are about 9,000 manufactories here, with a capital of nearly $250,000,000, and giving employment to about 150,000 people, the product of whose labor is almost $450,000,000 annually. Its water privileges are unequalled by any other city—the Delaware River on its eastern line is of sufficient depth to float the largest vessels in service; it forms a wharfage front more than twelve miles in length. The Schuylkill flows through the centre of a large portion of the city. The general health of the city is better than any other city in the world. The real estate of the city, including the property not taxable, is valued at $633,592,093, it has over 400 public school buildings, in which more than 90,000 children are educated. Places of public worship number about 500, with a seating capacity of 400,000. About 2,000 city railroad cars, running over 300 miles of track, carrying passengers to almost every part of the city.

The city is lighted by 10,000 public lamps, supplied from nearly 700 miles of gas mains, while the 15,000,000,000 gallons of water used annually is forced through about 650 miles of water-pipe.

Post Office employs 227 carriers, who deliver to Philadelphians 17,891,736 mail letters a year, 9,760,824 local letters, and 8,693,361 newspapers. About the same number of mail letters are collected by carriers.

Having given a minute history of Philadelphia for the last two centuries, I cannot pass over it without calling atttention to the numerous public squares coufined within its limits, where strangers and those residing in the city may find a spot to enjoy the cool air and balmy breeze for a short time, during the hot, sultry days of summer, and be refreshed thereby.

The four principal and oldest squares, (as spoken of in the preceding pages,) are still in existence, and though long condemned to obscurity and neglect, they are now restored, and are fulfilling their mission as "breathing spots" for our citizens.

Washington Square is at Sixth and Walnut Streets; close beside what was once the State-House Yard, now called the Independence Square, in grateful remembrance that in it liberty was first proclaimed to the people. This square was once used as a "Potters Field," many soldiers, victims of the small-pox and camp-fever, were buried here during the revolution.

Independence Square, between Fifth, Sixth, Chestnut and Walnut Streets, was formerly the property of the State, and was conveyed to the city with the proviso, that it should be kept open as a public square.

Franklin Square is between Sixth, Vine, Race, and Franklin Streets. A handsome square, with a beautiful fountain in the centre.

Logan Square, bounded by Race, Vine, Eighteenth and Nineteenth Streets.

Rittenhouse Square, between Walnut, Locust, Eighteenth and Nineteenth Streets. In the neighborhood of these last two squares are many elegant private residences.

Penn Squares were situated at Broad and Market Streets. The court house and offices of the officers of the city and county are being erected here. It was so intended by William Penn, and in accordance with the wishes of the majority of the citizens, who voted in favor of it.

Norris Square, given to the city by Isaac Parker Norris, is bounded by Susquehanna Avenue and Hancock, Diamond and Howard Streets.

Jefferson Square, west from Third Street and south from Washington Avenue.

There are a few more smaller ones in different parts of the city, but not of much note.

But the grandest spot of all, and one that Philadelphians may well be proud of, is "Fairmount Park." I shall not dwell upon its beauties here, but will devote a separate chapter to it in another part of this book, and give a full description of it by means of illustrations, which will convey a better idea of its grandeur than I could write.

PENN'S TREATY.

Almost the first effort of Penn after he reached these shores was to bring together the Indians from various parts, to form a treaty of peace and friendship. In this he was successful. They met in Philadelphia, and made the treaty at a spot which is now called Kensington, under an elm tree. Upon the spot where stood that tree is erected now a monument to the memory of Penn, known by all residents as the "Penn Treaty Monument." This treaty was never broken.

315

WM. PENN'S FIRST COTTAGE
Penn's first residence in Philadelphia, situated in Lettia Street between Chestnut and Market, and Front and Second Streets.

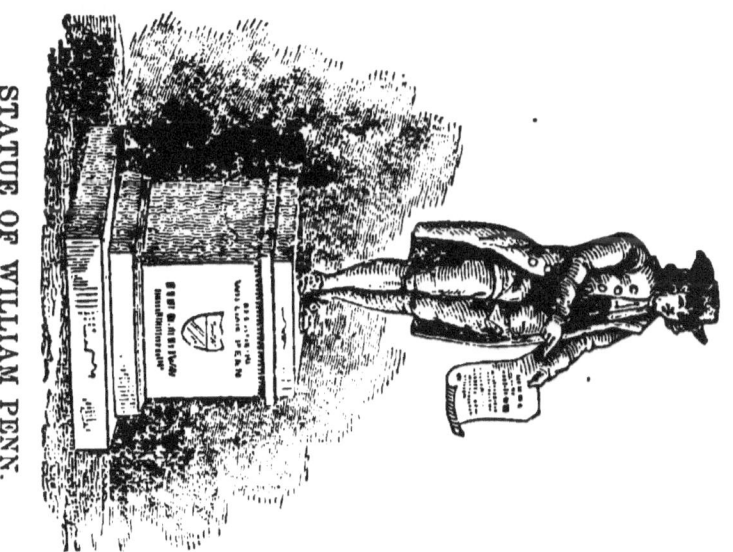

STATUE OF WILLIAM PENN.

This statue stands in the yard of the Pennsylvania Hospital, Ninth and Pine Streets. It was presented by his grandson, John Penn, in 1801.

This is the oldest Church in Philadelphia, having been erected in 1700. In 1677 a log house was built on the present site of this Church by the Swedes. This relic of olden times is situated on Swanson Street, below Christian.

CHRIST CHURCH.

Christ Church is located on Second Street above Market, west side, built in 1695. The first pastor was Rev. Mr. Clayton. The steeple is one hundred and ninety-six feet in height. It has eight chimes of bells, made in London, brought over in the ship "Myrtilla." Washington and Franklin each had a pew in this Church, and regularly attended with their families at divine worship.

GEORGE WASHINGTON
Was born in Westmorland Co., Virginia, near the banks of the Potomac, February 22d, 1732.
Died peacefully, December 14th, 1799.

MARTHA WASHINGTON
Wife of Gen. George Washington.
Her maiden name was Martha Dandridge, Married to "Col." Washington, January 6th, 1759.

Carpenter's Hall is located in Carpenter's Court, running south from Chestnut Street, a few paces east from Fourth Street. On the 5th of September, 1774, the first Continental Congress met in this Hall and commenced their deliberations, which, on the 4th of July, 1776, ultimated in declaring the colonies free and independent.

BIRTH-PLACE OF LIBERTY.

In the second story front room of this house, (located at South-West Corner of Seventh and Market Streets,) Jefferson drafted the Declaration of Independence.

321

BUILDING IN WHICH FIRST AMERICAN **FLAG** WAS MADE.

This Building is located at 239 Arch Street. The cut is an exact fac-simile of the building as it appeared at that time.

SIGNING THE DECLARATION OF INDEPENDENCE.

INDEPENDENCE HALL IN 1776.

Independence Hall is located on Chestnut Street, between Fifth and Sixth Streets, commenced in 1729 and finished in 1734. It was built by Edmund Wooley, Robert Smith being the architect. The Continental Congress first met in this building May 10th, 1775.

INDEPENDENCE HALL IN 1876.

GIRARD COLLEGE.

STEPHEN GIRARD.

Girard College is located on Ridge Avenue above Nineteenth Street. The grounds cover 41 acres. The main building is 111 feet wide by 269 feet long. The columns are 55 feet in height; 10 feet in diameter, surrounded by capitols 8 feet 6 inches high. The total height of the building is 95 feet. The main door entrance is 32 feet high by 16 feet wide.

BENJAMIN FRANKLIN.

FRANKLIN'S GRAVE.

The remains of Benjamin Franklin and his wife Deborah are laid in Old Christ Church Burial Ground, located at the South-East Corner of Fifth and Arch Streets.

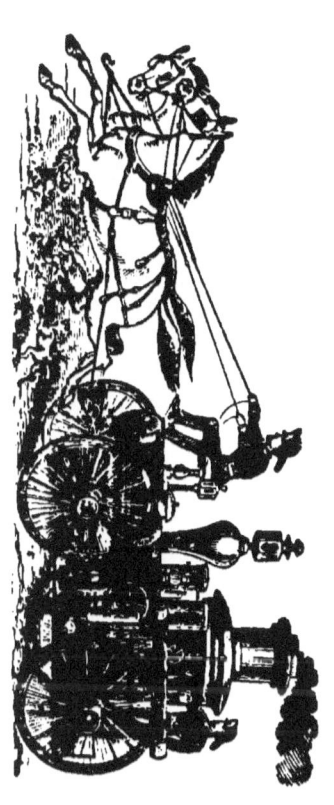

FIRE APPARATUS in 1876.

"The way they go it now."

FIRE SCENE in 1776.

Ancient apparatus—the Pump and Bucket.

FARMERS' MARKET HOUSE.
INTERIOR VIEW.

Located at North-East Corner of Twelfth and Market Streets.

MARKET STREET FERRY.

Located at foot of Market Street, on the Delaware opposite Camden, N. J. Five minutes time allotted for crossing the river.

PENNSYLVANIA HOSPITAL.

This Institution stands on the square bounded by Spruce and Pine Streets, and by Eighth and Ninth Streets.

PENNSYLVANIA COLLEGE.
Located on Ninth Street, below Locust Street.

NEW ACADEMY OF NATURAL SCIENCES.
Located at Nineteenth and Race Streets.

COLLEGIATE.

MEDICAL.

HOSPITAL.

BUILDINGS OF THE UNIVERSITY OF PENNSYLVANIA.

PENNSYLVANIA HOSPITAL FOR THE INSANE.—Haverford Road, West Philad.

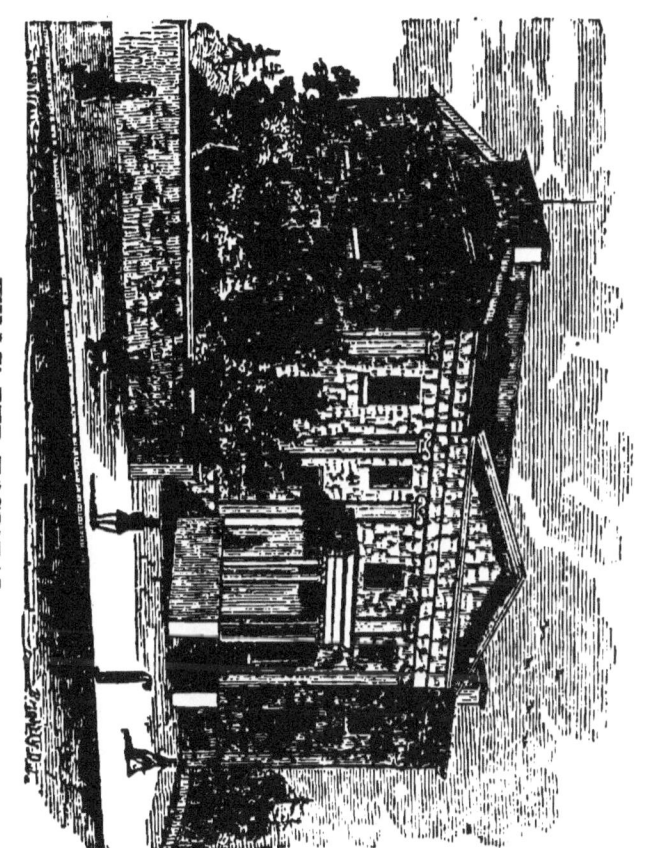

WILLS' EYE HOSPITAL.

This Institution for the cure of diseases of the Eyes and Limbs, is located on south side of Logan Square, on Race Street between 8th and 19th Streets.

It was founded by JAMES WILLS, who bequeathed for the purpose 108,396. Commenced in 1832 and finished in 1834. Since which time nearly 52,000 patients have been treated.

PRESTON RETREAT.

This elegant building designed as a Lying-in Hospital for indigent married women, was founded by bequest of Dr. Jonas Preston. It is located on Hamilton Street, between Twentieth and Twenty-first Streets. It is one of Philadelphia's noblest charities.

INSTITUTION FOR THE BLIND.

This Institution is located at Twentieth and Race Streets. It was founded in 1833. It has now accommodation for 225 pupils. During last year, over 55,000 brushes, brooms and whisks, were made by

INSTITUTION FOR DEAF AND DUMB.

This Institution is located at Broad and Pine Streets. It was founded in the year 1820. The original cost was $80,000.

The Cemetery is situated at Ridge Avenue and Lehigh Avenue. This engraving represents the main entrance on Ridge Avenue.

ODD FELLOWS' CEMETERY.

This Cemetery is situated at Twenty-fifth and Norris Streets.

ATHENÆUM.

Located at Sixth and Adelphi Streets. The Historical Society of Pennsylvania have an interesting museum in this building.

NEW LIBRARY BUILDING.

South Broad Street.

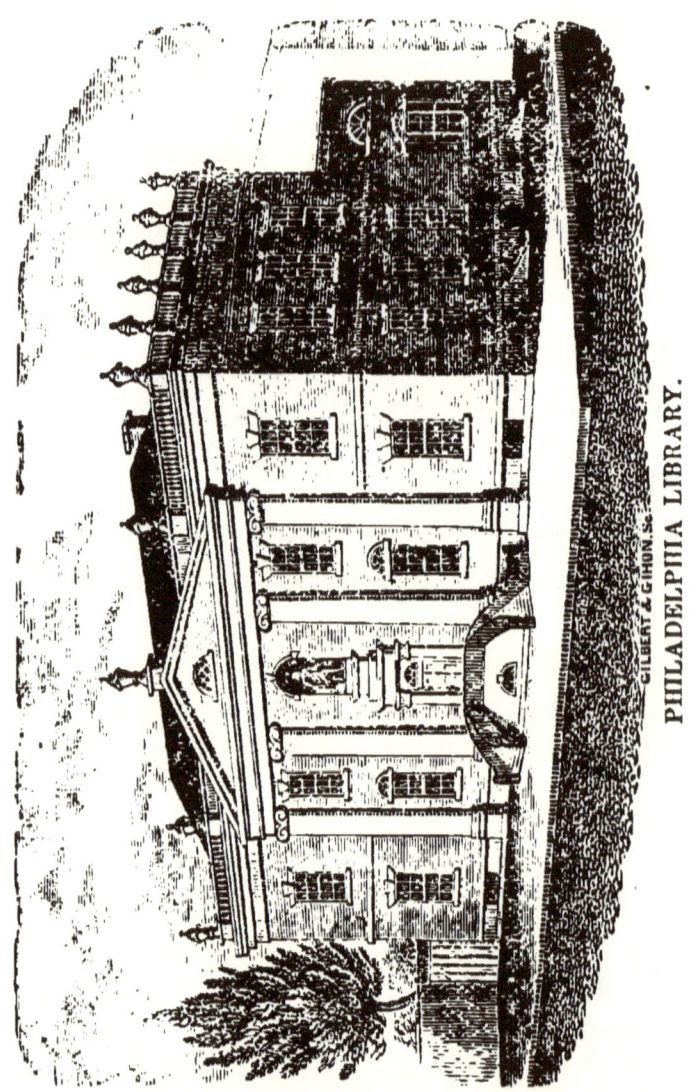

PHILADELPHIA LIBRARY.

Located at Fifth and Library Streets.

ACADEMY OF MUSIC AND HORTICULTURAL HALL.

Located at Broad and Locust Streets, nearly adjoining each other. he Academy is one of the most magnificent of modern opera ouses. It has a front of 140 feet on Broad Street, and a depth of 33 feet on Locust Street.

ACADEMY OF FINE ARTS.

Located on Broad Street, corner Cherry Street.

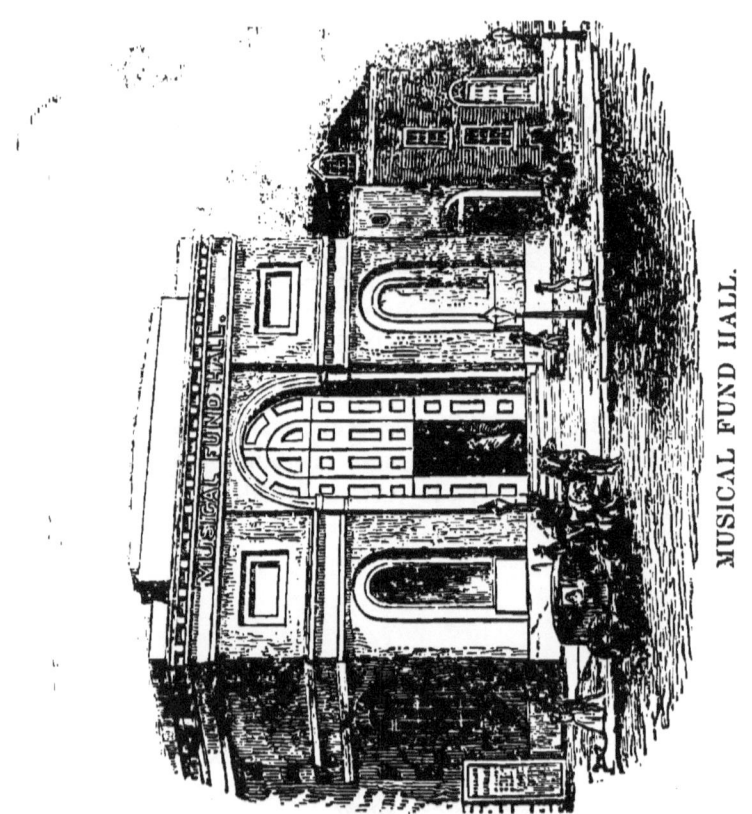

MUSICAL FUND HALL.

Musical Fund Hall located on Locust Street, above Eighth, founded in 1820, for the relief of superanuated musicians, the cultivation of skill and the diffusion of taste in music. The Hall seats 2,000 persons.

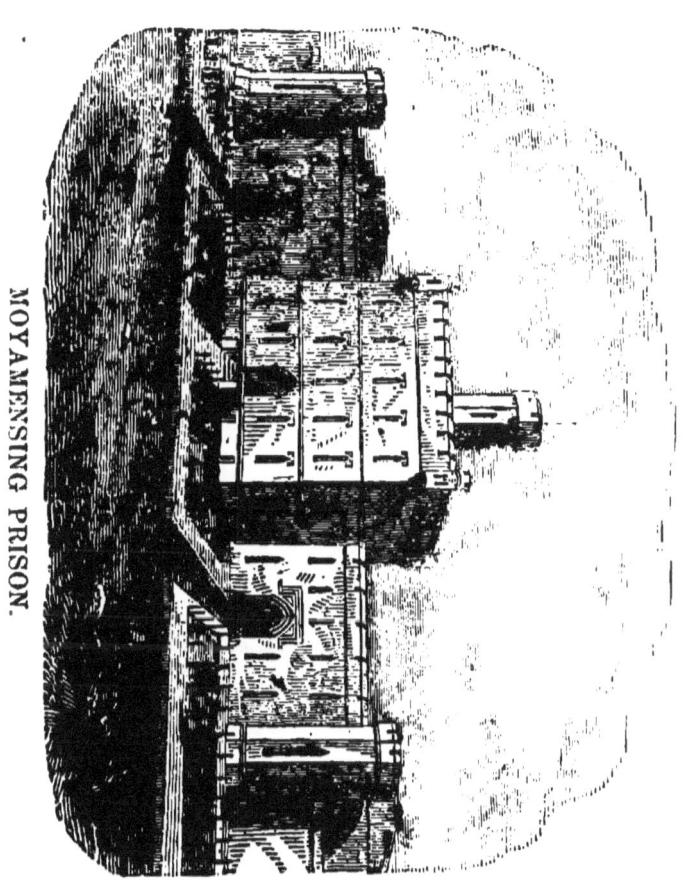

MOYAMENSING PRISON.

Moyamensing Prison is located on Passyunk Avenue, below Reed Street. It is built of Quincy granite, in the Tudor style of English gothic architecture. It was first occupied in October, 1835. It contains nearly five hundred cells.

EASTERN PENITENTIARY.

Located on Fairmount Avenue, west of Twenty-first Street. Original cost, $600,000.

U. S. NAVAL ASYLUM.

Located on Gray's Ferry Road, below Bainbridge Street. Surrounded by a beautiful park containing 25 acres.

OLD COMMERCIAL EXCHANGE.

Fronting on Walnut, Dock and Third Streets. To the extreme right may be observed the old Girard Bank.

NEW COMMERCIAL EXCHANGE.

Located on Second Street, below Chestnut Street, on the site of the "old slate roof house" (erected in 1700, and demolished in 1868). This building is one of the finest which adorns Philadelphia. It is built of fine brown stone and brick. Our heaviest merchants in flour, grain and high wines, meet daily here, and make exchanges to the amount of millions. The Government Signal Service is located in the tower of the building. The Philadelphia Produce Exchange, dealers in butter, eggs, cheese, etc., meet daily in one of the principal chambers of this building, and barter and make exchanges on a very extensive scale; this Exchange is still in its infancy, but it is in a very successful condition at present, and bids fair to rival the older one.

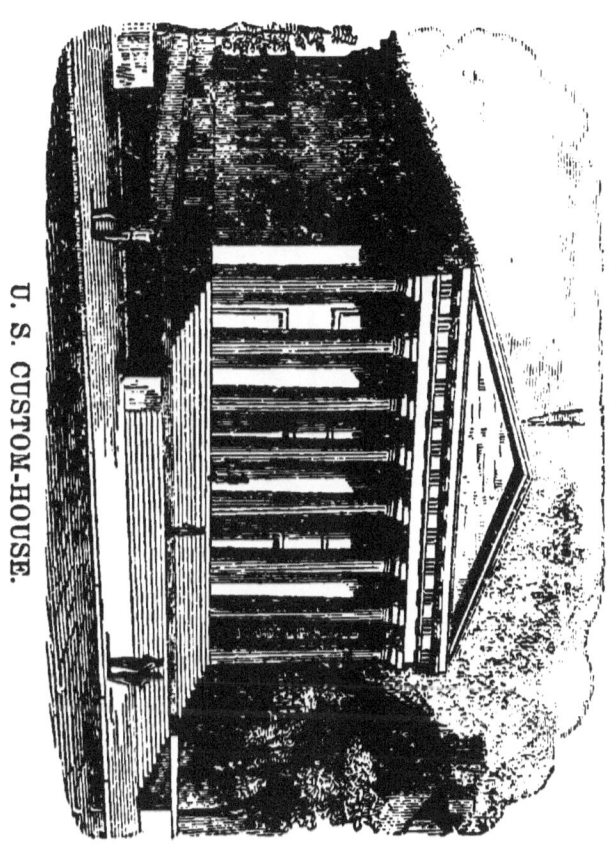

The Custom-House stands on the south side of Chestnut street, between Fourth and Fifth. It has two fronts, one on Chestnut, the other on Library Street, each ornamented with eight fluted Doric columns, 27 feet high and 4 feet 6 inches in diameter, supporting a heavy entablature. It is in imitation of the Parthenon at Athens, and is one of the purest specimens of Doric architecture in the country. The building was completed in 1824, having cost $500,000, and was formerly the United States Bank. It is now used by the United States Sub-Treasury and Custom-House officers.

U. S. MINT.

Located on Chestnut Street, below Broad.

CHESTNUT STREET BRIDGE.

Spans the Schuylkill River at Chestnut Street. Commenced September 19th, 1861, finished July 4th, 1866.

UNION LEAGUE BUILDING.

The Union League Club was formed in 1862, for promoting friendly intercourse among loyal people. The building is located on Broad Street, near Walnut. The cost, including furniture, was $200,000.

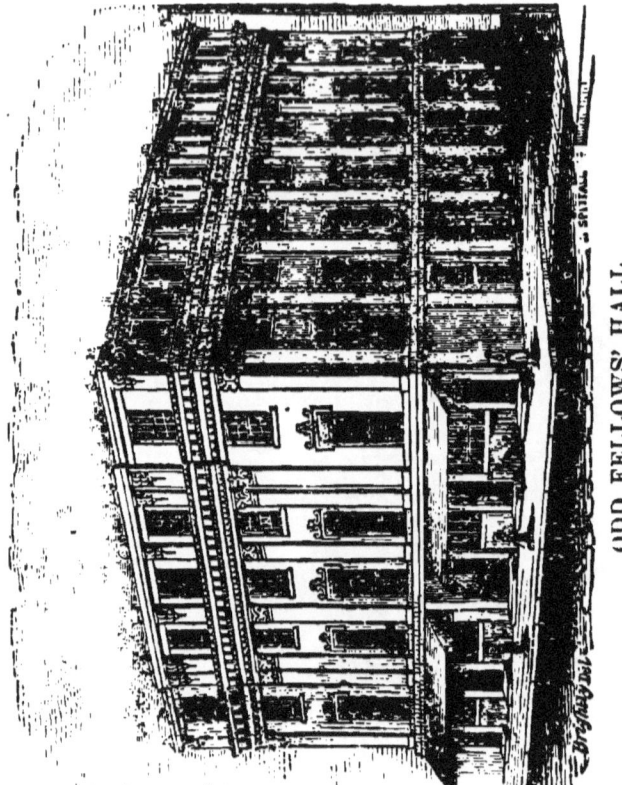

ODD FELLOWS' HALL.

Located at Sixth and Cresson Streets. The first Order instituted in this city, about the year 1823. Cost of hall and furniture $90,000. The office of the Grand Secretary is in the hall. There is one large Encampment room. The Grand Lodge and Grand Encampment, Trustees of the Hall Association, Trustees of Odd Fellows' Cemetery Company, one Degree Lodge, forty-seven Subordinate Lodges, and twelve Encampments, hold their meetings in it.

NEW MASONIC TEMPLE.

The New Masonic Temple is located at Broad and Filbert Streets. It is the grandest building of its kind in the world. It is a granite structure, 250 feet long and 150 feet wide; three lofty stories in height. The tower is 230 feet high. The building contains nine lodge rooms, together with the officers' and library rooms. The Temple was dedicated in 1873, in the presence of 50,000 members of the fraternity. The cost of the structure was $1,540,000.

NEW PUBLIC BUILDINGS.

These buildings are now in course of erection at Broad and Market Streets. They will be six years in course of completion. They will be 470 feet from east to west, and 486½ feet from north to south, covering an area, exclusive of the court-yard, of nearly four and a half acres. It will be larger than any single building on this continent. The cost of the whole structure will be about $12,000,000.

FOUNTAIN IN FRANKLIN SQUARE.

This place of resort is located at Sixth and Race Streets. It is named after the printer, patriot and philosopher—Benjamin Franklin.

LOGAN SQUARE.

Located at Eighteenth and Race Streets. During the civil war, there was held here one of the largest Sanitary Fairs that the world ever beheld.

SHIP IN FULL SAIL.

RIVER STEAMBOAT.

These boats may be seen gliding up and down the Delaware River at all hours of the day, loaded with passengers residing in towns on the Delaware banks, or with Philadelphians seeking health from the cool breeze of the river.

355

U. S. CAPITOL AT WASHINGTON, D. C.

Fairmount Park.

FAIRMOUNT PARK, at Philadelphia, is the most extensive, and in natural advantages, the most attractive, among the pleasure-grounds of Europe and America.

It borders and includes the Schuylkill River for a distance of over seven miles, and the Wissahickon, a tributary stream, for a distance of over six miles. It begins at Fairmount, a point on the Schuylkill distant about one and a half mile from Broad and Market Streets, and terminates at Chestnut Hill, on the Wissahickon, a distance of nearly fourteen miles.

Of the two principal sections of this Park, the one bordering the Schuylkill contains 2240 acres. The one bordering the Wissahickon contains 450 acres. The entire Park comprises nearly 3000 acres. It will require for access to its several portions more than fifty miles of carriage road, and one hundred miles of road-way, paths, and connections.

The Park contains 115 springs of pure cold water, and twenty small streams, tributaries of the Schuylkill and Wissahickon.

The ground selected for the site of the Centennial Exhibition in Fairmount Park is west of the Schuylkill River, and north of Girard and Elm Avenues, on a plateau ninety feet above the river, heretofore known as Lansdowne. The boundaries of the Exhibition are: South, Elm Avenue, from Forty-first to Fifty-second streets; West, the Park drive to George's Hill, with the Concourse; North, Belmont drive from George's Hill to the foot of Belmont; and East, Lansdowne drive from Belmont to Forty-first street.

Some of the principal points of interest in the Park are: The Art Gallery; The Water Works; Lincoln's Monument; The Fountain; The Mineral Spring; Lemon Hill; Grant's Old Log Cabin; (his headquarters at the time of Lee's surrender) Zoological Garden; The Ravines; Monster Pines; Sedgely Park; Belmont; Strawberry Mansion; Lansdowne; Egglesfield; George's Hill; Tom Moore's Cottage and Wissahickon Creek and Scenery.

The Park, in addition to its natural beauties and artificial adornments, has a halo of historical interest; its grounds were traversed by many of the historic personages of the Revolutionary period. On the banks of its principal stream Tom Moore probably wrote the lines

>   I knew by the smoke that so gracefully curled
>   Across the green elms, that a cottage was near,
>   And I said if there's peace to be found in this world,
>   A heart that is humble might hope for it here.

ENTRANCE TO FAIRMOUNT PARK, AT GREEN STREET.
Lincoln Monument and drive around Lemon Hill.

ENTRANCE TO WEST PARK, BY GIRARD AVENUE BRIDGE.
Also Penn'a R. R. Bridge, and the landing on the Schuylkill at Zoological Garden.

FAIRMOUNT BASIN, WATER WORKS, DAM, AND OLD WIRE BRIDGE.

GIRARD AVENUE BRIDGE.

Length, 1,000 feet; width, 100 feet. Opened for travel, July 4th, 1871. Cost $1,404,415.

361

LEMON HILL AND BOAT HOUSES OF THE SCHUYLKILL NAVY.

FOUNTAIN NEAR MINERAL SPRING, LEMON HILL.

363

COLUMBIA BRIDGE OVER THE SCHUYLKILL, FROM THE RUSTIC BRIDGE IN THE WESTERN PARK.

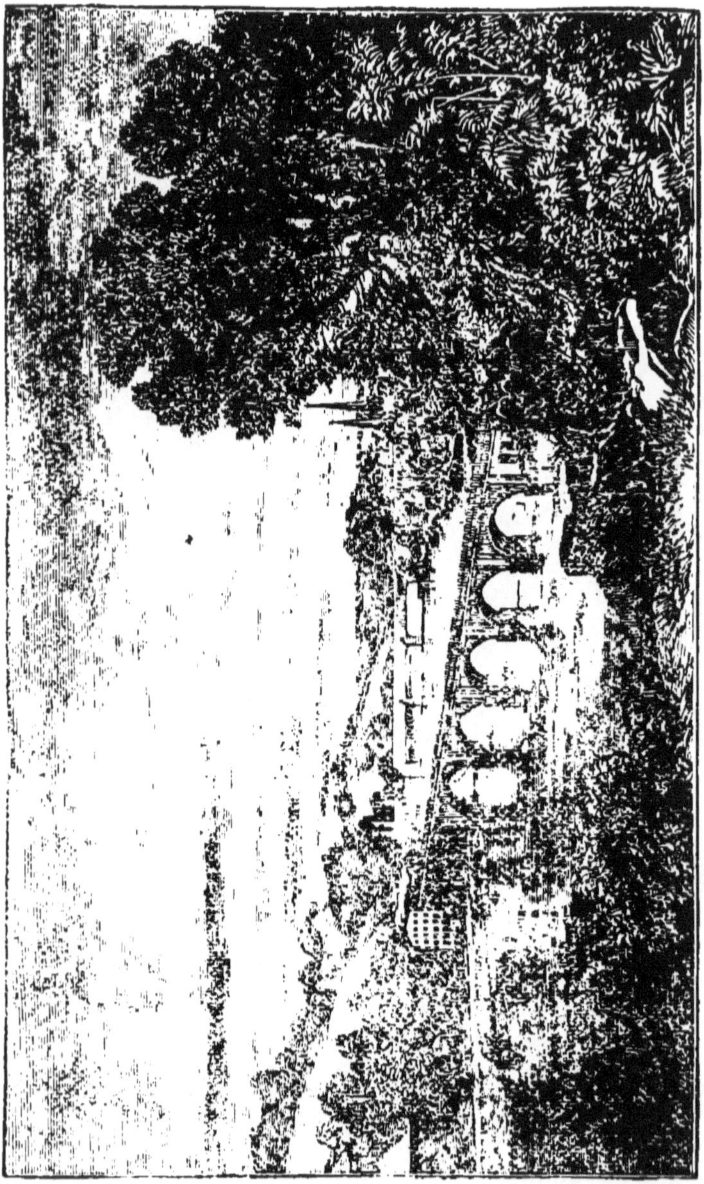

VIEW OF THE SCHUYLKILL FROM LAUREL HILL.

365

LAUREL HILL CEMETERY.
Landing on the Schuylkill.

STRAWBERRY MANSION.
Popular summer resort in East Park.

VIEW FROM BELMONT.
In West Park.

THE HERMIT'S POOL.

MONSTER PINES IN WEST PARK.

RAVINE IN WESTERN PARK, SWEETBRIAR VALE.

THE DRIVE—WISSAHICKON.

DRINKING FOUNTAIN ON THE WISSAHICKON.

ON THE WISSAHICKON DRIVE.

BRIDGE OVER WISSAHICKON, NEAR MOUNT AIRY.

BRIDGE OVER THE WISSAHICKON AT VALLEY GREEN.

HEMLOCK GLEN ON THE WISSAHICKON.

Exhibition Grounds.

THE INTERNATIONAL EXHIBITION
OPENS MAY 10th, 1876.   CLOSES NOV. 10th, 1876.

The Exhibition Buildings proper are five in number, and occupy about 60 acres at the foot of George's Hill, in the West Park. Two hundred and thirty acres have been enclosed for the purposes of the Exhibition. Thirteen ornamental edifices will be erected by the foreign commissions, to be used as offices, parlors, etc. Thirteen of our States will put up similar structures. About 150 buildings will be erected on the ground, and each one of a different style of architecture, and of a very attractive and imposing appearance.

This Exhibition is the largest ever held, exceeding in area of ground the Vienna Exhibition of 1874, by over four acres.

Area of enclosed grounds, 236 acres.
Lineal number of feet of the enclosure, 16,000.
Number of entrances, 13.
Dimensions of Main Building, 1,880 feet by 464 feet—21.47 acres.
Memorial Hall or Art Gallery, 210 feet by 365 feet—1¾ acres.
Machinery Hall, 360 feet by 1402 feet—11 acres.
Horticultural Hall, 160 feet by 350 feet.
Agricultural Hall, 820 feet by 540 feet.
United States Government Building.
Office for the United States Commission, 80 feet by 334 feet—¾ of an acre.
Judges' Hall, Length 152 feet by 115 feet wide.
The Women's Pavilion covers an area of 30,000 square feet, and is formed by two naves intersecting each other, each 64 feet wide by 192 feet long, on end of same a porch 8 by 32 feet.
Avenues and walks, 7 miles.
Length of proposed horse railway, 4 miles.
Average distance between the buildings, 550 feet.

OFFICERS OF THE U. S. CENTENNIAL COMMISSION.

PRESIDENT.
HON. JOSEPH R. HAWLEY, of Connecticut.

VICE-PRESIDENTS.
ALFRED T GOSHORN, of Ohio.   JOHN D. CREIGH, of California
ORESTES CLEVELAND, of N. J.   ROBERT LOWRY, of Iowa.
ROBERT MALLORY, of Ky.

SECRETARY.
JOHN L. CAMPBELL, of Indiana.

DIRECTOR-GENERAL OF THE EXHIBITION.
ALFRED T. GOSHORN, of Ohio.

ASSISTANT SECRETARY.
COL. MYER ASCH, of Philadelphia.

SOLICITOR-GENERAL.
JOHN L. SHOEMAKER, Esq., of Philadelphia.

375

CENTENNIAL MEMORIAL MEDAL.

MEMORIAL HALL OR ART GALLERY.
365 feet long. 210 feet wide.

HORTICULTURAL HALL.
350 feet long. 160 feet wide.

MAIN EXHIBITION BUILDING.
1880 feet long.   464 feet wide.

MACHINERY HALL.
1302 feet long.   360 feet wide.

THE JUDGE'S HALL.
152 feet long. 115 feet wide.

U. S. GOVERNMENT BUILDING.
360 feet long. 300 feet wide.

WOMEN'S PAVILION.
192 feet long. 64 feet wide.

AGRICULTURAL HALL.
820 feet long.   540 feet wide.

THE UNITED STATES.—THE ORIGINAL THIRTEEN.

Connecticut,	settled at	Windsor,	in 1633
Delaware,	"	Wilmington,	" 1638
Georgia,	"	Savannah,	" 1733
Maryland,	"	St. Mary,	" 1634
Massachusetts,	"	Plymouth,	" 1620
New Hampshire,	"	Dover,	" 1623
New Jersey	"	Bergen,	" 1624
New York,	"	Manhattan,	" 1614
North Carolina,	"	Albemarle,	" 1650
Pennsylvania,	"	Philadelphia,	" 1681
Rhode Island,	"	Providence,	" 1636
South Carolina,	"	Port Royal,	" 1670
Virginia,	"	Jamestown,	" 1607

PRESIDENTS AND VICE-PRESIDENTS OF THE UNITED STATES.—1789-1876.

YEAR.	NAME.	Where from	TERM OF OFFICE.
1789	Geo. Washington,	Virginia,	8 years.
1797	John Adams,	Mass.	4 "
1801	Thomas Jefferson,	Virginia,	8 "
1809	James Madison,	Virginia,	8 "
1817	James Monroe,	Virginia,	8 "
1824	John Q. Adams,	Mass.	4 "
1829	Andrew Jackson,	Tennessee,	8 "
1837	Martin Van Buren,	New York,	4 "
1841	W. H. Harrison,*	Ohio,	1 month.
1841	John Tyler,	Virginia,	3 years, 11 months.
1845	Jas. K. Polk,	Tennessee,	4 "
1849	Zachary Taylor,†	Louisiana,	1 year, 4 months, 5 days.
1850	Millard Fillmore,	New York,	2 years, 7 months, 26 days.
1853	Franklin Pierce,	New Hamp.	4 "
1856	James Buchanan,	Penna.	4 "
1861	Abm. Lincoln‡	Illinois,	4 years, 1 month, 10 days.
1865	Andrew Johnson,	Tennessee,	3 " 10 months, 20 "
1869	Ulysses S. Grant,	Illinois,	4 "
1873	Ulysses S. Grant,	Illinois,	

*Died in office, April 4, 1841, when Vice President Tyler succeeded him.

†Died in office, July 9, 1850, when Vice President Fillmore succeeded him.

‡Assassinated April 14, 1865, when Vice President Johnson succeeded him.

VICE PRESIDENTS.

YEAR.	NAME.	Where from
1789	John Adams,	Massachusetts
1797	Thomas Jefferson,	Virginia
1801	Aaron Burr,	New York
1804	George Clifton,	New York
1813	Elbridge Gerry,	Massachusetts
1817	Daniel D. Tompkins,,	New York
1824	John C. Calhoun,	South Carolina
1833	Martin Van Buren,	New York
1837	Richard M. Johnson,	Kentucky
1841	John Tyler,	Virginia
1842	Samuel L. Southard,*	New Jersey
1845	George M. Dallas,	Pennsylvania
1849	Millard Fillmore,	New York
1851	William R. King,*	Alabama
1853	David R. Achison,*	Missouri
1855	Jesse D. Bright,*	Indiana
1857	John C. Breckenridge,	Kentucky
1861	Hannibal Hamlin,	Maine
1865	Andrew Johnson,	Tennessee
1865	Lafayette Foster,*	Connecticut
1866	Benjamin F. Wade,*	Ohio
1869	Schuyler Colfax,	Indiana
1873	Henry Wilson,	Massachusetts
1875	Thomas W. Ferry,	Michigan

*Ex-officio as President *pro tem.* of the Senate.

GOVERNMENT OF THE UNITED STATES.

PRESIDENT, Ulysses S. Grant, of Illinois.
ACTING VICE PRESIDENT, T. W. Ferry, of Michigan.

THE CABINET.

SECRETARY OF STATE, Hamilton Fish, of New York.
SECRETARY OF TREASURY, B. H. Bristow, of Kentucky.
SECRETARY OF WAR, Alfonso Taft, of Ohio.
SECRETARY OF NAVY, Geo. M. Robeson, of New Jersey.
SECRETARY of INTERIOR, Z. Chandler, of Michigan.
POSTMASTER GENERAL, Marshall Jewell, of Connecticut.
ATTORNEY GENERAL, Edwards Pierrepont, of New York.

UNITED STATES SUPREME COURT.

CHIEF JUSTICE, Morrison R. Waite, of Ohio, age, 49, appointed 1874
Asso. JUSTICE, Nathan Clifford,   " Maine, " 71,   " 1858
"   "   Noah H. Swayne,   " Ohio, " 70,   " 1862
"   "   Saml. F. Miller,   " Iowa, " 59,   " 1862
"   "   David Davis,   " Ill.   " 60,   " 1862
"   "   Stephen J. Field,   " Cal.   " 58,   " 1863
"   "   William Strong,   " Penn. " 66,   " 1870
"   "   Joseph P. Bradley,   " N. J., " 62,   " 1870
"   "   Ward Hunt,   " N. Y., " 64,   " 1872
REPORTER, Wm. T. Otto, of Indiana, appointed 1875.

UNITED STATES ARMY.

RANK.	NAME.	Head-quarters.
GENERAL	William T. Sherman,	St. Louis, Mo.
LIEUT. GENERAL	Philip H. Sheridan,	Chicago, Ill.
MAJOR GENERAL	W. S. Hancock,	New York.
" "	J. M. Schofield,	San Francisco.
" "	Irving McDowell,	Philadelphia.
BRIG'R. GENERAL	John Pope,	Fort Leavenworth
" "	Oliver O. Howard,	Portland, Or.
" "	Alfred H. Terry,	Louisville, Ky.
" "	E. O. C. Ord,	San Francisco.
" "	Christ. C. Auger,	Omaha, Neb.
" "	George Crook,	Prescott, Arizona

UNITED STATES NAVY.

RANK.	NAME.	Where serving.
ADMIRAL	David D. Porter,	Washington.
VICE ADMIRAL	Stephen C. Rowan,	"
REAR ADMIRAL	Chas. H. Davis,	Naval Academy.
" "	John Rodgers,	Mare Island, Cal.
" "	Augustus L. Case,	Europe.
" "	Alexander M. Pennock,	Asia.
" "	John L. Worden,	On leave.
" "	John J. Almy,	North Pacific.
" "	James H. Strong,	On leave.
" "	William Reynolds,	Washington.
" "	Wm. E. LeRoy,	South Atlantic.
" "	J. R. M. Mullany,	North Atlantic.
" "	C. R. P. Rodgers,	Washington.

COAT OF ARMS OF THE STATE OF PENNSYLVANIA.

INDEX TO COOKERY.

PART FIRST.

		PAGE			PAGE
Bread, Art of Making		1	Beef, Boiled		124
"	Apple	4	"	Corned	125
"	Brown, Boston	5	"	Cold, Hashed	126
"	Currant	4	"	Fricassee	122
"	French	5	"	Heart, to Dress	128
"	Graham	3	"	Kidneys, Stewed	127
"	Indian	3	"	" Toast	127
"	Potatoe	4	"	Liver, Fried	128
"	Rye	2	"	" Broiled	128
"	Unleavened	3	"	Marrow Bones	128
"	Wheat, American	2	"	Potted	125
Biscuit, American		6	"	Patties, from under done	
"	Almond	9			[Beef 127
"	Common Sense	5	"	Palates	129
"	English	6	"	Roast, American	121
"	French	6	"	" Sirloin, English	121
"	Fruit, Wheat Meal	7	"	Stewed with Carrots	122
"	German	7	"	" " Raisins	122
"	Ginger	8	"	Steak and Oysters, Stewed	122
"	Graham Soda	9	"	" with Onions	124
"	Orange	8	"	Spiced	126
"	Soda	7	"	Sausages	126
"	Sour Milk	7	"	Tongue, London	124
Buns, Caraway		11	"	" American	125
"	Centennial	12	"	" French Roast	125
"	Citron	12	"	Tripe, to Fry	127
"	Tea	11	"	" Fricasseed	128
Buckwheat Cakes		14	Beer, Art of Managing		177
"	Griddle Cakes	15	"	Essential Oils	187
"	Short Cakes	15	"	Ginger	186
Beef, Art of Choosing		120	"	Lemon Pop	186
"	a la Daub	121	"	Molasses	187
"	a la Mode	123	"	Mead, Excellent	187
"	Broiled	123	"	Pop	186
"	" rare	123	"	Spruce	186

INDEX.

	PAGE
Beer, Sarsaparilla	186
" Silver Top	187
Brandy, Blackberry	184
" Cherry	184
" Raspberry	183
Cake, Corn Dodgers	16
" Flannel	15
" Green Corn	16
" Indian Corn	16
" Johnny	15
" Pan	17
" Pan, Common	17
" " London	17
" " French	18
" Rice	17
Cakes, Art of Making	22
" Almond	24
" " Garlands	25
" Apricot	27
" a la Polonaise	27
" Apple	32
" Cinnamon	24
" Cocoanut	24
" Chocolate	29
" Drop	29
" Frosting for	33
" Honey	29
" Josephine	28
" Jumbles	31
" Lemon	27
" Little White	29
" " Short	30
" Lady Kisses	30
" Pound Plum	23
" " Fruit	23
" Plain Pound	23
" Poor Man's	31
" Queen	25
" Rich Seed	28
" Rice Cream	28
" Raisin	30
" Strawberry	25
" Sponge	25
" Sugar Drop	32
" Turkish	30
" Velvet	24
" Venetian, Small	26

	PAGE
Cakes, Vienna	27
" Washington	26
" Webster	26
" White Mountain	30
Cheesecake, Apple	43
" Almond	44
" Lemon	44
" Plain	43
Custard, Almond	46
" Baked	45
" Cream	46
" Lemon	45
" Mottled	45
" Rich	45
Carving, Art of	158
" Aitch Bone	160
" Breast of Veal	161
" Chuck Ribs	160
" Calf's Head	161
" Duck	165
" Fillet of Veal	161
" Fore Quarter of Lamb	162
" Fowl	164
" Fish	166
" Grouse	165
" Goose	105
" Ham	163
" Haunch of Venison	163
" Hare	165
" Loin of Veal	160
" Leg of Mutton	161
" Leg of Lamb	162
" Loin of Mutton	162
" " Lamb	162
" " Pork	163
" Leg of "	163
" Pig	163
" Partridge	165
" Pigeon	165
" Rabbit	165
" Sirloin of Beef	159
" Shoulder of Mutton	161
" Saddle "	162
" Shoulder of Lamb	162
" Tongue	160
" Turkey	164
" Woodcock	165

INDEX.

	PAGE
Coffee, as a Stimulant	173
" as made in India	175
" French Mode	174
" Milk	174
" Roasting	173
" to Make	174
Chocolate, Philadelphia Mode	176
" to Make	176
Cocoa, Prepared	176
" Shells	176
Cider, Champagne	185
" Method of Making	184
" to Keep Sweet	185
" " for Years	185
Cleaning and Scouring	200
" " Black Cloth	200
" " Ink Spots [on Clothes	200
" " Iron Moulds [on Linen	200
" " Mildew from [Linen	200
" " Spots on Silk	200
Doughnuts, Country	33
" Superior	33
Dumplings, Apple	50
" Baked Apple	51
" Oxford	50
" Peach	51
" Raspberry	51
Eggs, Art of Choosing	167
" a la Coque	167
" and Sausages	168
" " Bacon	168
" " Beet Root	168
" a la Sicilienne	170
" Boiled, Plain	167
" Baked	169
" Croquettes	169
" Omelette, aux Confitures	170
" " of Ham	170
" " of Tongue or [Sausage	170
" " and Rum	171
" " American	171
" " and Cheese	171
" Poached	169

	PAGE
Eggs, Pickled	171
" Preserved	172
" Sandwiches	168
" Scrambled	170
" with Onions	169
Fritters, Apple	19
" Oyster	18
" Plain	19
" Potato	19
Fish	95
" Black, Fried	106
" Choosing	95
" Cod, Boiled	103
" " Sounds, Dressed	104
" " Salt, Boiled	104
" " Curry to make	104
" " Cakes, to make	105
" Cat, Fried	106
" Carp, Boiled	109
" " Stewed	109
" Eels, a la Cream	106
" " Baked	105
" " Fried	105
" Flounders, Stewed	106
" " Fried	105
" Halibut, Boiled	96
" " Fried	97
" " Broiled	97
" " Smoked	97
" Haddock, Boiled	97
" " Fried	98
" " Baked	98
" " Broiled	98
" Herring, Smoked	101
" " Fried	101
" " Broiled	102
" Mackerel, "	102
" " Fried	102
" " a la Maitre de [Hotel	102
" Mullet, Red	108
" Maids, Boiled	108
" Perch, Boiled	98
" " Fried	99
" " White, a la daub	99
" Pike, Baked	107
" Rock, to Boil	105

	PAGE
Fish Salmon, Roasted	95
" " Broiled	96
" " Potted	96
" " Fried	96
" " Boiled	96
" Shad, Boiled	100
" " Roast	100
" " Broil	101
" " Baked	101
" Sturgeon, to Dress	103
" " Roasted	103
" " Boiled	103
" " Broiled	103
" Seabass and Tomatoes	107
" Soles, Fried	107
" " Fricassee	107
" Smelts, Fried	108
" Skate, to Prepare	108
" " Crimp	108
" Trout, Boiled	99
" " Fried	99
" " Broiled	100
" Thorback	108
" Shells	110
" Crabs, to Choose	110
" " a la Russe	112
" " Devilled	113
" " Cold, Dressed	113
" " Clam Soup	113
" " Soft Shell	113
" " " Stewed	114
" " Boiled, Boston	114
Ginger Bread, Hard	31
" " Soft	31
" " Snaps	32
Game, Art of Choosing	148
" Grouse, to Roast	156
" Hare, '	157
" Pigeons, Broiled	154
" " Roasted	154
" " Stewed with [Maccaroni	154
" Pheasants, to Roast	155
" Partridges, "	155
" Plovers, to Dress	156
" Reed Birds, to Dress	156
" Rabbits, Stewed	156

	PAGE
Game, Rabbits, Ragout of	156
" " to Roast	157
" Snipes, Roasted	155
" Teal, to Truss	155
" " to Roast	155
" Venison, to Roast	149
" " Hashed	149
" " Minced	149
" " Stewed	150
" Wild Ducks, to Dress	154
" " " to Stew	154
" Woodcocks, roasted	155
Ice Cream, Cocoanut	188
" Chocolate	189
" Lemon	188
" Pineapple	189
" Strawberry	188
" Vanilla	188
Jelly, Apple	60
" Blackberry	57
" Cranberry	57
" Currant	57
" Claret	58
" Calf's Feet	58
" Confectioner's	59
" Grape	57
" Green Gage	58
" Iceland Moss	59
" Orange	58
" Plum	58
" Quince	59
" Raspberry	57
" Strawberry	57
Jam, Blackberry	60
" Currant	61
" Codlin	61
" Cherry	61
" Orange	61
" Raspberry	60
" Strawberry	60
Lobster, to Choose	110
" to Dress	110
" Patties	110
" Sauce	111
" Cutlets	111
" Buttered	111
" Stewed	112

INDEX.

	PAGE
Lobster, Scalloped	112
" Broiled	112
Lamb, Art of Choosing	138
" Cutlets and Green Peas, [a la Royal	138
" Chops	139
" Leg, Roasted	138
" Lamb's Fry	139
" Quarter, Boned	140
" Shoulder, Roasted	139
" Stewed	139
Muffins, Corn Meal	13
" "My Own"	14
" Plain	13
" Toast	14
" Yankee	14
Mush, and Milk	16
" Fried	17
Mutton, Art of Choosing	135
" Broiled, Tomato Sauce	136
" Breast, in Ragout	137
" " Boiled	137
" Chops, Broiled	136
" Leg, Boiled	137
" Minced with Mashed [Potatoes	137
" Saddle, Roasted	136
" Shoulder, Roasted	136
" Stewed	137
Oysters, Art of choosing	110
" Fried, Washington [Style	114
" Loaves, to Make	115
" to Fry	115
" to Stew	115
" Stewed, New York	115
" and Chestnuts	116
" and Maccaroni	116
" Scalloped	116
" Fritters	116
" Pancakes	116
" Roast, Philadelphia	117
" Sauce	117
" Milk Stew	117
" Patties	117
" Vol-au-vent	117
" Panned	118

	PAGE
Oysters, to Feed	118
Pies, Art and Directions	35
" Apple and Quince	41
" Blackberry	37
" Cherry	37
" Currant and Gooseberry	38
" Codlin	41
" Cherry	41
" Dried Apple	40
" Green Currant	36
" Gooseberry	36
" Grape	37
" Green Apple	39
" Glazing Pastry	50
" Lemon	37
" Mince	42
" " Lent	42
" " Lemon	42
" Orange or Lemon	41
" Prune	38
" Peach	39
" " Pot	39
" " Dried	39
" Pumpkin	40
" Plum	40
" Rhubarb	36
" Raisin	43
" Scotch Apple	40
" Tomatoe	37
" Whortleberry	38
" Yankee Mince	43
Puffs, Cream	44
" French	44
Pies, Meat and Vegetable	48
" Oyster	49
" Pigeon or Game	49
" Rabbit or Hare	49
" Turkey Patties	50
Pudding, American Christmas	54
" Bread	54
" Baked Apple	56
" Cup	53
" Cocoanut	55
" Fruit	52
" Plum	52
" Plain Rice	54
" " Suet	55

INDEX.

	PAGE
Pudding, Ragon's Cream	53
" Swiss	56
" Tapioca	55
" Victoria Battter	53
" Winter	56
" Yorkshire	53
Preserves, Clarify Sugar	63
" Cherries	66
" Crab Apple	67
" Green Gage	66
" Grapes in Brandy	68
" Peach	64
" Plum	65
" Pear	65
" Quince	65
" " whole or half	67
" Raspberry	64
" Rhubarb and Orange	67
" Strawberry	66
" To Keep	63
" Tomatoes	64
Pickles, Asparagus	70
" Barberries	70
" French Bean	71
" Green, to Make	71
" Onion	70
" Peach	69
" Plums, like Olives	69
" Red Cabbage	70
" Radish Pods	71
" Tomatoe	70
Pork, Art of Choosing	140
" Chops	142
" Ham, to Choose	140
" " to Toast	142
" " to Stuff	142
" " to Boil	142
" " Smoked, to Keep	146
" Hog's Head Cheese	144
" Leg, Roast, with Stuffing	140
" Olives	142
" Pudding, Holland	143
" " American	145
" Pickled	146
" Spare Rib, to Roast	141
" Sausage, Genuine Country	143
" " Bologna	145

	PAGE
Pork, Soused Feet	145
" " in Ragout	146
" Sausage, Fried	146
" Tongues, to Prepare	147
Pig, Baked	141
" Roasted	141
" Cheek, to Boil	144
" Feet and Ears	144
" Head, to Roast	143
" " to Boil	143
" Kidneys	144
Poultry, Art of Choosing	148
" Chickens, to Roast	151
" " Boiled with [Tongue	152
" " to Broil	153
" Capons, to Roast	153
" Duck, to Roast	153
" " to Stew	153
" Fowls, Devilled	151
" " to Roast	151
" " to Fry	152
" " to Stew	152
" " Croquettes of	152
" Goose, to Roast	153
" Turkey, Roast, with [Chestnuts	150
" " " American	150
" " " Fricasseed	150
" " " to Bone	151
" " " Devilled	151
Rolls, Breakfast	9
" Boston Buttermilk	10
" Cranberry	9
" Economical	10
" English Cheshire	10
" French	10
" Graham	10
" German Sausage	11
Rusks, Italian	13
" New York	12
Sauce, Auvin	72
" Apple	73
" Cranberry	73
" Caper	74
" Lobster	73
" Maitre de Hotel	74

INDEX.

	PAGE
Sauce, Mint, for Roast Lamb	74
" Oyster	73
" Plum Pudding	72
" Red Wine	72
" Wine	72
Salad, American Chicken	75
" de Bœuf	76
" French Chicken	75
" Lobster	76
Soup, a la Cardinal	77
" Clam	78
" Green Turtle	81
" Maccaroni	79
" Mock Turtle	81
" Noodle	79
" Oyster	78
" Ox Tail	79
" Pea	79
" Rice or Barley	80
" Stock for	77
" Vegetable	78
" White Maigre	78
Shrimps, to Serve	118
" to Pot	118
" Sauce	119
Starch, Art of Making	197
" Gum Arabic	198
" Shirts, Glossy	193
Toast, Buttered	20
" Egg	21
" French Milk	20
" Ham	21
" Sandwich	20
Tarts, Apple	47
" Black Currant	47
" Cranberry	47
" French Raspberry	46
" Plum	48
" Strawberry	47
Tea, Art of Making	175
" Ordinary Mode	175
Vegetables, Art of Preparing	82
" Artichokes, to [Dress	86
" Asparagus, to [Dress	91
" Beans, to Dress	88

	PAGE
Vegetables, Beans, French, to [Dress	88
" " Shelled, to [Dress	88
" " Fricasseed	88
" " Kidney, Boiled	89
" " Lima	89
" Beets, to Prepare	91
" " Pickled	91
" Carrots, a la Maitre do [Hotel	85
" Carrots, American Style	85
" Cauliflowers, to Dress	86
" Cauliflowers, in White [Sauce	86
" Corn, Green, Boiled	90
" Corn, Green, Roasted	90
" Cabbage, Red, to Stew	91
" Cabbage, with Onions	92
" Cabbage Sprouts, to Boil	92
" Celery, to Stew	93
" Cucumbers, to Stew	93
" Egg Plant, to Prepare	89
" Greens, to Boil	92
" Lettuce or Salad, to Pre- [pare	92
" Mushrooms, to Stew	92
" Onions, to Boil in Milk	92
" Onions, to Stew	92
" Oyster Plant, to Prepare	93
" Potatoes, to Broil	82
" " to Roast	88
" " to Fry	83
" " Sarato. Chips	83
" " to Mash	83
" " Puree of	83
" " Balls	83
" " with Bacon	84
" Potatoes, Mashed with [Onions	84
" Potatoes, Oyster Balls	84
" " Sweet Stewed	84
" " Sweet Baked	85
" " White Baked	85
" Parsnips, Fricassee of	86
" Parsnips, Mashed	86
" " Fried	86

INDEX.

	PAGE
Vegetables, Peas, to Dress	87
" " Green, to Stew	87
" Pea Pods, to Stew	88
" Rutabagas, to Prepare	87
" Spinach, with Gravy	85
" Spinach, Beignets of	85
" Succotash, to Prepare	90
" Squash, to Dress	93
" " to Stew	93
" Turnips, White, to Prepare	87
" Tomatoes, Baked, [American	89
" Tomatoes, Stewed	90
" " Scalloped	90
Veal, Art of Choosing	129
" Breast, to Stew	130
" " Ragout of	132
" Brains, to Fry	134
" Cutlet, a la Maitre de Hotel	130
" Calf's Feet to Fry	133
" " to Stew	133
" " to Clean	135
" Calf's Head, Baked	133
" " Boiled	133
" " to Clean	135
" Calf's Heart, Roasted	134
" " Pluck, Dressed	134
" Fillet, Baked	131
" Fricando of	132
" Hashed	134
" Liver, to Stuff and Roast	132
" " Broiled	132
" Neck, to Stew	130
" Olives	131
" Potted	135
" Roast	129
" Scollops, Scotch	131
" Sweet Breads, to Fry	134
Vinegar, Cider	190
" Raspberry	189

	PAGE
Vinegar, Sugar	190
" Whiskey	190
Waffles, American	19
" Plain	20
" Rice	20
Wine, Art of Managing	177
" Apple	183
" Blackberry, "My Own"	181
" Cherry	180
" Damson	180
" English Sherry	178
" Elderberry	181
" Grape	179
" Ginger	182
" Mixed Fruits	180
" Orange	178
" Parsnip	182
" Raisin	178
" Raspberry	179
" Red Currant	179
" Red Gooseberry	179
" Rhubarb	180
" Sherry, How to Imitate	183
" To Improve Poor	182
" To Restore Musty	182
" " Flat	183
" To Rack	183
Washing, Art of	192
" Calicoes	196
" Flannels	193
" Hints on	192
" Lawns, and Starching	195
" Muslins	193
" Occupying One Hour	197
" Piques	193
" Point Lace	195
" Quilts	196
" Shawls, Woolen	194
" " Merino	194
" Silks	195
" Woolens	193

INDEX TO FAMILY MEDICINES.

PART SECOND.

	PAGE		PAGE
Asthma Remedy	215	Cramp, in Stomach	232
" Mixture	215	Costive Habits, Pills for	232
Apoplexy	225	Cholic, Painters', Cure for	238
Bronchitis Remedy	215	Cold Cream	242
" another Remedy	215	Chilblains	242
Boils, Cure for	218	" another Remedy	242
Bruises, "	221	Corns, Cure for	243
" Swelling, to Prevent	221	Corns, Soft, Cure for	243
Burns, Cure for	222	Corn Plaster	243
" or Scalds	222	**Deformities** and Distortions	207
" " another Cure	223	Dropsy of Abdomen	217
Blood Spitting	230	" Excellent Remedy	218
Bladder Strictures	233	Deafness, Cure for	227
Back Pain, Cure for	236	" Another Remedy	227
Bunious, Cure for	243	Diarrhœa, Cure for	231
Child after birth, Treatment of	204	Dysentery, "	231
Children Clothing, Rules for	206	Diptheria, "	234
Cholera Infantum	210	Dyspepsia, "	235
Convulsions in Children	211	" Centennial Cure for	235
Cough, Soothing Syrup	212	Debility	235
Croup, in Children	212	Drowning, to Restore	239
" another Remedy	213	**Exercise,** Children	209
Chicken Pox	214	Erysipelas, Cure for	215
Consumptive Cough	216	Earache, Cure for	226
Cough, Shortness in Breath	217	Eyes, Soreness, Cure	227
" Excellent Remedy	217	" Weak, Strengthen	227
Catarrh or Cold	217	" Speck or Ulcers, Cure	227
Cancer, to Cure	219	**Family** Medicines	203
Consumption, German Cure	221	Full Instructions for Infants	204
" another Cure	222	Flames, A Body in	223
Coughs, Spitting Blood (Syrup)	230	Fever, Billious	224
Chin Bleeding	230	" Typhus, Cure for	224
Cholera Morbus, excellent remedy	231	" and Ague "	224
Cholera Mixture	231	Feverish Thirst, Drink	224
Cramp, Cure for	232	Fever, Intermittent	224

INDEX.

	PAGE
Felon, Cure for	225
" Safe Remedy	225
Fits, Falling, Epilepsy	232
Flux, Cure for	230
Frost Bites	242
Feet, Frost Bites, Itching	242
" Offensive, Cure for	243
" Swollen, "	243
Griping in Children	211
Gout, Rheumatic	223
Gravel, Remedy	233
Hoarseness, Cure	216
Headache, Nervous	226
Hair, To Promote Growth	226
Head, Baldness	226
Hydrophobia, Cure for	229
Hysterics, Cure for	232
Hiccoughs, "	234
" Powder for	234
Heartburn, Cure for	234
" Lozenges	235
Hands, Chapped	241
" " Another Cure	241
" Numbed or Trembling	241
Itch, Cure for	220
Intestines, Inflammation	229
Jaw Ache	227
Jaundice, Cure for	239
Kidneys, Remedy	232
Lock Jaw Relief	214
Lungs, Soundness	221
Liver Complaint	229
Lungs, Bleeding at	230
Languor, Nervous	236
Lightning, Struck, to Restore	240
Lip Salve	241
Mouth, Sore, Children	211
Measles and Scarlatina	213
Mad Dogs, Dr. Stoye's Cure	228
Mumps, Cure for	234
Nipples, Sore, Ointment	209
Navel, Soreness, Child	210
Nipples Inflamed, Child	211
Neuralgia, Cure for	226
" and Pain Killer	226
Nose Bleeding, to Arrest	230
" Another Remedy	230

	PAGE
Night Sweats, Cure	239
Proud Flesh, to Remove	219
Pile Ointment	220
" Another Remedy	220
" Liniment for	220
Poisons, Antidotes or Remedies	237
Painters' Cholic	238
Quincy, Cure for	233
" Gargle for	233
Ring Worms, Cure for	219
Rheumatism Cure for	223
" Chronic, Cure for	223
" Inflammatory	223
Rattlesnake, Poison of	237
Sick Room Chamber	201
Sleep for Infants	206
Sick Chamber, Purify the Air	208
Summer Complaint	210
Scurf on Head, Ointment	211
Scarlet Fever Remedy	213
Small Pox, Cure for	213
" Pitting, Prevent	214
Salt Rheum	216
Skin Blotches, Cure	218
Salve, Deshler's Original	218
Scrofula Remedy	220
Sprains, Remedies	221
" Liniment	221
Scalds, Cure for	222
Summer Complaint, Cure for	231
Spirits, Depression of	235
Sunstroke, Cure for	236
" Another Cure for	236
Snake Bites, Remedy	237
Stings, Hornets, Wasps, Bees	238
Teething, Children	20
Throat, Sore, Cure	216
" " Infallible Cure	216
Tetter, Cure for	219
Turn of Life	225
Teeth, Filling Decayed	227
Tooth Ache, Cure for	228
" Drops	228
Toes, Ingrowing Nails	242
Urine, Incontinence	233
" Another Remedy	233
" " "	233

INDEX. 397

	PAGE
Vaccination, Children	207
Visiting the Sick	208
Vermin in Hair	212
Weaning Children, Rules	205
" " Food After	205
Worms in Children	212
" Another Remedy	212
Whooping Cough	213
Whooping Cough, Another Remedy	213
White Swelling at Joints	214
" Another Remedy	214
White or Hard Swellings, Dissolve	215
" " " Another [Remedy	215
Wen, Cure for	225
What shall we eat	244

INDEX TO FARMING.

PART THIRD.

	PAGE
Art of Farming	247
Bees	295
" Art of Managing	295
" Honey, Taking, without [Killing	295
" Honey, to Purify	296
" Miller, to Destroy	296
Buttercups, to Prevent Growth in [Grass	257
Butter, Art of Making	259
" Churning	262
" Coloring of	265
" Improving Strong and [Rancid	265
" Milking of Cows	261
" Milk Room, Temperature of	261
" Packing and Shipping	265
" Rolls and Prints	265
" To Freshen	265
" Working	263
" Washing and Salting	263
Cheese, Art of Making	267
" Cream, to Make	268
" Dutch, "	269
" Material in Making	266
Cheese, Milk, to turn	266
" " Temperature	267
" " Preparation of	267
" Rennet, to Prepare	266
" Room for Curing	269
" Sage, to Make	269
" To Preserve Sound	269
Cows, Summer Pasture for	260
" Winter Food for	261
Cows and Cattle	271
" Art of Selecting	271
" Administering Medicine	272
" Bleeding, Rules for	273
" Bowels, Inflamed, Remedy [for	274
" Black Tongue, Remedy for	275
" " Leg, "	275
" Bee and Hornet Stings, [Remedy for	276
" Bite of Poisonous Snakes, [Remedy for	276
" Choking, Remedy for	273
" Colic, "	275
" Eyes Inflamed, "	276
" Flesh Wounds, "	273

398

INDEX.

Cows, Hoven or Swelling,
[Remedy for 274
" Hollow Horn, " 275
" Hide Bound, " 276
" Lice, " 274
" Lock Jaw, " 276
" Loss of Cud, " 276
" Physic for............... 272
" Purging Drink for............ 273
" Poison, Remedy for............ 273
" Red Water, " 274
" Teats, Sore, " 276
" Tar Water for............... 272
" Yellows or Jaundice,
[Remedy for 275
Caterpillars on Trees, to Destroy... 252
Canary Birds............... 293
" Asthma Remedy for 294
" Bowels, Inflamed,
[Remedy for 294
" Costiveness, Remedy
[for 294
" Diarrhœa, Remedy
[for 294
" Epilepsy, Remedy
[for 294
" Voice, to Restore..... 294
Dig Deep for Gold............... 247
Dried Fruit, to Protect............... 256
Dairy, Instructions for............... 259
Early Potatoes in Spring............ 249
Evergreens, to Make Grow
[Compact 254
Frozen Potatoes, Remedy for.... 249
Fruit, Premature............... 252
" Trees near Barn Yards......... 252
" " to Preserve from Mice 253
" " Preventive from
[Insects 253
Flowers, to Expand............... 255
Grain, Musty, to Correct............ 249
" to Preserve............... 249
Grafting, New Method............ 253
Grapes, Quickest way to Procure.. 255
" To Preserve............... 256
Horses............... 282
" Advice in Selecting......... 283

Horses, Asthma............,............... 286
" Ankle Sprain, Remedy
[for 288
" Botts, Remedy for 287
" Cold or Cough " 285
" Canker in, " 286
" Colic, " 287
" Distemper, " 285
" Epizooty, " 285
" Eyes, Sore, Wash for...... 286
" Founder, Remedy for..... 287
" Frog Ail, Remedy for 288
" Gripes, Remedy for......... 287
" Galled Backs, Liniment
[for 289
" Hoof, Ointment for......... 289
" Knee, " 288
" Lampass, Remedy for..... 286
" Liniment............... 290
" Poll Evil, Remedy for..... 286
" Purging, to Check........... 287
" Purgative Mixture......... 288
" Powder, Excellent for
[Horses and Cattle 290
" Ring Bone, Remedy for... 289
" Surfeit in, " ... 281
" Scours, " ... 285
" Staggers, " ... 286
" Swellings, " ... 288
" Spavin, " ... 289
" Scratches, " ... 289
" String Halt, " ... 289
" Sand Cracks, " ... 289
" Tongue, Sore, " ... 284
" Thrush, " ... 288
" Wind, Broken, " ... 287
" " Galls, " ... 288
Mice, To Drive from Fields........ 257
Orchard, Six Reasons for
[Planting 250
" General Hints on
[Planting 251
Peach Worm, To Destroy......... 252
Potato Bug, To Destroy............... 255
Plants, To Free from Leaf Lice.... 255
Poultry............... 290
" Art of Selecting..... 290

AND GENERAL GUIDE.

	PAGE		PAGE
Poultry, Cholera in	292	Sheep, Pelt Root, Remedy for	277
" Dressing and Shipping, Instructions for	293	" Poison, Eating	278
		" Protection from Dogs, Foxes and Wolves	279
" Eggs, To Distinguish Sex of	291		
" Fowls, to Fatten Shortly	291	" Rot, Remedy for	277
" Flux or Looseness, Remedy for	292	" Staggers, "	277
		" Scours in, "	278
" Gapes, Cure for	291	Swine	279
" Hens, to Lay in Winter	290	" Advice in Selecting	279
" Insects, To Destroy	293	" A Pig, How to Choose	279
" Lice on, " "	29	" Brain, Inflamed, Remedy for	280
" Legs, Scabby,"	292	" Black Teeth, . "	280
" Pip or Gapes, Cure for	292	" Blind Staggers, "	280
" Turkeys, To Fatten [Shortly	291	" Colds and Coughs, "	280
		" Itch, Scab or Mange, "	281
Rose Trees, To Clear of Blight	255	" Measles, Remedy for "	279
Rats, To Keep from Corn	257	" Pox, "	281
Seed Required per Acre	248	" Quincy, "	280
Sound Logic	248	" Sore Throat, "	279
Straw, Mixed with Clover	249	" Throat Swelling, "	280
Shrubs, Flowering, To Prune	254	" Universal Remedy,	281
Standard Weights of Grain, Seed, [&c.	258	Trees, To Protect from Hares	253
		Tulips, To Expand	255
Sheep	277	Tobacco, Growing	256
" Costiveness, Remedy for	278	Vegetables, To Preserve all [Winter	250
" Foot Rot, "	277		
" Foul Noses, "	277	Vines, To Stop from Bleeding	253
" Lice and Ticks on, "	277	" To Destroy Insects in	253
" Lungs, Inflammation of	278	Weeds, To Banish	257
" Mouth, Sore and Swollen	278		

INDEX TO MISCELLANEOUS RECIPES.

	PAGE		PAGE
Ants, To Expel	300	Breath, To Purify	305
" on Barrels, Preventive for	301	Butter, To Extract Rancidity	307
Apple Butter, To Make	306	China, To Mend	297
Boils, Remedy for	298	Children, Burning, To Protect	298
Blacking, for Shoes	299	Composition, Waterproof, for [Boots and Shoes	299
Baldness, To Prevent	301		
Butter, Yellow, in Winter	302	Cologne, To Make	301
Bed Bug Poison	305	Cattle, To Prevent Bloating	301

INDEX.

	PAGE		PAGE
Colors, To Wash	303	**Mildew** in Wheat	297
Cement for Glass and Wood	303	Mould, in Ink, Prevent	300
Castor Oil, Best Way to Take	304	Matches, Composition for	300
Canary Birds, To Clean	304	Meat, To Preserve in Hot Weather	301
Cream, Substitute for	304	Metals, Paste for Cleaning	303
Corn Seed, Soaked in Saltpetre	305	Mosquito Bites	304
Carpets, To Clean	305	Moths, To Keep from Clothes	304
China, Method of Cleaning	306	Milk, Turning Sour, To Prevent	306
Collars, Linen, To Glaze	306	**Nightmare**, To Prevent	301
Crape, Rusty, To Restore	307	**Onion**, Smell on Breath, To Remove	306
Dyeing, New Acid for	306		
Diet, for the Sick	307	Oats, the Best, the Cheapest	306
Eggs, To Color	303	**Plated** Ware, To Clean	298
Frost out of Fruit, &c	297	Passover Cake	298
Furs, To Preserve	298	Potatoe Crop, To Increase	300
Furniture Varnish	298	Paint, To Extract from Cotton, [Silk, &c.	300
Freckles, To Remove	298		
Feathers, To Curl	298	Paint, for Brick Houses	301
Fish, in Living State, To Preserve	299	Poultice, for a Fester	302
Fever Diet	300	Plums, To Keep	303
Feathers, White, To Clean	301	Potatoe Salad	304
Fleas, on Dogs, To Destroy	302	Poultice, Mustard	307
Fire, To Extinguish	302	**Rust** out of Steel	297
Fruit Spots, To take out	303	Rats, To Expel from House	298
" To Color Yellow	304	Rose Pomatum	299
Flowers, Faded, To Restore	305	Ribbons, To Renew	300
Grass, in Yards, To Prevent [Growing	299	**Shaving** Soap	297
		Sealing Wax, To Make	299
Grease Spots, To Extract from [Paper	299	Straw, To Bleach	301
		Soup, from Scraps	302
Grapes, To Keep	303	Scarlet Fever, Cure for	303
Gilding, upon Silver	303	Stains, To Take, from Mahogany	303
Herb Bitters, Superior	297	Stoves, To Polish	304
Hard Water, To Soften	297	Seidlitz Powders	305
Hair, Grow Rich, Soft and Glossy	298	Shingle Roofs, Washed with Lime	306
" To Increase Growth	301	Syrup, Raspberry	307
House on Fire, To Escape from	302	**Toads**, Benefit of	298
Hair Dye, Liquid	306	Tea Kettles, To Prevent Crust	299
Ink, To Extract from Floors	299	Tomatoe Ketchup	300
" To Make Good	299	Tooth Powder, to Make	301
Iron Stains, out of Marble	300	Teeth, To Fasten	306
Ink, Red, To Make	302	Tea, Flaxseed	307
Iron Castings, To Bronze	305	**Warts**, To Remove	297
Japan, Black, for Leather	300	Wagon Grease, To Make	302
Jockey Club, American	302	Wounds, To Prevent Mortifying	304
Knives, To Clean	303	Windsor Soap, Genuine	305
Lamps, To Prevent Smoking	302	Whitewash, Adhesive	307

NOT CLASSIFIED.

	PAGE		PAGE
Beef Tea	79	**Peach** Marmalade	62
Broth, Chicken	80	Peaches, To Spice	71
" Veal	80	Pepper Pot	80
Beefsteak Dumplings	124	**Sour** Crout	94
Crullers, Excellent	34	**To** Iron Clothes	198
Floating Island	48	**Water** Ices, To Make	189
Green Turtle, To Dress	61	Weights and Measures	191

INDEX TO EVENTS AND ILLUSTRATIONS.

PART FOURTH.

	PAGE
Academy of Natural Science, (New)	330
Athenæum	339
Academy of Music	341
Academy of Fine Arts	341
Agricultural Hall	382
Birth Place of "Liberty"	320
Building where first American Flag was made	321
Benjamin Franklin	326
Bridge over Wissahickon, at Valley Green	372
Bridge near Mt. Airy	372
Coat of Arms, United States	303
Christ's Church	317
Carpenters' Hall	319
Chestnut Street Bridge	348
Columbia Bridge over Schuylkill	363
Centennial Memorial Medal	375
Coat of Arms of State of Pennsylvania	386

	PAGE
Drinking Fountain on Wissahickon	371
Drive on the Wissahickon Creek	371
Events, Landing of Penn	309
" Arrival of Swedes and Friends	311
" Present Wealth and Population	312
" Squares in the City	313
Eastern Penitentiary	344
Entrance to Fairmount Park at Green Street	358
' Entrance to West Park by Girard Avenue Bridge	358
Exhibition Grounds, Information	374
Franklin's Grave	326
Fire Scene in 1776	327
Fire Apparatus in 1876	327
Farmers' Market House, (Interior View)	328
Fountain in Franklin Square	353
Fairmount Park	356
Fountain in East Park	357
Fairmount Basin	359
Fountain near Mineral Spring	362
George Washington	318
Girard College	325
Girard Avenue Bridge	360
Government of the United States	384
Horticultural Hall, (Broad Street)	341
Hermit's Pool	367
Hemlock Glen on Wissahickon	373
Horticultural Hall	377
Independence Hall in 1776	323
" " 1876	324
Institution for Blind	335
Institution for Deaf and Dumb	336
Judges' Hall	379
Laurel Hill Cemetery	337
Logan Square	353
Lemon Hill and Boat Houses	361
Laurel Hill Cemetery	365
Martha Washington	318
Market Street Ferry	328
Musical Fund Hall	342
Moyamensing Prison	343
Monster Pines in West Park	368
Memorial Hall or Art Gallery	376
Main Exhibition Building	378
Machinery Hall	378
New Library Building	339
New Commercial Exchange	346
New Masonic Temple	351

INDEX.

	PAGE
New Public Buildings	352
Odd Fellows' Cemetery	338
Old Commercial Exchange	345
Old Girard Bank	345
Odd Fellows' Hall	350
Old Wire Bridge	359
Officers of United States Centennial Commission	374
Old Swedes' Church	316
Philadelphia, History of, from 1609 to 1876	309
Penn's Treaty	314
" Statue	315
" First Cottage	315
Pennsylvania Hospital	329
Pennsylvania College	330
Pennsylvania Hospital for Insane	332
Preston Retreat	334
Philadelphia Library	340
Pennsylvania Rail Road Bridge	359
Presidents of United States from 1789 to 1876	383
River Steamboat	354
Ravine in West Park	369
Signing Declaration of Independence	322
Stephen Girard	325
Ship in Full Sail	354
Strawberry Mansion	365
Sweetbriar Vale	369
The Original "Thirteen" United States	383
United States Naval Asylum	344
University of Pennsylvania	321
United States Custom House	347
United States Mint	348
Union League Building	349
United States Capitol at Washington, D. C.	355
United States Government Building	360
United States Supreme Court	385
United States Army	385
United States Navy	385
View on Schuylkill from Laurel Hill	364
View from Belmont in West Park	366
Vice Presidents from 1789 to 1876	384
Will's Eye Hospital	333
Water Works and Dam	359
Wissahickon Drive	370
Women's Pavilion	381

www.ingramcontent.com/pod-product-compliance
Lightning Source LLC
Chambersburg PA
CBHW050851300426
44111CB00010B/1216